/

THE BALANCING ACT II

THE BALANCING ACT II

JAYME CURLEY

SHARON LADAR

LINDA MATTHEWS

ANNA SIEGLER

JANE GREENGOLD STEVENS

Chicago Review Press
CHICAGO

Copyright © 1981 by Chicago Review Press, Inc.
All rights reserved
Printed in the United States of America

First Edition
First Printing

Published by
Chicago Review Press, Inc.
820 North Franklin Street
Chicago, Illinois 60610

Library of Congress Cataloging in Publication Data

The Balancing Act II

1. Mother and child — Case studies.
2. Mothers — Employment — United States — Case Studies.
I. Curley, Jayme.

HQ759.B262	306.8'7	81-38524
ISBN (clothbound edition) 0-914091-07-7		AACR2
ISBN (paperback edition) 0-914091-08-5		

Cover design by Joseph Essex
Book design and typography by Claire J. Mahoney

Contents

Acknowledgments   5

Introduction   7

I
Linda Matthews   15

II
Jayme Curley   63

III
Jane Greengold Stevens   107

IV
Anna Siegler   169

V
Sharon Ladar   207

Conclusion   259

Acknowledgments

Our special thanks to Mary Munro, editor of *The Balancing Act II*, for her many valuable suggestions, her enthusiasm, and her hours of hard work.

We also like to thank Sydelle Kramer for her help in editing the original *The Balancing Act*.

Introduction

We are five professional women in our mid-thirties who six years ago, in *The Balancing Act*, described why we chose to have children, the assumptions and expectations with which we approached motherhood, and the impact of our first babies on our working and private lives. At the time our decisions to have children were made, each of us was seriously engaged in the development of a career and enjoying the productivity and fulfillment such activity brings. Each of us was committed to the ideal of maintaining her career to the fullest extent possible throughout the demanding process of pregnancy, birth and motherhood. *The Balancing Act* recounted in detail our struggles to realize that ideal in practice, and we made every effort to be candid about our failures as well as our successes.

Now, in *The Balancing Act II*, we bring our accounts up to date. Our original essays are retained, but in addition each of us has described, though in somewhat less detail, the shifts in priorities and attitudes, the problems and rewards that come as children grow older, families grow, and we become more experienced in balancing work with family life.

JAYME CURLEY is a ceramist. She has a B.A. from Wellesley, an M.A. from the University of Chicago, and an M.F.A. from the Art Institute of Chicago. She taught art for several years before devoting herself exclusively to her own work. She has been awarded prizes in many regional and national ceramic and craft shows, is often represented in galleries, and has many pieces in museums and private collections. Her husband David has a PH.D. from the University of Chicago in South Asian economic history. Their daughter Shona was born in December 1973, followed by a son, Jonathan, in July 1978.

SHARON LADAR* is a visual designer and an associate professor of design at the University of Kansas. She has a B.S. and an M.S. in Design from the Institute of Design at the Illinois Institute of Technology in Chicago. Between college and graduate school she worked professionally as a designer. She has published articles in several design journals and is an editor of *Visible Language*. Her husband Rex is an architect. Their son Scot was adopted when he was a week old, in November 1972. A second son, Jay, was born in June 1976.

LINDA MATTHEWS is an editor at Chicago Review Press. She has a B.A. from Reed College and a graduate degree in English from Tufts University. She taught English at Northwestern University and has owned and managed a small bookstore in Chicago. Her husband Curt is president of Chicago Review Press. Their daughter Sarah was born in October 1973, their son Joe in July 1976.

ANNA SIEGLER received a PH.D. in history from the University of Chicago in June 1980. During graduate school she taught college courses in humanities and the social sciences. For the past two years she has taught English part-time at a local private school (grades five through eight). Her hus-

---
*Pseudonym

band Mark, an Associate Professor of Medicine at the University of Chicago Medical School, has devoted his career to the practice of general internal medicine and to the study of medical ethics. They have twin daughters, Alison and Dillan, born in December 1972, and a son, Richard, born July 25, 1981.

JANE GREENGOLD STEVENS is an attorney and an artist. She works three to four days a week for a federally-funded legal services program in New York, and has had four one-woman shows in a cooperative gallery in SoHo since returning to New York in 1975. Her husband Ken is a designer now working to establish an independent design practice. Their twin daughters, Vanessa and Rachel, were born in June 1973 and their son Aaron in April 1978. They are expecting their fourth child in January 1982.

The five of us are white, middle class, well-educated married women living in traditional nuclear families. We rely for childcare on private paid help or various forms of school and group daycare rather than on unpaid help from friends or extended family. None of us is a five-day-a-week, nine-to-five professional. We have established schedules flexible enough to permit us to combine career with motherhood instead of sacrificing one to the other; we are as actively involved with our children as we are with our careers.

We fear that we may be accused of self-indulgence in writing about our lives, when other women face constraints of poverty and limited choice that we can only imagine. But we also believe that thousands of women share our situation, and that we like women of all classes need to re-examine our positions. We do not deny that we have had advantages: being able to work in our chosen fields and to establish flexible schedules; being able to afford childcare; and being free of absolute considerations of money. Yet even with this head start toward ordering our lives by choice rather than necessity, we still find ourselves confronting limitations. Precisely because we have been able to do so much, our efforts to be honest about our problems illuminate issues that might otherwise remain obscured.

Partly because our commitments to our children are as involving as our commitments to work, combining career with motherhood has been difficult for us all. We have had few models to emulate in our efforts to be professionals as well as mothers, so when we first began to write, in the early 1970s, we turned to the literature of childrearing and of the women's movement for guidance and support. To our dismay, both were barren of information and advice for women attempting to do what we had in mind. The books on childrearing were adequate for diagnosing chickenpox, but they presupposed a mother whose time and attention were devoted almost exclusively to her children. Often they criticized mothers who left their young children to someone else's care. The literature of the women's movement occasionally touched on the dangers of domesticity, including motherhood, but it had little to say to a woman who wanted to add a child to an active, stimulating, and demanding professional life — an unrealistic omission, since women, even "liberated" women, will obviously continue to have children.

Women becoming mothers, or considering becoming mothers, have a much wider literature to refer to today than we did eight years ago, yet the need for information about motherhood, especially combining motherhood with career, is still great and perhaps growing. Recent census figures show a surge of births among women in their thirties who postponed having children while they established their careers. Newspaper and magazine articles as well as our own friends announce to us that young women are more aware than ever of their freedom to choose between various combinations of work and motherhood, and of their need for information, role models, and support as they attempt to make their decisions. We believe that our experiences are typical of women who, like us, care deeply and actively about their work even while wanting to have and raise young children.

That we have written this book reflects our conditioning as women. It is women who are primarily responsible for and involved with their children, and it is women who urge men to share equally in the demands and satisfactions of parenthood. We have all asked ourselves why we chose to devote our precious time to this book when we had theses to write, paintings to paint, courses to teach. But motherhood has forced us to confront certain issues time and time again: who takes care of the children and meets the daily crises? How has motherhood affected our work, our marriages, our sense of ourselves?

All of us have been surprised by the intensity and complexity of our responses to motherhood. We know now, as we did not know a few years ago, what it is like to change diapers, referee fights, and comfort wailing children, but we are still searching to understand what it means to us, as involved, committed professionals, that we are also mothers. Talking together and writing these essays has helped us to grope towards understanding. We offer them in the hope that our experiences will provide support and insight for others who, like us, are attempting to work out new patterns of parenthood.

I

My adjustment to motherhood has been strenuous, undeniably, because I am involved with my work as well as with my child. But what Sarah has taken away in freedom she has replaced in richness; my life is fuller and deeper because of her.

LINDA MATTHEWS

Linda Matthews

From the time I was a little girl, motherhood was on my mind and in my expectations. I babysat eagerly and played with dolls till I was ten or twelve. My friends and I learned about childbirth early, from books, and we once horrified my mother by staging a delivery on my front lawn, our dolls laid between our legs and we groaning in plain view of the neighbors and any passer-by. My period, which arrived just before my twelfth birthday, was a great satisfaction to me; it meant I really could have children, any time I wanted to. In high school, a friend and I spent hours constructing our futures as wives and mothers, elaborating on our husbands, our houses, how we would dress our children and where they would go to school. Throughout my adolescence, a life without parenthood was inconceivable to me.

This deep interest of mine came partly, I expect, from the domestic, conservative culture that dominated my childhood. My mother's friends, my older cousins and aunts, aspired to the culture of *Good Housekeeping* and

The Ladies' Home Journal. In most of the families I knew, a well-ironed blouse brought as many compliments as an A in English. At least half my high school classmates married at, or before, graduation. Of the girls who did go on to college, many joked openly about going for their MRS. degrees. That atmosphere almost insisted upon motherhood.

In part, also, my interest came from my parents. Not that they pressured me to think of marriage and babies — they never spoke of maternity as the proper goal for a woman, never suggested that a childless life need be unhappy. Though they supported my fascination with babies by giving me the dolls I asked for, they did not explicitly encourage me. My parents' influence was indirect and also positive. They enjoyed being parents, took obvious pleasure in each other and in my brother and me, and we were happy with them. My brother and I grew up hoping to find, as our parents had, happiness in domestic life and children.

A third factor, and I think the crucial one, is personal inclination. Some people find happiness in domesticity; some do not. My aunt for instance never married although she was clever, attractive, and much pursued by men. She received her latest marriage proposal only a few years ago, when she was past sixty. Children make her jumpy; she has always treasured her autonomy even when it has made her lonely from time to time. And she grew up in precisely the same circumstances as my mother, who got engaged her first year in college and has happily spent every day of her life for the last forty years living with my father.

But I have always thought in terms of happiness with children. While most of my high school classmates became mothers years before I did, few of them, to my knowledge, were as enamored as I of the prospect of motherhood. They took it for granted; I looked forward to it eagerly.

Why? I don't believe in astrology, I don't believe in fate, I think of the sun signs as primitive science, but — I was born under Cancer, the most domestic, the most maternal, the lunar sign. And domestic life has always held an enormous attraction for me.

It has not held an exclusive attraction, however. My interest in motherhood is balanced by a drive for worldly success and a conviction that I can do anything, given sufficient space and time. At the age of five I daydreamed of being a great ballerina, twirling across the stage in a purple tutu with my corps de ballet dressed in white. At nine I was reading Gray's *Anatomy* and bragging that I'd go to Harvard later on. My parents encouraged my ambition, if not my conceit, and in their way they provided models of the unconventional life I hoped to lead. They had waited twelve years to have children, and in those years both worked, my mother as a schoolteacher and my father as a civil servant. They had earned teaching certificates in the 1930s; when I was ten, they undertook night and summer classes, and in 1957 they graduated from the University of Oregon, the only parents I knew who had college degrees. They read everything, had dozens of hobbies, and when my mother went back to teaching they divided the housework equally between them — a liberated couple in 1955. Their education, their interests, their sharing of domestic responsibilities set them far apart from most of the adults I knew and colored my expectations for the future. As a senior in high school my goals seemed attainable and clear: I would make a happy domestic life for myself, and I would distinguish myself in some kind of profession or career.

I still think those goals are admirable. Unfortunately, as I continue to learn, they are very crude. My fantasy of being a doctor perished when, as a sophomore at Reed College, I got a D in Natural Science. I never replaced that fantasy, but trusted my conscientiousness as a student and my college degree to make my calling clear to me in good time. As a consequence, my senior year found me on the verge of graduation without the remotest idea of what to do afterward. I couldn't get beyond the gray cinderblock wall that bounded, in my imagination, the four college years. Instead of facing the uncertainty, I jumped at the first option that opened up. I got married, to a Reed alumnus two years older than I, already in graduate school at Harvard, and lonely. We made a rational decision to marry. I would finish my B.A. at Harvard and find a graduate school in Boston. We would work together, he as a linguist, I as a literary critic; and eventually we would have children. I told myself that the marriage would answer both my goals at once, and it did in fact resolve the issue of career. I went to graduate school in English, as my husband suggested, liked it, and decided to aim for a teaching position at a school like Reed — small and very good.

However, we did not achieve domestic happiness. Despite the unconventional surface of our marriage — both of us in graduate school, planning on careers — its premise was utterly traditional. We both assumed that I could not make my own decisions; my panic at college graduation seemed evidence enough of that. So my husband made them for me, and the result was misery for both of us.

Our unhappiness focused, eventually, on the issue of children. My husband was convinced that I could not handle both a child and a career. He was sure my professional goals would slip away the minute we had a baby. His attitude infuriated me; I was happy as a graduate student and deeply committed to my work as an English medievalist. I thought of a child as an addition to my studies, not as a substitute for them, and was never tempted to become a full-time mother. However, the history of my marriage put me in a bad bargaining position, and so, in retrospect, did certain facts. In the first two or three years of my marriage I talked confidently of combining motherhood with career, but my imagination persisted in separating the two roles from each other.

For example, during my second year in graduate school, I went to an evening meeting at my (woman) advisor's house. There was a tricycle on her porch and a pair of child-sized tennis shoes in the hall. I could hear a man and a child talking upstairs as I came in. I immediately concluded that my advisor and her husband were taking care of someone else's child for a day or two. It absolutely did not occur to me that my advisor herself could be a mother.

The next fall I was out of town for several months. As soon as I got back I rushed to school to see my advisor. She was sitting in her office, wearing a loose black jumper, obviously pregnant. I was astonished, didn't know what to say, said nothing, and for the next five months she and I, two married women, spent an hour a week discussing Middle English Literature without once mentioning the increasingly obvious fact that she was going to have a baby. It is true that my advisor was half responsible for this embarrassing silence. Or perhaps it was embarrassing only to me — further evidence for my husband's position that, whatever I said, I did not really believe that profession and motherhood could be combined.

Nevertheless, I believe that my husband was mistaken. While combining motherhood with career is more complicated than I expected it to be as a graduate student, I doubt that a child even then could have kept me from my work. My husband's attitude, however, might have. Though he never said so, I think his resistance to my wish for a child came partly from his own unwillingness to share the responsibilities of parenthood. I suppose some half-conscious understanding of that kept me from quietly getting pregnant in spite of him.

My advisor was the first woman I knew who was actively engaged in both profession and motherhood. (Even my mother had stayed home with my brother and me until he was eight and I was ten.) I kept visualizing myself in my advisor's place, lecturing to an English class over a huge belly: would my students take me seriously? Would *I* take myself seriously? People certainly took my advisor seriously — she had just gotten tenure, just published a book. I found myself terribly curious about her daily life, but she volunteered nothing and I never asked.

Fortunately, that same year, I made friends with a woman graduate student who had two small children. She was delighted to discuss her life with me. One day she missed class; she said afterward that her babysitter had been sick. Her explanation made me feel very odd. I knew in the abstract that children were restrictive, but it hadn't occurred to me to wonder where and when the restrictions might apply. I thought how awkward it would be to live as precariously as she did, yet at the same time I envied her.

Although I was deeply involved with my studies, particularly with my dissertation — a study of style in three Middle English poems — my life compared to hers seemed narrow and one-sided. I wanted to temper, as she did, my work with a child.

At the end of that year my husband and I left Boston for our first teaching jobs, his at the University of Chicago, mine at Northwestern. I was eager for my new professional life in Chicago and for the opportunity, now that my career was clearly under way, to really consider the possibility of a baby. My husband, however, had changed his mind neither about children nor about my ability to make decisions for myself. The strain between us grew throughout our first year in Chicago, and in August 1972, when I was 27, we separated.

We had been married six years, long enough for the emotional ties to run deep. I couldn't have left him without the security of my job and my independent friendships, especially the friendship of my present husband, Curt.

Curt was thirty when we met, an instructor at Northwestern like myself, divorced after three years of marriage. He and I were discussing parenthood virtually from the moment we met: how should one raise a child? What human need does parenthood fulfill? When our friendship grew into an affair, the question of children became immediate and personal. For the first time in my life I could not get myself to use my diaphragm; in January 1973 I was pregnant. Both of us realized it had been no accident but a confirmation of our relationship. Abortion was legal at the time, but the idea appalled us. In March my divorce was final, and in April Curt and I were married.

In someone else's life these events would astonish me. I would be muttering about rashness and confused motives, predicting disaster. And it is true that the sequence, so fast, of divorce-marriage-baby complicated our adjustment to Sarah's birth, especially with the career upsets I will describe later on. But I don't regret anything about that year. In fact, I enjoy looking back on it — passion and romance in the middle of MY life! The whole experience confirmed something I had been trying not to believe: that life decisions are made emotionally, not rationally. Throughout my first marriage I had resented not being free to have a child. I told myself that I was ready, waiting only for my husband to give the rational go-ahead, to say that circumstances were appropriate for us to become parents. But now I think that our rational disagreement was just a mask for the real difficulty. We trusted each other too little to take the risk of a child; the emotional climate between us was wrong for having a baby. When the emotional climate was right, with Curt, I acted very promptly indeed.

Emotionally, then, the pregnancy was well-timed. I trusted Curt's commitment to fatherhood and my own desire for a child. Practically, it created some problems. Teaching was a strain for the first two or three months. I was always sleepy, in imminent danger of dozing during my office hours and sometimes even in class. Hunger made me feel sick to my stomach, so the eleven o'clock classes were especially difficult. As lunchtime approached I got queasier and queasier, more and more disturbed. A couple of times I thought I'd have to leave the room. Then I began carrying hard candies in my pocket. From 11:30 to 12 I talked around peppermints and honey drops.

More worrisome was the matter of a maternity leave. I had a three-year contract at Northwestern; the baby was due in October of the third year, right in the middle of fall quarter. Obviously I wouldn't be able to teach that quarter at all. I went to see the Chairman of the department, intending to ask for a quarter's leave of absence, but expecting to have to resign. In a perverse way I almost wanted to resign: I could get used to the baby, finish my dissertation, and look for a more permanent job for the following year. When the Chairman offered me a leave of absence at half pay — a real maternity leave and a new precedent at Northwestern — I was very pleased with myself but vaguely anxious. Pregnancy was exhausting; wouldn't it be even more exhausting to work with a tiny baby at home?

As the Chairman said, however, I would look considerably better to prospective employers writing from Northwestern rather than from a stack of diapers. I accepted the leave and began to enjoy both my status as professor/prospective mother and the hidden controversies it inspired among my older colleagues. They were shocked, by my pregnancy in the first place, and by my paid leave in the second. I was sorry that the last months of my pregnancy fell in the summer. It would have been fun to let my big belly really rub it in. My younger colleagues, the ones I associated with, were supportive and curious.

The maternity leave was the last big issue I had to settle before Sarah was born. When it had been arranged, Curt and I were free to spend a quiet spring and summer working — he on his publishing, I on my thesis — and adjusting to each other and to the prospect of a baby.

We knew that money would not be a problem. Curt's family is wealthy; he has a private income large enough to support the three of us comfortably, with as much paid child-care as we think we need. Obviously this income was crucial; without it, we probably wouldn't have been able to have Sarah, let alone paid child-care. Curt's teaching contract had expired in June 1972, and he hadn't found another attractive position. We could barely have supported ourselves on my full salary at Northwestern. On the half-pay of my maternity leave, it would have been impossible. Curt would have had to scrounge up any job he could, or I would have had to get an abortion. His money protected us from that horribly unattractive choice. He was able to continue writing his dissertation and planning to start a small publishing company, and we were both able to look forward to the baby.

Nor did it look like our relationship would be a problem. As a husband Curt allayed many of the fears I brought with me from my first marriage. He went quietly about the household chores, shopping, cooking, washing the dishes. When we were both in the kitchen working, I felt immeasurably content. We talked a lot about the baby — how we should raise it, especially how we would deal with sex roles. It seemed to us both that if we could share so easily before the baby was born, we would have no trouble afterward. We disagreed about how complete our role-levelling should be. I insisted on overalls and dolls for both sexes, while Curt said he wanted to see his little girl in a dress from time to time. He maintained that the crucial thing was to act from emotional conviction, not from theory. I tentatively agreed, though it seemed to me one had to have the theories — surely they influenced one's convictions. Our arguments were fun, as airy as inexperience could make them. We really didn't worry very much.

The pregnancy did have some upsetting features. For one thing it changed our sexual relationship. We had been wonderfully amorous, with lots of good and tender sex. When I was feeling weak and exhausted in the first two or three months, my interest declined and Curt was understanding and accommodating. By the fourth or fifth month my interest waxed again, along with my belly, but Curt's waned. My belly unnerved him, he said; he was afraid of hurting the baby. Intellectually he knew this was impossible, but his feeling persisted. He reacted almost as if my pregnancy were an illness. This was not only reflected in his reticence about sex. He was also squeamish about following the course of the pregnancy in pictures, and he was less enthusiastic than I had hoped about feeling the baby move. The development of the fetus inside me seemed emotionally strange and unnatural to him, and it violated his sense of privacy. He didn't like making love with a third party so close by. Ironically, just as I was beginning to get too uncomfortable to enjoy sex, his interest picked up. It took him eight months to get accustomed to my belly. My own expectations, too, were unrealistic. I had read some stories about passionate love affairs being conducted throughout pregnancy, and reality even in a form more intense than we experienced it probably would have disappointed me somewhat.

A second problem was all my own, though it worked into the question of sex. I felt increasingly unattractive as my figure and clothing changed, and from time to time I was exasperated with the whole affair. I explained my discontent to myself in an odd way. I decided that my figure unnerved Curt and frustrated me because I wasn't really big enough to look pregnant; I just looked funny. It's true that I never got very big with the baby, but that couldn't have been the source of the problem. I had romanticized pregnancy far more than I realized. I expected to look and feel radiant; instead my feet and fingers swelled, I sweated, I was hot. Curt was never critical of my appearance. He gave me lots of compliments about my pink cheeks and growing bosom, and his jokes about my stomach were always loving and tender. But his gingerliness about sex heightened my apprehensions. It was a great relief when my body returned to its usual shape and size.

In spite of these discomforts, my pregnancy was a happy, reassuring time for both of us. By October, when Sarah was due, the miseries of our first marriages seemed far away and we were eager to be a family.

Sarah came early, in the middle of a dissertation chapter that I had hoped to finish before she arrived. Compared to the experiences of many of my friends, the birth was quick and easy. We got to the hospital at four-thirty a.m., and she was born at nine a.m. Compared to what I had expected, however, it was a shock. I had the idea, partly from our Lamaze classes and partly from my own ego, that my mind and body were going to lift me above the experiences of most women, that my baby's birth would be intense but not overwhelming, and that I would always, easily, be in control. Well, it was intense — in a way that I wasn't prepared for. The contractions kept getting ahead of me until I thought I would burst or scream or split in two, then subsiding just in time. I did the Lamaze breathing determinedly with Curt's help, but I knew that really my body was operating completely independent of me. The last part of the labor was like being under water. From time to time I surfaced: the nurse asking if she should change the bed position, me saying it didn't matter; the doctor asking if I wanted medication, me saying "No, watch this!" Ice chips, back rubs, cold washcloths. Curt counted, I breathed. The hands on the clock moved infinitely slowly.

Then the doctor said, "With the next contraction, push!" They flopped me onto a delivery cart, banged me onto the delivery room table, strung up my legs. I yelled: "It hurts my back! Just pull it out!" I felt something slipping inside me. Curt yelled "Look!" The doctor said "It's a girl!" I opened my eyes.

I wasn't prepared for the intensity of childbirth. To the extent that I was able to ask myself anything during labor, I asked, "Is this really the way it ought to feel?" But in retrospect, the intensity was impressive rather than frightening. I respected childbirth after Sarah was born, and right away began looking forward to the birth of our second child, hoping that the second time I would be less immersed in detail and more aware of the complete, developing experience.

The intensity of Sarah's first twelve weeks was a less positive surprise. Everything in those weeks felt unpredictable and formless. If Sarah started crying at six p.m., I had no idea when she might stop — at six-thirty, at ten? I remember the incredible frustration of wanting to go to bed at nine but being afraid to because the night before Sarah had cried to be fed at eleven; and I remember the incredible relief of waking to a light sky and realizing that she had slept five hours between feedings. There had been some unpleasant moments in the pregnancy and in the labor too, but they had been clear steps in a process that I knew would end. The pregnancy lasted nine months, the labor several hours, but Sarah's demands to be fed, changed, and played with seemed likely to go on forever.

Curt was as responsible as I was for Sarah in her first

few weeks. At every feeding he changed her, brought her to me, and put her back to bed. He bottle-fed her when I felt dry, walked her when she was fussy, and took her daily to the clinic for bloodtests (she had a mild case of jaundice when she was born). He should have been as vulnerable as I was to her demands, but it was I, not he, who cried at the four a.m. feeding, panicked at the thought of drying sterile nipples on an ordinary paper towel, threw out day-old formula because it might have gotten bad. I, not he, had trouble coping with parenthood.

Exhaustion was a big part of my problem. In the first weeks of Sarah's life I was like an old lady who could not escape from her physical self. In the hospital, nothing meant more to me than hot baths, meals, and sleep. It was pleasant to see Curt during visiting hours, but I didn't miss him when he was gone. Home seemed a thousand miles away, and I had to concentrate enormously when he spoke of our house or the dogs. It was the same with Sarah. I liked to hold her if someone gave her to me, but it was a relief when the nurse took her away. Once I thought she was choking. I floundered out of bed and tiptoed her to the nearest nurse (you can tighten your crotch muscles better on tiptoe). I was angry when she said Sarah was all right — I didn't want to have made that huge effort for nothing. On the third day, the pediatrician announced that Sarah had jaundice, and again I was angry. I had no energy for complications.

It was no different at home. My best hours were those when Curt and Sarah were out of the house, getting blood tests for jaundice at the clinic. I sat in the bathtub or lay in bed, luxuriating in the respite from responsibility. Sometimes I imagined that Sarah hadn't yet been born and Curt and I were still in our old routine. I wasn't sorry that Sarah had been born; often our house, often the bright blue cover on my bed, seemed like a peaceful island that only she and

I shared. But my exhaustion colored everything in those first weeks. When I heard Curt's footsteps on the porch, home from the clinic with Sarah, tightness gripped me. Once again I had to forget myself and become a mother.

Another problem was breast feeding. I had looked forward for several years to nursing my baby. I couldn't imagine what the sensation would be like, but I was sure it would be pleasant, and I liked the idea of feeding a child the natural, and less usual, way. I had also worried for several years that breast feeding might be difficult for me. The nipple of my left breast is inverted and I didn't see how a baby could get a grip on it. My mother, who also has an inverted nipple, had tried unsuccessfully to nurse me. Her experience made my worry seem plausible, but every doctor I spoke to assured me that an inverted nipple was no problem at all. I suppose I felt mildly vindicated when it turned out in fact to be a major problem.

Sarah couldn't nurse the left breast. At feeding after feeding in the hospital, she emptied the right breast, nuzzled gamely at the left, and burst into a wail of frustration when she couldn't get the nipple in her mouth. Curt and I concluded that Sarah got enough milk from the right breast to sustain her but not enough to fill her up. At home, no nursery protected us from her hungry wails. After a day and a night of Sarah's squalling, we agreed that Curt should offer her a bottle of formula. She downed three ounces greedily and went to sleep.

Up to then, the problem with breast feeding had been physical. My inverted nipple was interfering with Sarah's nursing; that was all. But when she accepted the bottle, the problem became emotional. I had hoped she would reject the formula; when she finished it, I was more miserable about her satisfaction than I had been about her hunger. I felt humiliated and guilty, as if I had failed at something that should have been easy to do.

Obviously, my response was extreme. Curt tried to point out to me that breast feeding is no sure measure of maternal love. He suggested, rightly, that my sense of failure came in good part from a private competition with my mother. His reasonableness, however, made very little impression. Emotionally, I felt that in accepting the formula Sarah had rejected me.

In desperation, I called La Leche League, which sent me a breast shield designed especially for inverted nipples. The shield was big, hard, and clumsy. Milk collected in it and then leaked out. It was conspicuous on and impossible to remove discreetly, but it seemed to work. By the third week of breast shield and breast-and-bottle routine, Sarah's feedings were noticeably better. The longer she stayed at the breast, the happier I felt.

One night after both breasts, Sarah didn't seem to want the formula. She spat the nipple out and got fussier and fussier, and finally Curt put her in her crib out of exasperation. Amazingly, she went to sleep. The next night Curt only went through the motions of offering the bottle. Again she went to sleep. Although for a week or more after that we lugged bottles upstairs for her night feedings, her need for formula was really over. By the end of the sixth week, Sarah was a breast fed baby.

I am glad I made the effort. Nursing was a satisfying, intimate, completely novel experience for all three of us, and it certainly taught me something about myself. At the time of that crisis I was physically drained. Every bit of energy for the effort was emotional. My self-image was at stake: I could not bear to see myself defeated by something as universal, and also as quintessentially female, as breast feeding. The psychiatrists will mutter about doubts of femininity. I am more impressed by my determination to succeed.

The experience also proved something to me about womens' doctors. Neither the pediatrician nor my gynecologist had ever heard of the breast-shield that La Leche League sent out, though it has been used successfully in England since before World War II. My gynecologist was mildly interested in it when I showed it to him, but he said he wouldn't prescribe it routinely for inverted nipples — too much trouble for the woman, he said. I bet he never mentions it, even to patients as eager as I was to breast feed. They really do see nursing as a pleasant frill, nothing to be taken very seriously.

The breast feeding crisis was the worst that confronted me after Sarah's birth, but the maternity leave was a close second. The leave began in September and lasted till January, the entire fall quarter. The first six weeks were no problem; my parents were with us, Curt had not gone back to work, the weather was still warm and sunny — it seemed, if anything, like a sick leave combined with vacation. But at the end of October everything changed. My parents left, the weather got colder, and we began to establish a new routine. Then the maternity leave really began, and it was difficult.

Again, the difficulty had to do with my image of myself. I had been accustomed to a busy life: classes, meetings, lunch with colleagues, evening work. At the end of October I suddenly realized that I had no outside commitments at all. I had plenty of work to do, winter classes to prepare and a dissertation chapter to revise, and since Sarah slept most of the day, I had plenty of time. But I didn't have a public way of reassuring myself that, baby or no baby, I was the same active, busy person I had been before. I began having trouble concentrating on my class preparations. Whole afternoons went by when I did no work at all, just stared at my books or my baby or my face in the mirror until Curt came home, or until it was time to nurse Sarah again. My inactivity was unpleasant and frightening.

Curt had been supportive during the breast feeding crisis, but in the maternity leave crisis he was part of the problem. At first he had been as involved with Sarah as I, and I had depended on him physically and emotionally for help with the baby. But at the end of October he had to get back to work. His publishing company was releasing its first book, his night school students were beginning to hand in papers, and a small magazine he helped to edit slipped into a messy and time-consuming crisis. Because he was busy and I was not, we fell more and more into a conventional domestic routine. The household chores we had previously shared fell more and more to me, and Curt fell more and more into a typical fatherly role. He dandled Sarah in his spare moments, held her during Sunday football games, watched her for a couple of hours now and then as a favor to me; but I was the one who fed, changed, and amused her and got up with her at night. It seemed to me that our old habit of sharing had vanished forever.

When I complained that all the domestic work was falling to me, Curt suggested that we start our babysitting arrangements a month or two early. I agreed, so in early November Mrs. Lowe began coming two days and one evening a week to take care of Sarah. Mrs. Lowe is an elderly black woman whom Curt had known for several years as the cleaning woman for his advisor's wife and then as his own weekly housekeeper. When we found I was pregnant we asked Mrs. Lowe right away if she would help us with the baby. She was eager to do it, and made a point of asking me to call her the minute we needed her. She was glad to come to work in November.

Sarah slept most of Mrs. Lowe's six-hour day, and when she woke I nursed her as usual. For several weeks Mrs. Lowe's only responsibility was to change Sarah and give her a bottle if I went out. I often asked myself if we really needed her, especially when I came home bursting with milk to find Sarah full and sound asleep. The babysitting did help my morale, however. Just getting out of the house was therapeutic. I made Christmas shopping my occupation, went downtown once or twice a week and spent more time and money than ever before or since on Christmas presents for our families and friends. I watched myself in store windows a lot and was reassured to find that I looked the same as I had before Sarah was born.

But babysitting was not the answer to my restlessness during the maternity leave. It didn't change the relationship between Curt and me, and that, increasingly, was the focus of my irritation. I began badgering him to share the baby care and household chores equally, every day. He refused; he said our arrangements should reflect the fact that he was busier than I. Finally we worked out a complicated schedule that gave him more domestic work than he had been doing, but not as much as me. It was only half successful because he was only half-committed to it. Fortunately, Christmas vacation put an end to all of it, and in January I went back to work.

The maternity leave was meant to be a time when I could recover from the birth and form a close relationship to my baby without having to worry about money and a job. It was a failure because what I needed most, more than a convalescence and more, even, than time with my baby, was reassurance that I still could do the work I liked to do, and that the formal outlines of my life — my comings and goings at work, the division of responsibility at home — had not changed. The maternity leave prolonged the disruptions of Sarah's birth, and I was miserable because of it.

My misery was not without its ironies. Sarah's care fell increasingly to me in part because of my success with breast feeding. There was no reason for Curt to get up in the night to change her if I was getting up to feed her anyway. More importantly, when she was tiny, nursing was the best way of making emotional contact with her. It was natural that when Sarah was fussy, Curt would bring her to me rather than trying to soothe her himself, and that Sarah would look to me rather than to Curt for comfort. If we had really wanted to share equally, we should have bottle-fed Sarah.

It may also be that the newness of our marriage complicated my adjustment to Sarah. Curt and I had established a pattern of domestic sharing, but it hadn't had time to become longstanding tradition. Had we been married longer when Sarah was born, I might have been less frightened of taking on extra domestic responsibility, more able to see the maternity leave as an exception rather than a new rule. It is also possible, however, that the shift in domestic responsibility during my leave — a shift that because of breast feeding and my not working, seems in retrospect inevitable — might have been even more disruptive if I had taken sharing completely for granted before Sarah was born.

Sarah's birth, also ironically, made me realize how deeply committed I was to working and how much I drew my identity from it. At the time of the maternity leave, exactly what I did by way of a job wasn't as important as the fact that I did something, that I had a commitment to something other than my home and family. I suppose having to defend my wish to be a parent in my first marriage made me play down my need for a career. I didn't altogether realize until Sarah was born that to be happy, I had to have both.

Though Sarah was the reason for my maternity leave and therefore, in a sense, the cause of my distress, I never blamed her or resented her for my unhappiness. My anger fell on Curt, as in the problem of domestic sharing, or on myself, as in my extreme reaction to breast feeding. Even now, two years later, I rarely blame Sarah for my frustrations. A child inevitably brings difficult moments;

if one isn't willing to accept that, one shouldn't have a child. Occasionally I have wondered whether we should subject ourselves to a second baby, but on that account too my reservations have been short-lived and mild. I know that a second child will be a shock just because babies are so incredibly demanding. I believe, however, that Curt and I have experienced and for the most part overcome the emotional trauma that a baby brings. If I felt that the second baby was likely to be as emotionally difficult as the first, my reservations would be stronger. The trauma was good for me once in my life. It showed me aspects of my character, such as my need for work and my fear of failure, that I hadn't fully recognized before. Twice in a life, on the other hand, would be too much.

The problems I have just described, exhaustion, breast feeding, the maternity leave, were all basically problems of becoming a mother. My identifying myself as a professional woman aggravated some of them, but I would have felt a loss of freedom and a disruption of routine whether or not I had had a career. The problems that followed, on the other hand, were basically problems of combining profession with motherhood. They were more practical than the earlier ones, long-term issues like child-care and how much time Curt and I spend with the baby. Happily, my last two quarters at Northwestern formed a bridge between one set of problems and the next. In those five months, Curt and I were busy, settled, and content.

It was enormously gratifying to get back to work. As the only mother on the English faculty, I got loads of attention from my colleagues and friends, and I gobbled every bit of it. For several weeks my baby stories took precedence over all other lunch-table gossip, including sports, which was an impressive achievement and a first for the department, I'm sure. I got an incredible high from teaching a class in Shakespeare and then reminding myself that Sarah was waiting for me at home. What a confirmation of my talents and abilities! If Sarah and I had a bad afternoon at home, I could escape next morning at work. If a class went badly, thoughts of Sarah comforted me. As I drove home from school I was flooded with contentment. I felt settled, organized, useful, and happy.

The readjustment in our life at home was partly responsible for my happiness. When I went back to teaching, Curt went back to sharing household chores and babycare. I was peeved at how easily he shared the work once he decided it was necessary, but I also enjoyed watching the closeness develop between him and Sarah. In April, when I weaned her, Curt and I really became equals as parents. Though I missed nursing at first, Curt's getting up with Sarah in the morning was a pleasant compensation. We both felt satisfied with the new routine. Our sense of family deepened; we were content.

Delightful as it was, the tranquility of those months could have lasted only at the expense of Curt's or my career. Our schedule then depended on a lot of flexibility and not much work to do. But Curt's publishing company became more demanding as it grew, and I knew I would soon have to again make time for my dissertation and some academic articles if I were to continue as a college teacher. Even if we had remained as publisher and teacher, we'd have had to make new decisions about schedules and child-care. Our professional changes only hastened the inevitable.

That spring was the end of my three-year contract at Northwestern. During the maternity leave I had applied for work at virtually every Chicago-area college with no appealing results. It looked increasingly as if I'd spend 1974-75 finishing my dissertation at home and looking for work the following year. While I was eager to return part-time to my dissertation, the isolation of full-time writing, and the likelihood that, being at home, the domestic work would again fall to me, was not attractive. I was also worried about finding a job when my dissertation was done. Though I wanted an academic career and, from my experience at Northwestern, seemed suited to it, I wasn't prepared to leave the Chicago area or to take a dead-end position teaching English Composition. With the job market as restricted as it was, I didn't know whether the kind of position I wanted would be available to me.

In the middle of my uncertainty Curt suggested that we buy a bookstore. His motives were partly selfish: as a publisher he needed experience in retailing books but he didn't want the responsibility of a full-time job in a bookstore or the burden of owning and managing a store by himself. They were also partly generous. I could work part-time at the bookstore until I finished my thesis and then I could decide whether bookselling or teaching offered the most promising career. I was startled by his suggestion; I distrusted business without knowing anything about it and had never imagined myself as a businesswoman. On the other hand, a store might give me the balance I wanted between study and work, and I could conceive of liking it. Before I had made up my mind, Curt found a store for sale, small, established, and in a good location. My reservations seemed petty in the face of his enthusiasm, and within a month we agreed to buy.

When it comes to life decisions, my imagination fails me. I foresee a thousand versions of the improbable, while the probable consequences of what I'm about to do elude me altogether. Curt and I carefully planned our new, post-bookstore schedule to accommodate his publishing, my thesis, the store, and the baby, all on three days a week of child-care. As summer and the new schedule approached, I confidently expected the store to fall into place behind my dissertation and Sarah to fit neatly around the edges of both. Perhaps I had the maternity leave in mind, when Sarah slept half the morning and most of the afternoon; perhaps I am just an incurable optimist. Whichever it was, I was certain that the coming months would be novel, productive, orderly, and fun.

In the beginning, before classes were over at Northwestern, my expectations seemed justified. Teaching was dull compared to the bookstore; I prepared my classes as quickly as conscience would allow and simply let them happen. If I felt any guilt, it vanished as I rushed home to find out what had happened that day in the bookstore. Thursdays I worked in the store myself. The hours were long, twice as long as an academic day. The work was physically demanding: lifting cartons, shelving books, standing up for hours. I wasn't used to it and at night my legs ached. But I liked my executive image — I was president of our three-person corporation — and it was reassuring to have pulled a new job out of nowhere. The six weeks before school was out were tiring but fun.

It wasn't until the middle of June that reality struck. Curt and I then began a six-day week, three each at work and three at home. But only on Friday was I free at home; Thursday and Saturday I cared for Sarah. I was appalled at how my time had vanished. At the back of my mind, regardless of the bookstore, I had expected the summer to open as usual before me. Instead, our daily routine swallowed me up: long days at the store; long days with Sarah; only bits and pieces of time grabbed in the evening, on Sunday, during her nap, to flesh out that pathetically short Friday. As I fell further and further behind the dissertation schedule I had set for myself, I became convinced that the bookstore had been a terrible mistake. Everything was a burden to me. I felt like a shopgirl in the bookstore, a maid when I was at home with Sarah. I felt trapped. I asked Curt to work in the bookstore a fourth day each week or to take Sarah all, not half, of Sunday. But he was feeling pressed for time himself. Out of desperation, I persuaded him that we should increase our babysitting. I first asked Mrs. Lowe to work five days a week instead of three. When she refused, I went to a neighbor whose babysitter, Mary, was looking for more work. Mary is a young, vibrant black woman; my neighbor recommended her highly. I hired Mary for two days a week on the spot.

That was even worse. Instead of using my new free time, I tormented myself with guilt over full-time care for Sarah. If she cried with one of the sitters, I was sure she was crying from neglect. If she was quiet, it had to be the quiet of despair. I rushed downstairs at every whimper to hold her or stroke her cheek, usurping Mary's or Mrs. Lowe's efforts to feed her, change her, get her dressed. I couldn't even trust her laughter. I was convinced that, for our own convenience, Curt and I were sacrificing Sarah.

As in all my crises of profession and motherhood, the issue behind my distress was one of self-image. Behind my fear that we were sacrificing Sarah to our careers lay the deeper fear that in buying the bookstore, I was sacrificing my "real" identity, my academic self, to an image in which I did not recognize myself at all. No one in my family had owned a business. I showed no trace of Curt's entrepreneurial expertise. The demands of the bookstore were unfamiliar and they went against the grain. What was I, the educated and literate college teacher, doing selling *The Joy of Sex* to conventioneers and *Fascinating Womanhood* to their wives? It seemed outrageous that the bookstore should crowd out my thesis, a higher-status enterprise, and one which represented an enormous investment of my time and energy. I wasn't about to give up that investment until I had another equally involving and satisfying one to take its place.

No matter how impossibly pressed for time I felt, I

never considered not finishing my thesis. The villain was the bookstore — or, increasingly, the money that allowed us to buy the bookstore. Instead of feeling relieved that Curt and I had the money to pay for more child-care and thereby to free me two days a week from the store, I blamed our income both for the store and for full-time care for Sarah. It didn't bother me that, strictly speaking, the money behind our child-care was Curt's and not my own. What bothered me was that the money, by making the bookstore possible, brought complexity rather than ease into my life. Many times I wished that we had no money at all, that circumstances would force me to choose between the store, my thesis, and the baby. Naturally I'd have had to choose Sarah, and in the back of my mind I knew that taking care of her full-time would make me miserable. Nevertheless, for a time I preferred the fantasy of giving up career for baby to the reality of splitting myself between thesis, baby, and bookstore. I told myself then that no career was better than two careers and a neglected baby. I suppose I half wanted Sarah to show signs of neglect so I could back out of the bookstore, cut our child-care to three days, and devote those three days to my thesis.

My distress was not entirely self-serving, however. There was a real concern for Sarah. It had been clear to me for years that I would have to have some child-care if I wanted to combine motherhood with career, but I had counted on the flexibility of an academic schedule, both for myself and for my husband, to make full-time care unnecessary. When Curt and I began discussing babysitters early in my pregnancy, we agreed that it was pointless to have a baby unless we wanted to spend a good deal of time taking care of it. I felt betrayed, and like a betrayer, in leaving Sarah to babysitters five days a week. Why had I become a mother if I could spare so little time for my baby?

Curt was sympathetic, with reservations. He felt that my

dilemma was of my own making: I had taken on too many responsibilities at once, and as a result, I had the added responsibility of balancing all of them. Although in the abstract he agreed that part-time care was preferable to full-time, he felt that full-time care was the obvious solution to my difficulties, and he had trouble understanding my reaction against it. His attitude reflected, in part, the class difference between us. His mother always had live-in maids and babysitters; he had grown up with daily child-care and had never felt neglected because of it. In my family, on the other hand, child-care was a luxury, and perhaps a faintly suspicious one. My parents rarely left my brother and me with sitters, evening or daytime. When my mother went back to work, he and I took care of ourselves after school. No one I knew, and no one I knew of, had daily paid child-care. Even when I myself needed it, it seemed outlandish and not quite legitimate to me.

Our attitudes about full-time child-care reflected our sex as well as our class, however. It was dismaying how quickly the traditional assumptions surfaced when we found ourselves so pressed: I felt guilty about leaving Sarah to go to work, and Curt felt guilty about leaving work to take care of Sarah. Again, our parents' households reinforced our attitudes. Curt's father and mine had worked a conventional week, and our mothers had been responsible for the children — in my case, until I was ten, and in Curt's case, until he grew up and left home. Fortunately, although our parents' sex roles were conventional, the partnerships were equal. In neither couple did one spouse dominate the other. Without that tradition of equality behind us, Curt's and my efforts to share domestic and professional life would be difficult indeed.

My distress over too little time and too much child-care lasted for six or eight weeks and then began to vanish. Circumstances didn't change, but my attitude did, partly because Sarah was so evidently happy, partly because full-time care put me back to work on my thesis. There were times even after that miserable summer when I felt that I never should have agreed to buy the bookstore, that in spite of the dwindling market for college teachers and my own exclusive standards, I ought to have found an academic place for myself. But as I grew more comfortable with the store and more aware of the difficulties that plagued my former teaching colleagues, that feeling eased. Now I find myself chafing at my thesis, resenting how it saps my bookstore energies and my time for Sarah. It may be, if my satisfaction with the store continues to grow, that ultimately I will put my thesis aside. To have put it aside in response to the first demands of the bookstore, however, would have been disastrous for me.

Buying the store would have brought some confusion even without Sarah. With her, it became a crisis: she consumed my time and energy when I had no reserves of either one. While in retrospect I agree with Curt that full-time child-care was the only practical solution to my distress, I continue to have serious reservations about it. Our baby-sitters now spend more time with Sarah than Curt and I do. Since they are loving, responsible women, I don't worry about Sarah's physical or emotional safety, nor do I fear that our sitters will teach her attitudes that conflict with Curt's and mine. We have been very lucky in finding women whose ideas about childrearing are similar to our own. As Sarah gets older, the opportunities for disagreement will surely increase, and Curt and I will have to be more alert about spotting issues early. At the moment, however, my objections are much more personal. With so much child-care I don't get to see enough of my baby. I have the sense of losing track of Sarah during the week, growing out of touch with her and then scrambling to renew the contact on Saturdays and Sundays. Though I am deeply absorbed in my work while I'm doing it, in the evenings, at lunchtime, at odd moments of the day, I am conscious of missing her. And I can't help feeling that if I miss Sarah, she must miss me too.

Curt and I are planning to begin a four-day child-care week very shortly, when I complete a first draft of my dissertation. Our babysitter will come Monday through Thursday, and he and I will take turns spending Friday at home with Sarah. That will make more of a difference to Sarah than it will to me, but I think it will ease my dissatisfaction somewhat. It should also be a schedule that we can maintain indefinitely, since it reduces neither my working time nor Curt's very much.

I am curious to see how Curt and I respond to the new schedule, since full-time care has spoiled us in some respects. I, for instance, am no longer the stickler for equal sharing that I used to be. When we had only three days of babysitting a week, I kept close watch on Curt's time with Sarah. If he weaseled out of even ten minutes of his share, he had to put up with my resentment and anger. Now if he does less than I do, the best I can muster is an abstract dissatisfaction. Extra time with Sarah is, at the moment, a pleasure.

The same thing has happened with the household work. Our babysitters clean as well as take care of Sarah, so the only chores left for Curt and me to do are shopping, cooking, and weekend dishes. I generally do more of these chores than Curt — two-thirds to one-third, perhaps. Again, this bothers me only in theory. I worry about what will happen if suddenly we can't afford housekeeping; I wonder how hard it would be to return to our pre-baby pattern of equal sharing. In practice, however, the time and work involved now are so minimal that I can't muster the intensity of need for equal sharing that I felt when Sarah was tiny. If things should change for the worse, I'm sure that intensity will be back in full force. Until then, I can only shake my head at the ease with which theory is vitiated by circumstance.

We began our schedule of full-time child-care in July, and by Sarah's first birthday, in October, we were comfortable with the new routine. Now that she is approaching her second birthday, I am beginning to get some perspective on what it is like to be a professional and also a mother. Combining parenthood with career continues to be demanding. Mornings between seven and nine and evenings between four-thirty or five and eight o'clock are pretty much devoted to Sarah. We have a leisurely breakfast, as leisurely as any meal can be with a two-year-old, and then play with her until the sitter comes. Evenings are more hectic, since all of us are tired by the time Curt and I get home, but we usually get through dinner and bedtime without too much distress. Weekends Curt and I split the child-care so that each of us can do something besides watch the baby, and we try to work in a couple of family projects as well.

Even with our careful scheduling and our full-time childcare, however, time for ourselves is at a premium. I budget energy between baby and work the way most people budget money, virtually every minute allotted to one project or another and virtually none left over. Before Sarah was born I squandered whole hours in daydreams, remembrances, self-scrutiny. Now I compress all such thoughts into ten minutes, morning and evening, on the train to and from the bookstore. One result is that my night dreams, always vivid, are astonishing in their length and complexity. Another is that on vacations I can't get myself to plan anything at all. Curt feels the pressure to budget time somewhat less than I because he is more realistic about the number of projects he takes on, but he too complains of not enough time to lie in a hammock, taking stock of himself.

Sometimes, if I fall behind schedule on my thesis or on some bookstore project, or if Curt has to go out of town, or if our babysitter gets sick, really if anything happens to disrupt our delicately-balanced routine, I get furious at the precariousness of my life. My anger is doubly frustrating because the stronger it gets, the more it hampers me in returning to whatever project I want to do. At its worst, it convinces me that my efforts to be productive are ludicrous and doomed to failure, and that in combining motherhood with career I am missing out on the best parts of both.

Fortunately those fits of anger grow less and less frequent as I feel more and more familiar with the limitations and advantages of life with a child. Sarah is more fun as she gets older, and I am beginning to see that, in spite of setbacks, my work does go on. Life has been on a continuous upswing since the shock of Sarah's birth. My life is too busy to permit the obsession with detail that plagued me as a graduate student and as a teacher. Sarah forces me to relax. No matter how immersed I am in some intricacy of my thesis, when the babysitter goes home I have to put my work aside and think about something else. That has been good for me; I now see my work not as my whole life but simply as one of its parts. Sarah limits me, but she stimulates me too. She surrounds Curt and me with development, growth, and change; I am as delighted with her mastery of a new word or game as I am with an improvement in the bookstore or a new chapter of the thesis. Each of those accomplishments is a confirmation of ability, a sign of progress along her or my developing life, and I value them both. I also value the intimacy that Sarah fosters between Curt and me. Our enjoyment of her deepens our own relationship; we are closer because we share the strains and pleasures of parenthood and career. My adjustment to motherhood has been strenuous, undeniably, because I am involved with my work as well as with my child. But what Sarah has taken away in freedom she has replaced in richness; my life is fuller and deeper because of her.

▲

In the spring of 1975, soon after we had finished the first *Balancing Act* essays, Curt, Sarah and I moved to a new neighborhood and hired a new housekeeper/babysitter, Virginia. Virginia came to our house four days a week and did all the household chores except shopping, cooking, and paying the bills, and with her help our daily lives became perceptibly smoother. But in spite of the new, smoother routine, unresolved issues loomed large in my life. Would I finish my thesis or concentrate on the bookstore? Would we continue with full-time or nearly full-time childcare, or would one or both of us cut down on our working time to spend more hours with Sarah? When would we have a second child, and how would we arrange our schedules to accommodate a new baby? To me these issues were a daily, intangible harrassment. I remember describing myself to a friend as a sideshow juggler who was absolutely destined to drop a ball.

My thesis was the most harrassing of these issues, because it was the most extraneous to my daily life. I had no idea of returning to the academic world — finding a desirable teaching job around Chicago had become an impossibility — but for my own satisfaction I wanted to finish my thesis if I could. So in July of 1975 I arranged a three-week leave of absence from the bookstore and went every day to the Northwestern University library. I was determined to see what if anything I could make of my thesis, and how long it would take me to get it written.

The first few days in the library overwhelmed me with nostalgia. The summertime silence there, the sunshine pouring through the windows, the familiar pages of my books — it seemed that five years had telescoped into nothing behind me, and I was a graduate student again.

But the work did not go well. I tried piecing my chapters together every possible way, and again and again it appeared that months of research and writing would be necessary to draw the material together. I could not both write the thesis and run the bookstore. Even more than that, I found I did not want to make the effort to do the work. It would have been terribly difficult to get free of the store to write my thesis. It would have meant hiring a manager or, possibly, selling the store, both major propositions. Still, I could have managed one or the other. I could at least have tried. But the fact was, I did not want to try. The huge effort of disentangling myself from the bookstore, and then the effort immediately following of taking on the research, laboring through the material, writing it up . . .

It was too much. I put my thesis in a drawer on a Friday, and on the following Monday I was back at the store, as though I had never left. I have not forgotten about my thesis, and from time to time the thought that I did not finish it brings a pang of regret. But the circumstances had become too difficult. I did not want to battle them, and I did not want the issue to drag on any longer.

That was in the summer of 1975. Sarah was almost two and I was thirty. We had a reliable housekeeper at home and two excellent part-time employees at the bookstore, and with the thesis out of the way, Curt and I decided it was a good time to have another baby. Perhaps the prospect of a baby — a new project — helped to soften the disappointment of the thesis. In any case, the decision required no soul-searching; we wanted the children to be close enough in age to know each other and be companions. I became pregnant in November, and the baby was due the following August.

My second pregnancy was very different from the first in that Curt and I felt comfortable with my changing figure and with the idea that we were going to have another baby. The help I needed was practical rather than emotional, so I depended less on Curt for support than on the women around me — Virginia at home and my two part-time employees, both women, at the bookstore. Curt had moved out of the bookstore early in my pregnancy and as far as work was concerned he was completely occupied with his growing business. I didn't expect his help in the store during my pregnancy or afterward, during my maternity leave, and in fact he could not have helped very much if he had had the time. The three of us in the bookstore had our own routines, and Curt had not been privy to them for months.

It was the other women in the bookstore — a bookkeeper and a young salesperson — who made it possible for me to enjoy my pregnancy without worrying about complicated arrangements for a maternity leave. They both committed themselves to staying at the store part-time until the baby was born and full-time from late summer through Christmas. I would return to the store in January, and then their special obligations would be over. It seemed to be a solid, secure arrangement, made in quite a feminist spirit of mutual support and cooperation.

At that time the atmosphere in the store was one of competence and energy. The three of us worked hard, and we enjoyed each other. That spring I felt less uncertain about my commitment to the store than ever before. It was a time of very little tension at work or at home. Curt was solicitous of me, and I made few demands on him. On weekends there were few chores, and Sarah's three-hour nap freed me for whatever work I wanted to do. It was an easy, gratifying time.

However, in June some tremors of difficulty began to be felt. Not in my belly; that was fine. The difficulty was at the bookstore. The young saleswoman began to hint that she wanted to move to New York, in August. Finally, in July, she announced that she would go. The bookkeeper and I each argued with her, but she was unshakeable. I left the store on July 23 for my maternity leave, planning to spend the two or three weeks before the baby was due in looking for a new salesperson. But on July 24, our son was born.

The labor was relatively quick and easy, much like my first though less overwhelming because I knew what to expect. Curt was with me — it was another Lamaze birth — and he, the baby and I all came through the delivery well. I experienced none of that lost vagueness that enveloped me after Sarah's birth, and it was a good thing, as I spent the third day of my hospital stay on the telephone, trying to find someone to work in the bookstore. After many hours of conversation with people I had never met, I hired a young man to work full-time along with my bookkeeper, at least through Christmas.

That day I spent making phone calls from my hospital bed stands out in my mind as the one day of my life when my version of combining career with motherhood corresponded to society's image of the successful career woman / mother. I did not agonize over the calls, because I knew that whatever happened or failed to happen I was invulnerable to the bookstore for a couple of months at least. No one could drag me back to the store with a newborn baby to take care of at home. The phoning was actually fun. I performed, for my hospital roommate and her many visitors, as the glamorous working woman not to be distracted by the mere birth of a baby, and I enjoyed the performance because I knew it was just a pose. At heart, I was eager to spend many weeks at home without the complications of bookstore matters.

Those few days in the hospital were the last in more than two months when I felt connected to the outside world. At home I was engulfed by the emotions of new motherhood. There is something about having a baby that makes every nerve cell in me feel over-sensitized and vulnerable. For the first two or three weeks after Joe was born, tears came to my eyes at the slightest occurrence — when the baby cried, when Sarah spoke to me or cried or laughed. I felt defenseless before my own emotions, so that I could hardly distinguish the joy and pleasure I took in my children from my anxiety when Joe nursed badly or Sarah had a tantrum of jealousy over the baby.

In my first *Balancing Act* essay I explained this vulnerability as the result of physical exhaustion. Now I recognize it as my own version of postnatal depression, though "depression" is much too negative a word. This heightened sensitivity did not frighten me, as it had after Sarah's birth, and I did not try to escape from it. In a way I welcomed it. My sensitivity seemed to erase the boundaries between me and my children; I felt as conscious of them as of the parts of my own body. At night I woke before the baby, and as I waited and listened for his cry I could almost feel the hormones surging through me, re-arranging my physical and psychic chemistry completely independent of my control.

After two or three weeks this vulnerability subsided and I began genuinely to enjoy my maternity leave. In enormous contrast to my months at home after Sarah's birth, this second leave was a joyful and busy time. I no longer needed reassurance that in becoming a mother I had not somehow lost myself. Because I felt relaxed and comfortable, everything was easier. I felt strong and energetic earlier, and breast-feeding was only a minor problem that mended itself as the days passed and Joe became more skillful at nursing. Virginia continued to come throughout my leave, so I was not saddled with the household chores. I spent my time with the children, trying to learn how to be the mother of two.

That was a considerable task. In the beginning my loyalties to the children felt terribly torn. I wanted to cuddle and cherish both of them at the same time, but that was impossible. Joe always had to come first because he was the new, tiny one, and every time I had to put Sarah off I felt guilty and heart-torn. She was terribly jealous of my nursing the baby. If I was alone with the children when Joe had to be fed she would climb up beside me and try to pull him away, and when I scolded her she burst into the most pathetic tears. Curt helped when he was at home, and for weeks he came home early so that he could help. But since I was at home all the time, the burden of Sarah's jealousy fell on me, and I did feel it as a burden — or rather as a problem that absorbed many hours of my time and thought. I felt engaged in important work during that maternity leave, while our whole family, but especially Sarah and I tried to find new connections in our relationships.

So the weeks passed until the end of September, when my bookkeeper phoned from the store to say that she was going into the hospital on October 11 for gall bladder surgery, and she would not return to work until after Christmas, if at all.

That was a blow. My bookkeeper knew the store inside and out; she had made it possible for me to hire a completely new employee without returning to the store, and she was also the bookkeeper! I had no idea how to do her work, or even altogether what her work entailed. I brought up the possibility of hiring another bookkeeper, though even that could not have protected me from having to go back to the store. *Somebody* had to be there who knew the customers and the routines.

Still, I asked her if she could suggest someone to take her place, and then the second blow fell. She said, "Quite frankly, I don't think you can afford it." She said that business had been falling off since my departure and that the store would be hard-pressed to keep up its accounts even without the drain of a bookkeeper's salary. She apologized for the news, and then she hung up.

I was crushed. Not so much that the bookstore was failing, though that was bad enough. No, the really bad news was that I could not afford a bookkeeper. I would have to go back to work; Joe would have to learn to take a bottle for at least one feeding a day, and I would have to go back. But how could I exist in the store without a bookkeeper? Sitting at that cramped desk all day, totalling up figures on the adding machine was a dismal prospect. I did not know how to do the work, and I did not want to learn.

Nevertheless, after many hours of debate with Curt and with myself, I decided I would have to learn. We discussed hiring a bookkeeper out of our own pockets — an expense of about $3,000 over the six months between October and April, when our lease expired—and we agreed that we would do it if I could not manage the accounts myself. But the store was my responsibility, I had agreed to buying it and I had agreed to run it. Much as I disliked the idea of going back and tackling the bookwork, I knew I had an obligation to try.

I returned to the store in mid-October, halfway through my maternity leave, when Joe was ten weeks old. I worked three, and then as Christmas approached, four days a week, leaving home at about ten in the morning and walking out of the store at four pm without fail. Joe usually missed just one feeding in my absence, and I was able to nurse him until he was seven months old. By objective measure my schedule was not onerous. In fact it was almost exactly the schedule I had returned to so gladly after Sarah was born. But though I felt it was my obligation to be back at the store, and though I gradually unravelled the mysteries of our accounts, I did not want to be there. I hated being there.

So Curt and I discussed the matter for the thousandth time, and we decided to sell the store if we possibly could. I insisted that if we could not sell it, we would go out of business at the end of April, when our lease expired. Curt did not hold this decision against me. He had hoped that I would like the bookstore and that the business would be a success, but he had known very well that we were taking a risk on both counts.

We did everything we could think of to sell the store that fall, with no success by Christmas. After Christmas I set myself to closing out the business, returning the books, holding sales, spending Saturday afternoons at home in the study, trying to make sense of our miserably overdue accounts while Curt babysat hour on hour. It was a dispiriting time, relieved only by thoughts of that magical date, April 30. I visualized our last day in business a hundred times that winter — the dusty shop empty around me, my embarrassed explanations to what few customers might wander by — but in late February, a miracle occurred. A customer said she wanted to buy the store, and buy it she did. It seemed unbelievable. On the twenty-fourth of March I was buried as usual among the ledgers, bank statements and sheafs of unpaid invoices, and on March 25, it was all over.

In *Passages*, Gail Sheehy talks about steps taken sideways along one's career path. The bookstore was one of those sideways steps. It was not all bad as an experience; it gave me a daily structure, somewhere to go and something to do, and it gave me a new set of skills. It had been pleasant, even exciting to work with the other two women to make the store reflect our tastes and to bring the sprawling business routines into good order. But contrary to what I had always believed, there are some kinds of work that I do not enjoy and cannot do well. I am a terrible salesperson. I hated catering to tastes that were not my own, and I never overcame the feeling that the customers were interrupting me, no matter how trivial the task that occupied me when they came in.

The bookstore also taught me something about the relations between employees and employers. That almost heady atmosphere of mutual support and mutual effort in the store lasted only as long as the work remained convenient to the employees. It collapsed at the first suggestion of conflict between loyalty to me and the store or loyalty to some private concern. I had regarded the women as friends, and I had depended on them to protect me from full responsibility for the store. But as Curt pointed out, it is hard to be altruistic on $3.50 an hour. The responsibility for the store was mine, whether I wanted it or not, and finally I had to accept every painful bit of it.

It was over this question of responsibility that my roles as professional woman and as mother collided head-on. In my three years at the bookstore I was continually having to decide which of my responsibilities — those at home or those at work — could most easily be handed over to another person, and my responsibilities at home almost always lost the toss. My maternity leave with Joe is the best example of this, but there were many times even in the best days of the store when business infringed on my hours at home. I always resented this and felt guilty about it. It seems to me that some careers are simply not compatible with parenthood — at least not with the kind of parenthood that involves a real commitment of time and energy at home — and running a retail business is one of them. When we sold the store, I was determined to find some kind of work for myself where responsibility for the day-to-day existence of the company did not belong to me.

There had been one final reason for my reluctance to return to the bookstore early. In the course of my weeks at home I had spent many hours with our housekeeper / babysitter, Virginia, and I had not been satisfied with what I saw.

Virginia was a large black woman whose priorities in childrearing were very different from Curt's and mine, but before Joe was born this seemed like an advantage. Every day she fixed a hot lunch for Sarah and herself, and she always dressed Sarah prettily to meet Curt and me when we came home. But she did *not* like to go to the park and would do so only if I specifically asked her to. Nor was she physically demonstrative. She showed her affection for Sarah by doling out peppermints from her pocket (I set a limit of two a day) and holding Sarah on her knee while they watched whatever soap it was that came on at 12:30 pm. She taught Sarah to put herself to bed at naptime and to push the bundles of dirty laundry downstairs to save Virginia the effort of climbing the stairs herself. At first it surprised me that Virginia would ask so young a child to do these things, but then it occurred to me that Sarah's efforts to be helpful contributed to their relationship. Sarah took her small tasks very seriously, and Virginia thanked her for doing them. In turn, when the laundry was finished Sarah thanked Virginia for washing and folding her clothes. There were a few occasions before Joe was born when I thought that Virginia's brusque manner intimidated Sarah, but in general Curt and I both thought it was a good thing for Sarah to experience a way of caring so different from our own.

All this changed after Joe was born. It was not that Virginia's manner toward Sarah changed, but that her way of handling Joe provided such a dramatic contrast to it. She doted on Joe, lavished attention on him, couldn't get enough of him, but toward Sarah she was as undemonstrative as ever. This was especially distressing because after Joe was born Sarah needed extra support and reassurance so badly. Curt and I were on the point of firing Virginia when the bookstore crisis came up, and then we changed our minds.

Virginia was familiar and reliable, and I had very little time to look for someone else. I was afraid of coming up with someone worse.

So Virginia stayed. That fall Sarah went to nursery school three mornings a week, where she had a wonderful time, and on the fourth morning I tried to arrange for her to play with the neighbor children instead of staying home. She did not spend hours every day feeling slighted by Virginia, and though Curt and I thought she seemed more subdued than usual during those months, she showed very little genuine unhappiness. Neither of us has been able to see any long-term effect on Sarah from that time. She certainly seems to have no unpleasant memory of it — lately she has been asking to visit at Virginia's house. But I regret having kept Virginia without trying to find a replacement. We gave her notice on the day that the store changed hands, and I felt that we had shed a year of bad situations all at once.

So in March, 1977, my life changed radically once again. For the first time, I was "just" a mother. It was exactly what I wanted to be. At home with my children, no longer any buffers of housekeeper or work between us, I felt that I was at last experiencing the pure facts of my life, and I was determined to let my future decisions about working and childcare be molded by those facts. I promised myself that I would not make a commitment to anything, not a job, not even to hiring a cleaning woman, until I was dead sure it was a commitment that I wanted to make, and one with responsibilities I could control.

That spring and summer passed in an atmosphere of supreme relief on my part, tinged with moments of nervousness about the future that I more or less successfully suppressed. The children and I took long walks to the park, looked up friends, and Sarah helped me fold the laundry outside at the picnic table while baby Joe played on the grass. It was instructive to be doing all the housework. I had never realized how much work it was to run our household, and a little flicker of sympathy stirred for Virginia. While I was working at the bookstore I had enjoyed my whole days with Sarah and Joe, but often in the morning of a day at home I had felt a flutter of apprehension — how would the time pass? Would the children be happy or cross? Would they nap well so I could have some time to myself? Now that feeling vanished. The days rolled by easily, and we all seemed to relax and thrive. I began to understand some of the attractions of a life without a career. It was low pressure in a way that we had not experienced since before Sarah was born, if ever.

But all that time — and this has its comic aspect, I know — a certain phrase kept repeating itself in my head. I did not consciously invent the phrase; it just welled up and spoke itself to me in odd moments, as though a Victorian great-uncle were lodged somewhere in the back of my brain. The phrase was, "That most commonplace of individuals, the woman of promise who comes to nothing." It was a distressing phrase, pompous but hard to dismiss. Was I really coming to nothing? (That I was a woman of promise I did not for a moment question.)

I had been trying to write during the children's naptimes, little bits of stories, ideas for magazine articles, even the very rough outline of a very short book. But none of those writing schemes ever got past stage one. After the initial interest of sketching out the idea, they bored me. The days began to seem long and lacking in stimulation. It was lonesome at home with no other adults around. Slowly it became clear that I could not put off considering the future any longer.

It was then, in the fall of 1977, that Curt asked me to think about working at the publishing company. He timed his offer very well, and he made it carefully, much more carefully than he had made the bookstore offer three years earlier. And I considered it carefully, from every possible (and some impossible) angles. We discussed salary, responsibilities, the pros and cons of working together as husband and wife, and then I meditated all of these on my own time, laboriously. I really tried as hard as I could to make a responsible, rational decision, and I am left with my old conviction that such decisions are finally not rational. Finally, we end up doing what we want.

A manuscript arrived at the office that fascinated me. Curt was interested in publishing it, but it was a mess, and no one at the office had time to put it into shape. *I* had time, and I wanted to do it — I was dying to do it. The children and I investigated childcare possibilities together. Joe was a charming but inarticulate one-year-old; Sarah, at four, an active participant. We inquired at numerous agencies, senior citizens' centers, and community groups, where, as I tried to maneuver Joe's stroller through the door, Sarah would walk up to the counter and announce, "We need a babysitter!" After two weeks of deadends, I stumbled across a situation where Sarah and Joe could spend the day together, with a faculty wife who had set up a daycare center in her home while her own children were small. The arrangement was ideal. We agreed on a modest starting schedule of 2½ days a week, and in November, 1977, I went to work at the company.

I joined the company as editor, but in the past four years my responsibilities have proliferated, and now I deal with manuscripts, authors, typesetters and designers and also with bookstores who are negligent about their overdue bills. At its best, my job draws upon my strongest skills, reading critically, writing a little, organizing detail. At worst it is not intolerable, because even the most routine task is crucial to the survival of the company. I like the flexibility in scheduling work hours and in taking on new responsibilities that is possible in a small business, and I like working with a small group of people toward a common objective. I feel as loyal and committed to the press as I think I am capable of feeling toward any business or institution.

My working schedule has varied from year to year, but now that Sarah is in second grade and Joe in an all-day nursery school, I have been working twenty-five to thirty hours a week, depending on what I can arrange for Sarah after school. With the help of a weekly cleaning woman and —the great luxury of my life—a college student who spends Thursday mornings washing and folding our clothes, everything that absolutely has to get done does in fact get done, both at work and at home. This to me is a triumph of scheduling.

After the upheavals that these two essays largely describe, it would be pleasant to conclude that life is easy, that all the conflicts have been resolved. Of course that is not true. I still get angry at Curt when I feel he is putting in too little effort at home; our marriage is a continuing history of policy statements, the airing of grievances, negotiation and compromise. I am still very busy, and pockets of leisure are still few and far between. But there is no doubt that life is far less stressful now than it was when our children were babies, and that I am no longer dominated by the problems of combining work with motherhood.

Sometimes I think that those first few years were difficult because of the career complications that descended upon us just when we were having our family. More often I am convinced that some such struggle is inevitable, that there can be no easy transition from work to working motherhood. However carefully one ponders the issues before a baby is born, the reality of that child is overwhelming. And I maintain that none of us, men or women, can speak with absolute confidence of our principles, attitudes, and assumptions about family life until we actually are in the midst of that family.

Before Sarah was born I knew that I wanted both parenthood and career, and I thought I wanted Curt to share the responsibilities of parenthood equally with me. It took me four years to realize that I want to spend less time at work than Curt does, and more with the children. And it has taken me more than four years to acknowledge this without suffering a flood of embarrassment at being, after all, so conventional.

What would have happened had Curt been as anxious as I to spend time at home? Would we have divided the household tasks amicably between us? Would I have been enough reassured by his capable handling of domestic matters to become more involved than he in outside work? Would we have competed over household responsibility? This last seems as possible to me as any of the others. However, social expectations are at least as deeply ingrained in Curt as they are in me. He has always been willing to share in some domestic responsibility, but equal sharing is not one of his goals. And I am startled to see how negative my youthful feminism was, to regard motherhood as legitimate only if its responsibilities were shared equally by men.

Now when I step back to survey my life, I am most curious about what it means to be involved in a family business. Certainly our work draws Curt and me together, so much so that on Saturday mornings, when our shop talk drives the children upstairs to the television, I have sometimes felt that we exclude them. However, friends who grew up in family businesses assure me that as the children get older they make a place for themselves. Lately, I have been imagining Sarah and Joe as teenagers, putting in summers at the warehouse, coming down on the train to meet us for dinner in the city, helping with office errands at busy times of the year — pleasant daydreams of opportunities I think I would have loved, and that I hope will someday appeal to them. We have made a small start by spending Saturdays at our new office, where Curt and I clean and paint while the children climb on the boxed-up pyramids of books.

Joining the company has also given a great boost to my more relaxed attitude toward time at home. When I first thought about combining work with parenthood, I envisioned a pressured, head-on conflict for time between my husband and myself, to which equal sharing of household duties would be the only possible solution. To some extent we experienced that conflict when Curt was running the business and I was trying to finish my thesis and manage the bookstore. But since I joined the company, our business and domestic lives feel to me like a continuous round, a single mutual effort. It is hard for me to weigh accomplishments at work very differently from accomplishments at home, or to feel that one has enormous precedence over the other. At the same time, my spending extra hours at home gives me the sense of a separate domain, an area of separate effort, which is gratifying after all the hours we spend in the office together.

The company has also given me a new idea of success. As a young woman with high ideals and ambitions but only two years' work experience as very junior faculty member, I associated success with creative, individual effort, such as that involved in writing a thesis or teaching a class. Success at the publishing company, on the other hand, is a team success. Our sales have doubled, tripled and quadrupled over the past few years, and our books have received, if not national acclaim, certainly national respect and recognition. I can claim a share in both of these achievements, and I am proud that our small business has survived and flourished at a time when so few do. But working on these *Balancing Act* essays has reminded me how pleasant it is to finish an individual project, to exclaim, "It's mine! I've done it!" Perhaps under the impetus of *The Balancing Act II*, I'll take on another, larger editing and writing project of my own.

II

I am reassured that when my basic home and family security is re-established, my artistic drive will revive, probably in new arrangements. But now I am content to be just a mother.

JAYME CURLEY

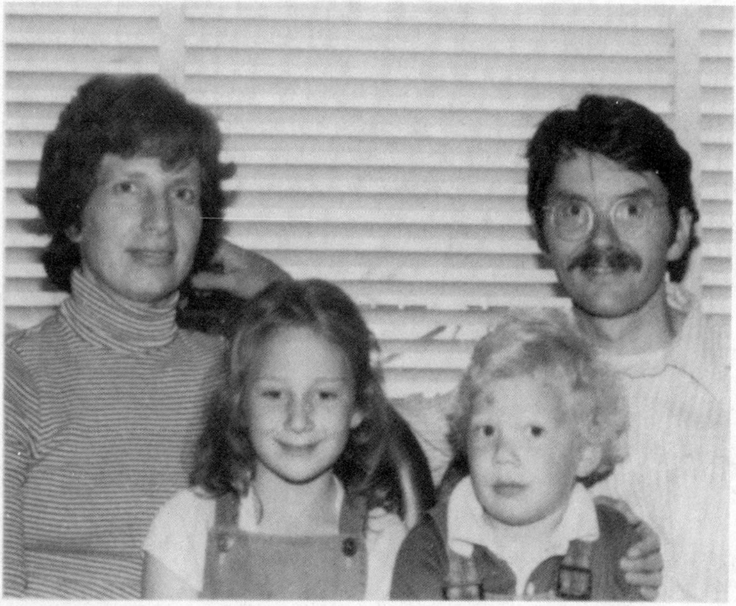

Jayme Curley

I am a thirty-two year old parent, spouse, and artist with short but intense and varied experiences in trying to combine these roles. My personal history is a fitting prelude to an adult life of uncertain outlines. Growing up, I tried hard to please far too many people, and I suspect I still tend to do that. While I was possessed with the energy of a teenager, I polished my ability to be sensitive and artistic to please my mother. I was an eager disciple to my father's knowledge of nature, money, and politics; virginal, musical, and obedient to please the older cousin who raised me from the age of five until I left for college; able to earn money and get good grades in school to please her husband. To keep up with my two much older and married sisters, and to please all of my family, I tried to be a reasonable prospect for upper middle class housewifery and motherhood, but I had little grasp of or talent for the actual qualities that would demand. The general feeling was that a career would be acceptable if I failed at marriage and raising children (and that failure appeared to be a distinct possibility), but the career should certainly give way to those other more important jobs if I managed to secure them.

I married when I was twenty-nine, by which time I'd been deterred from this primary goal of mine long enough to explore some of the alternatives, which I still felt were second-best. I had earned a B.A. in art history, a Master's enabling me to teach art (which I did for three years), and later a Masters in Fine Arts. The process of getting that last degree resulted in a commitment to sculpturing which I think of as my career. My husband, David, was working toward his Ph.D. in Asian Studies at the University of Chicago.

Before Shona was born, our lives together seemed to require little adjustment. We continued our separate careers, kept our finances separate, took turns doing the chores, and had time for hiking, camping, tennis, talking — being together. We tried to establish the habit of bargaining about household responsibilities. We alternated jobs rather than dividing them, so there were no "man's" jobs or "woman's" jobs. One person shopped and cooked one week, cleaned house the next.

Usually my work seems relevant to my personal preoccupations. I draw the imagery of my sculptures and drawings from some flow of continuous half-consciousness at the back of my head. For example, I made playful sexual pieces and marriage monuments when David and I were first married; incubating potatoes growing through a satin quilt as we were deciding to have a child; buckled things unbuckling, valleys being split, nests, eggs, pillows, clouds, and a cookie jar lady with great bare breasts as the birth approached. I usually worked on several pieces, each at different stages, some being built from slabs of wet clay, some needing a coat of colored slip, some to be loaded into or pulled out of the kiln, some needing underglazes, glazes, drawings, lustres, or decals on their surfaces. Often I was under pressure to dig up packing boxes and foam rubber, and to fill in forms to send a piece to a competition or ceramic show. There were trips to get supplies and deliver pieces to galleries or Railway Express, or to pick them up.

I enjoyed meeting deadlines for shows and the large hassle of preparing for an art fair every summer. Friends from the Art Institute and art-related activities gave me an informal bunch of colleagues, and becoming a member of one of the cooperative women's art galleries in Chicago provided me with a source of stimulation, moral support, and liveliness.

During my last year of sculpturing, before I got pregnant, I became involved in a competition between graduating students of the school of the Art Institute which, if I won, could result in admittance to a loftier competition to be exhibited in the Art Institute itself, and in possible prize money. To enter one had to prepare and present a professional-level show of work. This required an intense build-up of involvement in a project. There were hours of preparing the setting for my pieces; canvas stretched on large frames and starched taut to make temporary uncluttered walls; risers borrowed or built or painted, appropriate to each piece; hauling, arranging. The show was the culmination of three years of work for me, and I succeeded in it: I won the first competition and, later, the second. My career seemed well under way.

But there was a complication looming on the horizon. Early in our marriage, David and I had agreed that we wanted children sometime. I assumed our equal-sharing would continue in some slightly altered form after we had children. This was an easy assumption to make since for David, sharing was (and is) vitally important. He said that he didn't want to miss out on the home side of life as many American fathers seem to do, that he wanted to be "rescued" from burying himself in his work and perhaps also from the competitiveness of an all-absorbing career. And he wanted a partner who had commitments outside of the home, parallel to his, a source of intellectual liveliness which he could share. For all of these reasons, he was happy to give up some of his work time to free me to do my art. In fact when I, for one reason or another, was avoiding my career, I felt considerable pressure from David to get at it again. This entirely satisfactory attitude on his part, combined with our solid history of sharing, allowed me to avoid certain realities as we considered having a child. I didn't ponder the warning that a child was a full-time job, and that that meant there could only be one full-time or two half-time jobs between us. I didn't squarely face the fact that we could each have only a partial career, would be handicapped compared to colleagues with more time, and would have to relinquish full-scale competitiveness. I vaguely figured that his academic career and my art career could each be compressed to make room for parenting. I didn't bother finding anyone who had done that. I was not thinking of our lives as one whole, but as two separate entities. I did not foresee how having a child would force us to share a much larger portion of our lives and make us much more dependent upon each other. In short, I didn't consider the probable situation very concretely or seriously. I wanted children and our lives could just fit around that. A baby (or two) would just be fitted into our secure twosome like an extra cat or dog. We'd divide the extra chores in half as we'd always done. I'd bring home some of my work, so could David, and we'd do it while the hypothetical baby slept.

Careless with the future of our careers — or my career. Despite our avowed equality, I covertly held intact the assumption I was raised with: David's career came first. If we ran out of time or money, I would be ready to give up my work to allow David his. I had chosen an unstructured career which could survive (I hoped) interruptions and fallow periods. In fact, before we married, I decided on my own, and announced to David, that if he went to India sometime in the future (a likely prospect, given his area of study) I would drop whatever I was doing and go with him. I used this voluntary concession to his career to get him, a year later, to agree to the crucial decision to have a child before, rather than after, our now certain trip to India. I won the right to have a baby (at the expense of both our careers), while David won the right to further his career by taking us all to India (at the expense of my career).

Since at the time of our decision to have a child I had one year's work still to do for the M.F.A., and David had four to do for his Ph.D., and since we were dependent upon grants, some income from a trust, and a little from my ceramic sales, both our careers and our finances would have been better established if we had waited to have the baby until after the trip. However, I would have been thirty-three years old by that time, and that fact influenced me strongly in favor of having a child sooner rather than later. David was less sure that this was sound and would rather have waited, although he couldn't see that any future time would be that much easier or better. In order that a child be old enough to survive India, we would have to hurry up and get our baby under way even before I left art school. Again I put something — in this case, my physical safety and comfort and that of our hypothetical child — ahead of the smooth advancement of my career. (Ironically, India provided us with a wild assortment of discomforts, illnesses, and distresses probably much more difficult than any that would have resulted from having our first child a few years later.) I also figured that India would be such a disruption of my sculpturing that I might as well combine it with the disruption of having a first child. This mode of thinking effectively sabotaged my career.

Trying to override David's hesitations, I offered to give up more and more of my working time to assure him his. He felt that I was "just saying" this, that I didn't actually believe we would come to such a time squeeze. He was correct. One night, however, he pressed me so persistently that I cried out that I was being pushed into a corner. I had to promise that I'd do *all* the baby care if necessary. Finally he felt I took his concern with time seriously. He realized that it would never be too difficult to bargain time from me in a pinch. He knew that in the short run, he would be saved from our equal sharing by the trip to India. And he also knew that he had made it clear to me that his career was the most important thing to him, while having a baby was the most important thing to me. This difference in priorities continued, in fact, even after the baby arrived. A common breakfast-time confusion during our first few months of parenting illustrates this. I would ask David which shift he wanted — morning or afternoon — meaning which Shona-shift he wanted. He would assume I was asking which part of the day he wanted free to work.

Once our time problems and priorities were as settled as they could be, we began to try to have a child. I became pregnant quickly and was enormously pleased. During the first three months I would gladly have taken advantage of the necessary physical adjustment and the sleepiness to slack off in my work and revel in being pregnant. But since I had succeeded in the first Art Institute competition, which had been held before I got pregnant, I was forced to maintain the pace and prepare for the final one. I had now to produce four or five additional pieces to sharpen and fill out my collection of sculptures. It was a demanding and satisfying time. However, I was beginning to withdraw from some of the more strenuous things David and

I had always done together (jogging, tennis, hiking, etc.). David had to give up some of his expectations of me and, at the same time, give me extra support (such as taking over the bulk of the cooking when food smells became unpleasant to me) and extra understanding (such as accepting my gluttonous desire for sleep).

No sooner was the final competition over, me garlanded with acclaim and a prize and many sales, than I dove into the setting-up of a studio/workshop with a friend. I also began illustrating two children's books. I was riding a big crest, to be followed later in the year by the inevitable backwash and what-next crisis. David meantime had had much less reward for his labors and began to feel pressure to finish most of his academic work before the expected arrival in six months' time of our child. He, at least, anticipated a severe reduction in his career time and energy. I blithely ignored such considerations and continued committing myself to projects and shows for after the baby's arrival. I ignored the probability that having to push myself after we had a baby might result in my getting sick and/or in infringements upon David's fair share of free time and energy. I assumed I had reservoirs of strength which, as it turned out, I did not have.

With our studio set up, the competition successfully behind me, and a gallery I respected taking my work, I sailed light-heartedly into the enjoyment of pregnancy. The future looked rosy, especially as I was so easily able to ignore the realities of becoming a parent. I did however feel a slight warning jolt when, at six months, the nurse lecturing to our class of parents-to-be began referring to "your baby." This phrase sounded so actual and concrete. David was upset too. That night he drove through a red light. We went directly to an ice cream parlor to recover ourselves. He redoubled his efforts to get his big papers, exams, and interviews done.

I began excusing myself from some of the creative demands of my work, (I now see) and falling back on older ideas and techniques. I began to ask my studio partner to shoulder some of my teaching responsibilities in return for doing chores which didn't require that I drive at night when I was exhausted. My continuing quantity of production lulled me into thinking pregnancy was not interfering with my work. In fact, a lot of my psychic energy was turning inward. I made things for "our baby" and began pressuring David to make furniture, not realizing how carelessly I slighted my work, or how I assumed he should do the same. Somehow he did meet all of these demands without ever losing his temper. He even left us a week or so together, pressureless, before the baby was due. By then I was working only half-days and concentrating on the amazing changes within my body.

Shona's birth was momentous and wondrous and exciting beyond anything either of us had anticipated, an experience which soldered us together and simultaneously flung us miles apart. After the event, which was as uncomplicated as the examples in the Lamaze handbook, I settled down excitedly in the congenial hospital with our eight-pound, red-faced cuddly baby, and David went home to a departure-scrambled, empty apartment. For five days, he was just a hospital visitor. But once we were home he became as much her parent as I was, aside from the fact that I nursed her while he (somewhat later on) fed her a bottle. Thus ended our leisure.

For the first eight months of Shona's life, we were at home in our four-room, third-floor apartment. We were "at home" as we'd never been before — at least two of us at a time for most of the twenty-four hours of the day. Taking Shona outside in the winter (she was born about Christmas-time) was not easy or fun. The apartment was getting much more use than before and got dirtier. More cleaning up. More meals at home. More laundry, which was tricky as the machines were down three flights of stairs, a walk outside, and through three locked doors — all with the laundry under one arm and the baby under the other.

There was a quick end to fancy or laborious meals and to all bread-making. Tidiness, which was my particular interest, crumbled. Entertaining vanished, to resurface months later as Sunday brunches (evenings we were usually tired and frazzled.). We clung to our equal sharing, but out of twenty-four hours in a day, we could each only muster three to four hours to do work out of the house, and that was on a good day. There were frequent not-so-good days when Shona would have a cold and require extra patience and care from us, or I would have a cold (or worse). And since even with four hours free, some part of those hours were spent getting where we were going, and some in settling down to work, we each got less than half the time to work that we were accustomed to. I felt as if the pregnancy had prepared me for this in a way, forcing me to adjust, slow down, the baby absorbing my energy and attention. Those nine months had cranked my gaze away from outside concerns and focused it on the spot where Shona amazingly appeared. It was with some reluctance and resentment, and a rigid urge to prove I could do it, that I cranked it back around to sculpturing for three hours each day.

Here are some excerpts from the diary I kept after Shona's birth:

4/17 A friend is in Chicago for a week with her baby a month and a half older than Shona. She is doing all the care for him. I feel a twinge of jealousy. Isn't it a woman's *right* to stay home with her children, withdraw from the competitive professional "man's" world?

Sometimes I long for the security of the traditional female role despite the fact that I've made a definite choice not to have it. Actually I would resent having to do the house and child work that David does now. I'd feel stagnant and confined. My ambivalence.

5/23 I'm greedy for Shona's dependence on me. Notice myself trying (successfully) to steal her glances and smiles from David. Vying for her favors. Trying to stop this unhealthy competition. Something to do with my confusion over what my role in life should properly be. This confusion is exaggerated every time I go home and am partially seduced by the life I was raised to lead (full-time mother with wealth and leisure). Scanning our four-room apartment for signs of the wall-to-wall carpeting and housekeeper I deserve. Where is the time to play tennis? Why should I take my sculpting seriously? Isn't it more important for me to have pleasant mornings than productive ones? Wrap my baby around my life. I need to shore up my confidence in the life David and I have worked out for ourselves.

David had some difficult adjustments to make too:

4/23 David describing himself sending me off to work in the mornings: gets out of bed and changes the baby's diapers and hands her to me to nurse; hurries in to make our and her breakfasts; spooning cereal into her mouth as he fixes the coffee; calling me in to eat (me all dressed, he in his pajamas still); he holds the baby and tries to eat; I leave; he drinks another cup of coffee. Househusband. Waiting for my return with news of the "world."

But despite the obvious fact that his work was drastically cut down by his parental responsibilities, he never shirked them:

> 5/27 David said today that he's re-evaluating his life goals, accepting the prominence of family life and the resultant lowering of career ambitions. When Shona and I were gone last week, he realized how important his family life has become to him; felt maybe the sixteen hour work days he has been missing are no longer essential to him. I'm glad.

We both shared an ambivalence about our new life, but on the surface things continued to be productive. In the first seven months of Shona's life, David made good progress on his thesis, and I worked on a series of new and larger (up to five feet long) sculptures. I participated in five shows, exhibited entire groups of pieces in two of them and in a summer art fair. Classes continued (anemically) at our studio, although I didn't teach as often as before. I felt that I was fully engaged in my work. However, when I began to take a serious look at where I was, prior to leaving on our trip, I began to doubt the quality of the work I'd done. Another excerpt from my journal:

> 5/3 Looking at the sculptures I've produced during the last four months in painstakingly eked-out two-hour stretches, it doesn't seem worth it. They are not spectacular successes. And three months (the three immediately following the baby's birth) just isn't such a huge chunk of time to relinquish. Next time I will be more relaxed and drop out.

And in a long, painful talk with the woman who had shown faith in me by asking me to show some pieces in her fine ceramics gallery, we both agreed that my last year's work did not have the vitality and integrity we'd hoped for.

When I examine my journal for an explanation, I find that it contains almost no entries directly concerning my work plans or experiences. Although I had originally intended it to specifically address the problems of combining motherhood and career, I wrote instead about logistics (how to get away to the studio, how to keep my breasts from bursting while I was there) or of fantasies during the drives to and from the studio, and not the work itself. The journal is, however, crammed full of my feelings about and observations of Shona, and the new snarls, tangles and intricacies in David's and my relationship resulting from her birth.

Once David's research trip became definite in April, I withdrew even more energy from my work to prepare for this further momentous change. I kept at sculpturing only in order to make a body of work for an important show at the cooperative women's gallery in July. Those were the last pieces I made, and I have not discovered many germs for further pieces in them. My sketchbook at that time was devoid of new ideas. Instead, it contained lists of the ninety-eight pounds of things the three of us could take for our sixteen months in England, India, and Bangladesh. I managed with difficulty to finish the last few illustrations for a book I'd been working on with a friend. I had a few illustration projects in mind to do as we traveled. Otherwise, my career was in mothballs. And I was relieved.

I just didn't have the energy to cope with my pre-baby life as well as with the demands of the new baby. I forced myself to continue working at a reduced version of my career partly because of my need for an exoskeleton of orderly routine, a sort of emotional girdle which I tried desperately to preserve after Shona's birth despite (perhaps because of) the drastic changes brought on by parenting. In fact, however, my emotional focus had begun to shift away from my art and toward motherhood even before Shona was born.

For instance, when I was pregnant I felt an unprecedented urge to become affiliated with a church, and began attending Quaker services. The first time I went, a phrase came to me: ". . . to surround the child within me with love."

That nest-building instinct extended outside David and me into our community and our families after Shona's birth. From my journal:

> 2/20 Thinking about how our having Shona has put the whole human race in a different light for me. Sharing this with many other people. I see people on the street and speculate about their infancy, whether or not they are parents, what that might mean to them. I have an immediate physical response to babies, feel I could mother any one of them. Last September, talking with my sister, saying I was a misanthrope. Change must be due to the concreteness, intimacy of having my own child.
>
> 3/26 A vault over the line between generations; unsuspected affinities with our parents. Unmarried people and couples without children seem substantially different from us. I feel protective towards friends who are pregnant now.

I felt a new bond with people in general that I had never felt before.

And Shona's birth definitely changed my attitude towards the role of order in my life; my need for order had to yield under the pressure of her demands. Although at first I spent energy trying to keep our increasingly used and dirty apartment tidy, the job was endless and I eventually relaxed. Likewise, although I did despair of the messiness of untimely leaking breasts (often during the drive home from the studio, or when I felt unusually sorry for some adult, or during the night — milk-wet sheets upon waking), I gradually became more tolerant of basic bodily disorder as well:

2/24 Messiness, the anathema of the visually tidy. Blood, sperm, milk, sweat, saliva. All the messy elements are pertinent to babies. Yesterday, I walked home from the butcher's with, among other things, a pound and a half of raw liver trimmings for the cats. When I got upstairs, I realized the liver had leaked blood through the paper which had run through my mittens and all down my jacket and pants. I was amazingly unperturbed.

I discovered a "psychic tidiness" in myself through its disruption.

3/5 Time —
doling it out with precision
harboring it
balanced/measured
down the drain!
It all flows together — no important boundaries —
let it go.
Recover sleep when you can't resist it any longer.
Naps.
The fragile structures I've always protected. Got to get eight hours of sleep a night. Got to eat three solid meals a day. Got to be on time. Got to keep clothes neat, clean. Got to maintain visual order around myself. All I've got to do now is make do!

I never felt (or allowed myself to consciously feel) resentment towards Shona for the discomforts of these relinquishments, but my occasional blow-ups measured the strain.

Ironically, I noticed my need for order and control in sex as that very need diminished. (I find I discover these things about myself only when I am forced to change them, or when I suddenly see that I have in fact changed them.) Theoretically, if ours was a marriage of equals, our sex life should have been no exception. However, some insecurity had made me be more comfortable as the more passive partner. But my sexual self-assurance got a marked boost when I accomplished the womanly feat of becoming pregnant. I felt less self-conscious and obliged to demonstrate my pleasure to David. As a result, I enjoyed it all much more. And once we resumed sex, I noticed that giving birth had increased this effect. I caught sight of the tail end of the orderly attitude which had been replaced when, one time, I noticed myself not keeping track of my surroundings and suddenly knew that I always had. I must always have kept the scaffolding of "where I am," "What's on the stove," "are the sheets tucked in," firmly in place between David and me during our lovemaking because at that moment I saw it all melt away. That was good, and got better. But I wore myself to such a physical frazzle during the first half year of Shona's life that I was often too tired to enjoy this happier sex. My exhaustion began to make the emotional demands of mothering and wifeing seem too great. My sexual appetite sagged. Sometimes I resented David's enthusiasm. I felt already used up.

Part of what used me up was breast feeding. I had always assumed I'd nurse our child. Both my older sisters and my friends had nursed their children and were enthusiastic. I assumed it was the easiest, healthiest, and most natural way to feed a baby. And, in fact, breast feeding Shona was basically a cosy and loving process, highly satisfying to the two of us. David also liked seeing us at it. I felt directly responsible for and proud of Shona's voluptuous abundance and cheeriness.

On the other hand, the very worst moments of those early months were due to problems with breast feeding. I was unprepared for anything to go wrong with it. My gynecologist apparently was too. Or at least he was unprepared to deal with any difficulties by means short of instant weaning. I have since talked to women who learned simple, direct ways of taking care of plugged ducts (wet heat, massage, rest, lots of nursing, and an antibiotic to prevent infection); but when I developed a plugged duct, my doctor gave me conflicting advice (dry heat for two days, then ice packs for two, don't touch it, treat it like a sprained wrist), and no realistic sense of what was going on or how it was likely to develop. I was sick for nineteen days. It was a frightening experience. I got such a high fever that I was slightly delirious. It was unnerving to have the doctor predict "recovery in twenty-four hours" and not to have improved at all by then. He suggested that I immediately stop nursing. But I'd heard from friends that that was the most dangerous thing to do, that that could magnify the problem and even lead to surgery. It was a miserable, debilitating, three week experience. Two months later, when I felt the familiar warning tingles in the same breast, I panicked and decided to follow the doctor's advice to wean Shona. (You can't flog a dead horse," he said.) Given how run-down I was and the strenuous months of travel ahead of us, it was probably a good decision. But the process was horrible. I suffered badly from the suddenness of it:

> 4/24 A slow day. My breasts look like the fronts of Cadillacs and ache all the way under my armpits. I stopped letting them leak after talking to the doctor

again. (He called me a cow. Thanks.) He said not to touch them. Shona's pediatrician, whom I'd called about something else, said to leak them or else they'd pop. I love all this unanimity. I let them leak. Bliss. Two little jars on the dining room table, one under each gratefully dripping tit. Plop.

4/25 This weaning has turned out to be horrid and upsetting. My breasts are huge and hard and tender, and I can't cuddle Shona because of them, which makes it even harder to have given up the pleasures and closeness of nursing her eight times a day. I feel a mile away from her. She smiles at me from David's arms.

Finally, at breakfast, I burst into tears. Brutality of this process. Losing the special ability to feed and comfort my baby. David says now I'm no more special than a father.

While I was nursing, a lot of my physical energy had gone into just producing milk for Shona and being awake eight times a day to offer it. It was emotionally tiring too to be constantly aware of my function as cafeteria, as much when I was away at the studio as when I was at home. I enjoyed being so important to her, but I was also irritated by it, resenting the messiness and the intrusion into orderliness and tidiness of my self and surroundings. Sometimes I resented the lack of freedom to be physically absent. Of course, David was fettered by parenthood too, but I flattered myself that I was more inexorably so. Trying to get Shona's appetite, my milk supply, and our working times all coordinated was often frustrating:

3/21 Coming home from the studio with my breasts aburst, only to find Shona quite full enough. I somehow can't accept that and keep shoving her at the nipple. Suck. Holler. Jets of milk all over us both. Frustration! Have to give up and catch the leaks in little jars. Sigh.

Although I'm sure I'll nurse our next child, that will be all I'll do for the first few months. I just don't have the physical energy to take care of a baby and maintain my usual pace and life style.

Despite my hardships with nursing, I didn't consider giving up my work or hiring baby care, and as a result, my health suffered. It took us seven months to realize the kinds of prices we were paying to maintain equal sharing with no help and both of us working:

> 7/8 I'm acutely aware of energy drains: constant attention to Shona, nursing, sex, the less tangible demands of a partnership (moral support, interest in another's feelings, projects, needs), climbing stairs, getting organized to leave the house. The smallest efforts seem to count. I have no energy margin, just barely enough to do the minimum. Depressing. Even my walk has changed to a simply functional slumpy, unalert gait. Low. (Help.) How can I build up the reservoir of energy I anticipate needing to cope with our trip?

> 7/8 When I get sick (which is every few weeks lately), David's support soon wears thin. The burden is too much for him. I feel (and resent) pressure to make love and to resume my work duties and to pay him back for the extra work he has had to do, before I'm feeling well. I feel guilty for getting sick and dumping my share of the work on him, so I yield to all these demands and stay sick longer. Stupid.

7/16 Shona has caught the cold I have just recovered from. David and I were up six times with her last night, she sweaty and coughing. Of the 203 days of her life, she has been sick fifty days with colds, two with stomach aches. I've been sick seventy-four days with colds and the breast infections. David, fifteen days with colds. What a mess we've been.

David had to give up his rightful work time to prop us up during these breakdowns at precisely the time he was under pressure to prepare for his year of research. When unexpected crises occurred in my family on the West Coast, the effort of flying out with Shona and dealing with them left me totally depleted. I had already plundered my energy reserves.

In the months after Shona was born and before our trip to India, we could have conserved energy and provided more time for our careers by hiring someone to care for Shona. That would have been a financial strain, but our reluctance was more complicated than just a lack of money would indicate. Our family backgrounds had, each in their separate ways, convinced us to care for our child without paid help.

David's mother had cared for her children by herself with limited help from her husband. She had maintained her major outside interest, an active religious affiliation, all through the raising of their three children. Outside baby care had been infrequent and in the form of leaving the children with a relative or friend for a specific occasion. (She thought regular daytime babysitters "ruined" children.) Mothering had been one of her major expectations and pleasures in life. The same had been true of my family, but this attitude was badly complicated by enormous crazy pressures to keep astride the unsteady new economic, academic, and social peaks in Seattle at the expense of simpler satisfactions. My mother was devastated by a series of breakdowns, often leaving the raising of us four children to housekeepers, and reluctantly gave up both her marriage and her children when I, the youngest, was five. Since then, she has tried to the best of her abilities and opportunities to resume her parental role. She had been accustomed to having household help, but thought of herself, I think, as primarily a mother. She wrote poetry, but didn't see it as a profession and has not pursued it. The cousin who then raised my next older sister and me was paid by our father for our upkeep. She did a large part of the job herself, albeit with household help, and kept her musical interests alive so that they've blossomed as parenting has lessened. So in both David's and my families, the women expected first to raise their children and to continue their other interests (not careers) as they were able.

I cannot help associating paid care (I keep wanting to call it "paid love") with my mother's frightening breakdowns and my imagined rejection by her. I also associate it with what I saw as my rejection by both my parents when we were sent to live with our cousins, and later, by my father's ultimate desertion— his death when I was seventeen. I feel negative about leaving Shona with people other than David or me because of these associations. I imagine that she'll feel rejected and abandoned as I did. I identify with other people's children who are routinely left with sitters, feel their imagined grief at seeing "too little" of their parents. I feel hostile towards hired sitters and "callous" parents.

> 4/3 Out for a walk. We saw a black woman pushing a stroller with a white baby in it. She came to the curb (we had been carefully lowering Shona in her pram off and onto the curbs) and WHAM, sailed right over,

PLOP BUMP, without breaking stride. David: "Mother's aide."

7/6 I feel hostility towards the one family in our apartment building where both parents work full-time. I see and hear (and identify with) their little boy's distress. On the other hand, I'm jealous of our friends who can afford daily substitute parents, to the extent that their children seem contented with this arrangement.

My journal from this time has an inordinate number of outraged descriptions of stray dogs struck down or in danger of being killed by cars on the drive to my studio. I've just realized these sad creatures represented the "abandoned children" of our society to me. I would not "abandon" our child.

My strong (irrational) feelings account for my surprising disinterest in figuring out a broader range of child-care arrangements before Shona arrived. But by the time she was six months old, I began to relax a little. David's reluctance centered around the state of our finances, but he was now under enough pressure that he also began to see how some babysitting could be worth the money. I was exhausted, and we had a hectic summer ahead of us. Before Shona was born, we had talked with friends about organizing "condensed" babysitting, with one or two adults at a time taking care of the four new children; but it proved to be too complicated to transport and synchronize our babies and ourselves. Our friends hired regular daytime sitters. Eventually David and I arranged to pay a neighbor, who had sat for friends and was trying to get pregnant herself, to take Shona for three hours twice a week. What a relief! Shona was quite content, and we had some breathing space. This was an entirely different magnitude of child care from that where both parents pursue full careers while the child is cared for by a professional sitter. It was the kind of child care that I could live with. Possibly, if we had been able to stay in Chicago and make those six hours of babysitting part of our ordinary routine, I would have pulled out of my exhaustion and revitalized my languishing interest in my work.

But two months into our babysitting arrangement with the neighbor, David, Shona, and I left for our sixteen-month-stay in England, India, and Bangladesh. The trip was even more disruptive than I had anticipated. The minute we reached England I became an all-day rather than a half-day parent. David's days were spent away from our succession of homes digging up material for his thesis. When we arrived in India, my continuing isolation from him and my sense of geographical dislocation were aggravated by illness, both my own and Shona's. Though a middle class *aya* came to our house for thirty-six hours a week, I never left for more than three hours at a time. Often I did not leave at all, or else I left with Shona, to take her to the doctor. I rarely felt comfortable enough or well enough to do even the few art projects I had brought with me.

Finally, when Shona was fifteen months old, the situation in India became intolerable. Her continual and increasingly serious illness terrified me (not without reason) and my ability to deal with it was undermined by my own sickness and by the burden of living in extremely alien surroundings. David and I decided that I would have to take the baby back to America to recuperate. One can easily imagine the intense feelings of defeat, guilt — and relief — that contended in my mind as Shona and I flew home, leaving David behind to finish his work.

For the last three months Shona and I have been living

near relatives on the West Coast, and I have been a twenty-four-hour-a-day mother. This period of isolation from David and from work has however given me an opportunity to think through my past experience of combining motherhood and career, and to confront the problems that will surely arise when David returns and a more normal life is reestablished. Some of my thoughts and conclusions surprise me.

To a certain extent, I continue to feel as I have always felt about even minimal child care: it seems like an abandonment of Shona. In fact, Shona has been cared for by babysitters quite a bit. She managed all right with the neighbor and the *aya*. The significant thing is that *I* have never felt confident enough to forget entirely about her. My role as mother now predominates.

It is a bit odd to be defending such an ordinary practice as mothering one's own child. And yet I feel guilty for wanting to mother Shona full-time, that if I do so I will be cheating my self-as-artist by favoring my self-as-mother. There is also the issue of my cheating David of his parental role. Perhaps this is a subtle revenge on him for leaving it all to me for so long while he did only his work? I would rather see myself as a single self merely choosing to change my contours for a while, but I am nagged by the suspicion that my motives are not so simple or straightforward. After all, I allowed my career to lose its momentum. To regain it now would mean David's reassuming his full share of the child-care and thus jeopardizing his competing for a college teaching job. Besides, in my present unsettledness, I crave the security of his having a job. I've retreated to conservative ground and taken a less critical look at the conventional lives my sisters, neighbors, childhood friends, parents are living. There are merits in their styles I had overlooked before.

Not surprisingly during this present chaotic time, when

I find myself unable to work, I'm having second thoughts about the practice of the idea of equal sharing itself. Despite my feeling that I want to work, I can't help but feel it would be less stressful for me to do most of the parenting for a while longer, to let that be my full-time job. Maybe it is too expensive of time and energy for us both to share doing everything, even if we have some paid help. Maybe we ought to specialize temporarily when coping with young children and/or getting launched professionally. I mean, maybe now I should specialize in rearing Shona while David gets into the job market. This arrangement instead of the reverse because that is our current tendency; why fight it just now? If we discover ourselves being split by our very different roles and interests, or if a feeling of inequality settles over our relationship, or if I begin to feel too distant from my career, we could change or adjust our roles again. The trick, of course, is that David would have to remain psychologically prepared to withdraw part of his energy from his career to spend on child and home care, and I to do the opposite.

An argument in favor of role division grows out of a pattern of parenting that began early in our experience of equally sharing care of Shona. I noticed that longer stretches spent with her were more relaxed and easier than shorter ones.

> 4/12 Enjoyed having Shona alone for a long stretch yesterday. In touch with her. No interruptions or distractions. The daily transition between working at the studio and caring for Shona sometimes seems strenuous. Switching channels. The drive to and from the studio helps (David's mile and a half walk to the university). Easy to care for Shona when I'm totally absorbed in her primitively perceived world; not preoccupied with my own work; in tune with her.

This effect was very noticeable when Shona and I returned to America and spent three months living alone together. I fit myself to her rhythms and pursued my own interests (other than household work, which I did while she was awake) as she slept. Her daily patterns became more regular and things seemed to run more smoothly. I felt less strained, although I also felt I'd shut down a large area of my personality.

I admit that if I cared for Shona full-time, over a long period of time I might aggravate the problematic aspects of my relationship with her. A significant part of the energy drain I felt after Shona's birth was due to my peculiar way of relating to her (and other children). I got more involved than is necessary for an adult to be. In psychological terms, I over-identify.

> 5/26 This morning, David and I talked about the disastrous state of my health since Shona's birth. I eagerly attribute this to trying to work while being broken in to motherhood. Shouldn't I therefore cut down even more on working? David says it's not the working which has caused the illness. Suggests it's the quality of my mothering. Too intense. Too much input. Sounds sickeningly familiar. I found that to be a problem when I was new at teaching. We tried to think up concrete things I can do when I catch myself putting on too much of a show for Shona, and demanding too much response from her.

This tendency of mine interferes with my relationship with David too. Early on, I caught myself sometimes trying to steal Shona's attention from him. Was I feeling excluded by their intimacy? Were my parenting abilities threatened by David's? The events of the last year have aggravated this tendency in that Shona and I have had only each other to be close to for three months. However, I have become much more confident in my ability to care for her by myself, and to be self-sufficient. To that degree, it should be easier to allow David and Shona their full relationship in the future.

I know, however, that the problem of overidentification is one I'm firmly stuck with. The best I can do is to try to stay aware of it and to turn it off. It helps to be around other adults (David or close friends) who feel free to comment on it when they feel it happening. It's undoubtedly good for Shona to be cared for by people other than me some of the time, in order to take part of the pressure to respond off her and to let her learn to be independent of me.

Another unresolved problem that Shona's presence has precipitated for both David and me involves our struggles with what we call our "demons" the instinctive, gut-level bias in our attitudes toward the raising of Shona. Aside from the incredible reorientation of time and energy, the hardest thing about becoming parents has been dealing with these. David finds himself demanding "discipline" as he remembers his father doing; I rush to grant Shona's every wish as my mother must have done for me. And we are made nervous by each other's attitudes. We are also nervous about our own attitudes, which seem beyond our conscious control and often undesirable. David's demon popped up sporadically right after Shona's birth, only to be vigorously attacked by me. Mine was more gradual and continuous: a sort of a general indistinctness, soft-edgedness, lack of separateness between Shona and me. Harder for David to attack and probably for Shona to react against:

4/2 David's worry: he takes perverse pleasure in seeing how long Shona can complain before she really howls. Mine: I hardly let her peep before guessing and granting her every wish. Conditioning her to have only two levels of commnication: the peep and the bellow.

5/30 David worries that I'll overfeed/overindulge Shona. I worry that he will starve/deprive her. We agree on most actual decisions, but we still distrust each other's attitudes. Because I'm worried that David is glad that Shona's weight gain has slowed down while she's sick, I do try to overfeed her. Because he is glad, and I do overfeed her, he tries to counteract my actions by disapproving them (which makes me worried).

My demon tells me that I should always be delighted with motherhood (in order to demonstrate how good I am at it?). It may also be a way of keeping an edge on David, a way of being the "best" of us two parents, the one who loves it most. My forced cheerfulness in the midst of much actual adjusting and strain has sometimes been difficult for David to live with.

5/31 Last night, all my anxieties and weariness (Shona had been up during the previous night again) and Shona's misery (a cold) conspired to get me so upset that I said I wished we'd never had a baby, and where was my "freedom"? (And my eight hours sleep?). I hated motherhood, and why had we (I forgot it had been largely *my* choice) ever decided to have a baby? David was so relieved that he laughed and laughed! I've spent the last five and a half months apparently treasuring every minute of parenthood, making him feel guilty for his periodic regret.

Our demons represent ongoing problems, issues which are still unresolved. It's pretty clear that David and I will have some adjustments to make when we get back to Chicago and begin to develop a lasting, workable routine for ourselves. Child-care, for instance: will we have it, and if so, how much? David and I still do not consider full-time care a possibility. We have considered hiring someone or swapping child-care with someone for three hours a day, five days a week once we settle down again. Our basic plan is for us to be doing the parenting a majority of the time. We depart from our families' arrangements in that David will contribute as much time as I will, giving me an equal chance to have a career. Our recent total separation and our division of roles for five months has given us exaggerated and firsthand experience of our parents' arrangements, a painful but not totally worthless education.

I know that redeveloping a stable, secure, and equitable framework for our lives will not be easy but I am optimistic, partly because I can see my present retreat from career into parenthood as a strategy for self-preservation, and not just as an evasion of work. Being an artist has been for me an unprescribed activity, basically self-directed, self-centered, structured by relatively unpredictable things (the materials I chose to work with, the shows and competitions and fairs I chose/didn't choose/was chosen to take part in, the ebb and flow of my ideas and fantasies and interests, the growth of my knowledge of materials, skills, habits). Being a parent has been structured and methodical in comparison, and since Shona's birth, I have needed that structure. My time and energy now follow the baby's timetable, which is more or less biological and basically predictable. For the moment, my individuality has been replaced by the parental role. It has been a threatening switch, since I've always valued flexibility and individuality as major ingredients in my life; but I have had a certain freedom in being able to choose or adapt to a new kind of living at this difficult time in my life. I didn't make a very conscious choice, but I see that I indeed have "chosen" a new style of living, one which has steadied me during the multiple shocks of becoming a parent, leaving a familiar environment, and, for a few months, losing my spouse.

This month, just before flying back to London for the last five months of David's stay abroad, Shona and I have been in Chicago among friends. Talking to my studio partner about her involvement in clay, teaching and earning a living, talking to the woman I collaborate with on books, seeing my equal-sharing friends go off to work, seeing my sculptures in friends houses, seeing the person I was before our trip in my friends' attitudes toward me — all begin to rekindle my desire to work. I am reassured that when my basic home and family security is re-established, my artistic drive will revive, probably in new arrangements. But now I am content to be just a mother.

▲

FEBRUARY 1980

Considering that I am an orderly person concerned with structure, sequence, completion and security, how is it that each of these *Balancing Act* essays has caught me in the midst of upheaval? After four years of relative stability in Chicago, David and I have just executed another giant disruption in our lives. We have moved back "home" to the Pacific Northwest, in a gesture more poetic than practical, as seems to be our emerging style. Let me try to piece together the chain of events between 1976 and 1980 that led to this radical and disorienting act.

For the first year after we had returned from England and India in early 1976, David and Shona and I managed to lead a life somewhat like our pre-trip life. Supported for six months by David's academic grant, then by savings, and with the help of a local daycare center where Shona somewhat stoically spent four to six hours a day (it was adequate but not exciting), David worked on getting his thesis written up, and I plunged back into a very productive and successful year and a half of sculpturing. I loved the feel of the clay, and discovered no impediments to getting back into being a practicing artist. My ideas were as accessible as before. I visualize the process of creating partly as tuning into a stream of "stuff" in the back of my skull. I realized that this stream continues whether or not I'm currently plundering it to make sculptures. It's always there. I can use it whenever I decide to — to make art, to invent silly stories for my kids, to entertain my friends and David. I'm happiest when I'm using it, but it doesn't atrophy when I'm not. This is not to minimize the pleasures of actually working with clay and colors, and the challenges of making formal visual order. In 1977, I had my first one-person show at a downtown gallery, was in several group shows, held part-time teaching jobs and workshops, and finally had a second one-person show at a fine crafts gallery.

Earlier that year, in response to increasing pressures on our budget, David had begun working twenty hours a week at a community development bank. He worked during the hours Shona was at the daycare center, and then he went to the library to write his thesis while I spent the afternoons at home. Within a few months the bank asked him to work thirty hours. This cut deeply into his thesis time, but by then David had begun to see that the academic job market, especially in history, had become very tight. He had to face the possibility that even with a first-rate thesis, a publication, and several reviews, he might not get an academic job. He began working full-time at the bank, squeezing his thesis into evenings and weekends. I made one effort to get a job, so that he could continue to work part-time at the bank and part-time on his thesis, but I soon abandoned the effort. Our reasoning was that we would earn much less with two part-time jobs, and would lose many hours in combined travel time. My sculpturing time would pretty much vanish, leaving neither of us doing significant history/art. We could have arranged for Shona to spend longer hours at the daycare center, but we did not feel the center should be her "home" for more than six hours a day. Especially in retrospect, I'm glad that real home is where the major part of her young life was spent — that some of the best hours of my day were spent with her, not just the harried breakfast and dinner hours.

When David began to work at the bank our fifty-fifty sharing of child and house care came to an abrupt end. I was in charge at home and David earned money. I still had time to sculpt, thanks to the daycare center, but since David still made time to spend with Shona, his thesis time was cut to precious little. Our roles became increasingly different. We dressed differently, lived at different paces, were engaged in utterly different occupations. We often felt distant from each other.

At the same time I began to feel dissatisfied with being in the studio so many hours each day. I was surfacing from more than a year of intense sculpturing and it bothered me that my work brought in only a few thousand dollars a year beyond paying for itself. Compared to David's job / history ratio, I felt guilty for having so much time to spend on such a luxurious pastime. This feeling persisted despite David's insistence that is was better for one of us to be doing what we loved, than neither of us. I felt my sculpturing was too self-centered and isolated. I was not in touch with Life Out There and envied artists who organized neighborhood murals. Teaching art was the obvious way for me to earn money, but through earlier teaching experience I knew I didn't want to teach more than the low-key evening classes I led at a local college. I liked being an artist and a parent, but didn't relish the idea of trying to be an artist and a *teacher* and a parent. I felt the commitment to a teaching job would rob the other two by virtue of its more rigid structure.

On the other hand I couldn't picture promoting my work more aggressively through building social connections in art-buying circles. My social circle was university, Art Institute and neighborhood, and my evenings were with my family. I left the marketing of my art up to the galleries, and sales at the studio. This is the way I wanted it, and yet it bothered me that my art was not giving me much liveliness socially. A friend and I started a critique group of artists, which was stimulating and fun, but as rarified as my own work. I was growing restless and ready to tackle something broader-based and more a part of "Real Life."

In mid 1977, partly because of these feelings, and also because we wanted Shona to have a sibling and ourselves to have a family (not just a child), and due to my being thirty-four, David and I decided to initiate a second child. We had a lot of fun and no trouble in doing so. I intended to have a very active pregnancy. I agreed to a one-person show a few months before the baby was due, and continued evening jogging with a friend. It was not long before the jogging got fairly uncomfortable: bigger bouncing breasts and straining gut. Luckily winter arrived and provided a good excuse for not slogging anymore. And before much longer I began to get enormously sleepy. I spent many afternoons at the studio sacked out on an army cot during my sculpting time — waking up to the rumble of the forklift moving sacks of clay downstairs, or someone coming in to work. I'd walk back to Shona's daycare center and SIT DOWN waiting till the kids had finished their snack so we could go home and I could collapse. Finally even walking became uncomfortable. This baby seemed so HEAVY, pressing on my crotch and thighs. Sex was unthinkable. I barely remember the show I had in May, despite its success. The month of June was very hot and very long.

Being pregnant was certainly Real Life, and it took even more of an edge off my artistic ambitions. I made smaller, more light-hearted pieces. Curiously, they were very good and not only constituted an excellent show, but received some national attention and publication. But as my involvement in my work became less intense, I decided that I could not leave Shona in the daycare center so much. I was beginning to feel that I was missing out on raising her. She was rapidly approaching kindergarten age, when she would be gone for only two hours a day. To continue to do my art, I would soon have to find and pay for some way to care for her in the afternoons, or do more of that caring myself. I was ready to cut back on my sculpturing time in order to spend more time with Shona.

Shona was interested in my changing condition and much more anxious about its possible repercussions to herself than David and I suspected. Her alert daycare teachers let us in on her fears, which she probably felt freer to tell them than us. We were trying hard to encourage her to like the idea of a new baby, but we also tried to explain how difficult sharing her parents with a brother or sister would be. Once we made her understand that any reaction she had was acceptable to us, we got some anger and some fear. Then she and we relaxed, and in retrospect, Shona has put up with ensuing adjustments with tolerable, if sometimes acid, restraint.

When Shona was four and a half, Jonathan was born, at noon on his due date. Shona spent the night with our upstairs neighbors, who kindly took her to the daycare center in the morning. She weathered the event with poise. David and I got to the hospital in plenty of time and actually spent a few hours dozing together on the narrow bed while I dilated. Eventually things got under way and the hard work began. I felt well in control, and the birth was orderly. We had requested as much of a Le Boyer birth procedure as the hospital could accommodate. However, their version of the baby's gentle and harmonious entrance into the world was slightly off the mark. Our doctor had gone home to bed, and a colleague cheerily assisted our birthing by belting out "The Marseilles" (it was Bastille Day) as he eased the nine-pound, fifteen-ounce baby out of me. The nurse put on Elvis Presley's "Heartbreak Hotel" for the background accompaniment (I had envisioned Purcell), and laid newly-born Jonathan into a bath. David was the first to notice that the water was cold and the baby shivering. So much for our Le Boyer.

As in Shona's birth, I found it difficult to accept how much hard work it took to shove the baby out, and I depended on David's sympathy and support. The mirror was properly placed this time, and I made sure no one blocked my view into it of the emergence of Jonathan. He looked like a huge gray-pink building stone as he came out. And later of course he became a wonderful armful of uncurling baby! David had to leave soon afterward to pick up Shona, and for some damn reason the hospital wouldn't let me have Jonathan for twenty-four hours. I was furious despite the excitement of having our second child, and we were never given a satisfactory reason why I couldn't have him right away. Two weeks later I developed a colossal and debilitating breast infection which turned out to have been caused by special hospital staphylococcus, treatable only with special antibiotics costing seventy cents a pill, and no apologies whatsoever from the hospital or doctors. I am developing a certain amount of resentment towards the medical establishment I have relied on.

After Jonathan's birth I didn't visit the studio for six months, and I didn't miss it a bit. Because my ability to work had been unharmed by the sixteen-month hiatus of our India-England trip, I was confident that another break would not be disastrous, and I was right. I stayed at home, relaxed, and enjoyed my baby. Caring for Jonathan, I got to know the neighbors and community goings-on. Shona spent fewer hours at school, more at home. She and I both liked that. It was wonderful having a baby again. (Shona may have a slightly different opinion of this.) I loved being needed by the baby, and rediscovering how much Shona also needed me as she reassessed her place in our family. I loved seeing David and Jonathan together. Jonathan showed a marked preference for David's shoulder over all other roosts. I also loved being a full-time member of our neighborhood, although the particular area was too big-city for me. We made some new good friends and felt the excitement of being members of a lively community. One friend, whose baby boy was a day older than Jonathan, and I swapped babies fairly regularly to give ourselves a bit of breathing space. We were both nursing, and we discovered that if the boys got hungry, whoever was mothering at the moment could calm both babies by giving them one breast-ful each, until the other mother returned to give them each a second go-round. That was a friendly arrangement and made us all feel close. Jonathan was nicknamed the Vacuum Cleaner.

But my more relaxed schedule did not prevent hardships during Jonathan's first year. I was healthier than I had been after Shona's birth, due to being more at ease, but still had two bad breast infections. That winter was Chicago's worst ever, and both children had a series of ear infections, which we attributed in part to the drafts and uneven heat in our apartment. The ice and snow made David's commute to the bank horrendous. We talked about moving closer to the bank — my father had left me money in a trust with which to buy a house, and housing prices were skyrocketing. It was *the* time to buy, but I found I wasn't sure I wanted to settle permanently in Chicago. Then Shona's daycare center fell apart, as did the next pre-school she attended. Her debut into kindergarten and the infamous Chicago public school system was fast approaching, as was the end of David's thesis. The fragments of time he had managed to find for it had paid off, but the prospect of finishing brought his career dilemma very close.

As that winter ended and spring progressed, we found we were talking seriously about leaving Chicago. We wanted to be nearer our extended families. I wanted to be in a smaller city and closer to familiar salt water, islands, mountains, and I knew I was at a turning point in my art. David wanted to be jolted into a serious non-academic career search. In the early summer of 1979 he flew out to Seattle and Portland on a short and fruitless job hunting trip. Finally we decided just to pack up and go.

I had hired a sitter that winter, when Jonathan was six months old, to free me twelve hours a week so that I could finish a commissioned mural. Returning to the studio was fun, but when summer came and our sitter became ill, I didn't replace her. The move would be expensive, and I knew from past experience that I would do little productive work in a climate of disruption, and also, to what end? I'd have to sell most of my pieces before the move anyway. The hassle and expense of finding a good sitter did not appear to be balanced by the benefits. I finished the commission and two other murals and spent the summer with the children — cementing our family in preparation for the big move. David continued at the bank, then took two weeks to finish writing his thesis, and delivered it to his typist. The four of us spent time with friends we might not see again soon.

And then the scramble began. I had to finish and install the four large wall pieces, organize the rest of my sculptures to go to shows, galleries, or to be sold from my studio, dismantle the studio, and pack some favorite pieces to take along to prime the pump once we got settled and I began to work again. We had to sort, disperse, consolidate and pack our possessions. David had to get that thesis done. And all of this with no baby sitter, and David at the bank until almost the last minute. What a jumble. The last week we waited in frustration with the house packed up, but no movers in evidence.

Finally in October, 1979, Jonathan and I flew west to David's family in eastern Washington state, while David and Shona drove west, a memorable trip over the "Roke Mawtins," stopping with friends and relatives along the way. David then drove to Seattle to find a job, while the kids and I settled in with his folks to wait. Six weeks later, he and I found a house to buy during a very busy four days when Jonathan and I came over to Seattle to help look. Still no job. Undaunted by the disparity between income and outgo which this suggested, we moved into a summer cabin my mother had deeded to us on an island an hour and a half north of Seattle to wait for the city house to be ours and to see what job David would turn up. This stretch of time, although anxious, was lyrical and fresh. My days settled into the rhythms of the children's needs, with beach and forest walks as the main events. David commuted by ferry and car to Seattle to find a job.

Two days before Shona's sixth birthday and nine days before Christmas we took possession of our house, in an old modest neighborhood above Lake Union close to downtown Seattle. I'm writing six weeks later over a wreckage of holidays, cleaning, painting, pruning, patching, building storm windows, scrambled in with getting Shona launched in a new school and finding friends. David is facing an array of unfamiliar fix-up jobs centering on the plumbing, and Jonathan at age one-and-one-half is discovering much more about the possibilities and ramifications of the word "No."

We've also weathered two cases of the chicken pox, and a fever of 105.6° when Jonathan got yet another ear infection. Still no job. We have mountainous payments due to the bank for the house, which has revealed itself to be in need of almost every expensive repair an old house could require.

David and I are learning a sprawling range of the basics in home repair, and in psychic repair of each other: we reassure each other during the successive disappointments in the job-hunting process, support each other in dealing with the children and that other needy child, our house, all the while adjusting to living closer to our families and missing our Chicago friends. I'm eager to get beyond insulating, painting, guttering, tuck-pointing, roofing, porch-building, and furnace-replacing to: building a studio in the basement, buying a kiln and settling in to my next binge of sculpturing. My up-coming What Next? Crisis will be how to make my sculpturing lucrative, or how I can sculpt as well as provide income for our family. One way or another, this effort will force more connection between myself and the outside world and will be a significant growth for me. Fiscal responsibility. My entrepreneur Dad would have loved it.

In the meantime our anxiety is relieved by family, friends, the preposterousness of our predicament, Shona's intermittent, but greatly appreciated moments of pitching in and helping make things run smoothly, Jonathan's gorgeous smooches and hugs and tantrums, spring uncovering hundreds of blooming plants in our garden.

JANUARY 1981

Work on the house has ceased for the wet months. A year ago my only goal was to return to our former arrangements of David working and me running the household. But we've come up with a more dynamic arrangement, which unfortunately does not include much art time. Last March David stopped job hunting and we both took part-time jobs. He began working twenty hours a week at his father's orange juice company while I began working in the evenings doing telephone sales for a book publisher, two blocks down the street. In April I began to build a wholesale distributorship for vitamins and food supplements out of our home. With persistence, this business should free me from my evening job entirely. Already it has made our house a minor nerve center in the neighborhood, so I don't think I'll feel isolated working at home once I stop my evening job. I love feeling part of my community. David has joined our community council, we are both involved in Shona's school, and our immediate neighbors as well as our families have been supportive and helpful as we settle into our new life.

Since our move we have been sharing house and childcare again as we did when Shona was small. David now cooks most of our dinners since I am gone from five o'clock until nine on week nights. This is to everyone's benefit as he's a discriminating cook and I'm not. Jonathan and I contribute to mealtimes by baking bread together. David and I are both earning money, and that equality feels great, although it took dire necessity to force me to shoulder my share in that area.

David finished his thesis at the end of the summer and received his PH.D. He is hoping for a grant to co-author a book on five Bengali myths in the year ahead. Meanwhile, an Indian publisher, and possibly an American too, will turn David's thesis into a book. It is already being used by scholars in his field. To give himself the time to do the necessary rewriting, David gave up his job at his father's company in September and is now working at the same telephone sales job as I am. He works mornings; I nights. David is also trying to teach himself accounting as an eventual substitute for telephone sales, which is a convenient money-job but one which makes him feel uncomfortable. I rather enjoy my phoning skills and the camaraderie with fellow-phoners and also the skimming contact with People Out There over the phone. In addition, the ability to use the phone has been very useful in starting my home business. We're beginning to get a measurable income from that too.

When school started this year Shona was accepted into an accelerated public school program, and she has been loving the challenges and enjoying many friends. She seems really happy. David and I are proud of her help and competence within the family. Jonathan has become a sociable twerp, happy tagging along with Shona and her friends, but proud to have his own special friends too. He's working hard to figure out letters and numbers and is practicing jumping, dancing, running, making up stories and jokes, modeling with clay and drawing. Our extended families are very real to both children now, and they enjoy hearing stories about When Grandma, Aunt Sally, Papa . . . was a little kid. Jonathan and Shona seem to be thriving in this busy atmosphere. They are not getting smothered with parental attention to say the least, but we are always close by. This has been a change for Shona. She has developed her independence with projects and make-believe, and has taught Jonathan to play along with her. She often takes responsibility for Jonathan when we are busy. She's lined up a crew of female friends and is working on all sorts of prowess: roller skating, swimming, bike riding, sewing, reading and whistling.

This fall I met some clay colleagues through a woman who is writing a book on low-fire ceramic sculpture and that has led to an invitation to participate in a group show in April with some exciting women in my field. With David's help, I've finally got the rudiments of a studio in the basement. My oldest sister, who is a portrait sculptress, and I bought a kiln from my middle sister, and we installed it in my basement and began to work on a two-person show. I have some good pieces in progress right now for the group show in April, and swapping childcare plus two mornings of paid daycare should give me reliable chunks of morning time to prepare for the show. David and I each have two afternoons free a week. Money-work, my art, and David's history, children and home remain in a jumbly heap from which occasional signs of progress emerge.

We are too busy, and our budget is too tight. Our lives lack grace. We've worked out what feels like a "fair" division of responsibilities but it's less efficient and less remunerative than if one of us were working full-time while the other ran the show at home. Art and history are on hold while we work to achieve "escape velocity" and free ourselves from our telephone sales jobs. David would love above all else to teach history at the university level, but until such a situation materializes, our goal is to continue to work part-time — we hope at endeavors we enjoy more and earn more from than telephone sales.

Working for money has done more than just assuage my guilt about the self-indulgence of being an artist. There's the whole issue of the self-confidence gained by mastering an everyman's job and putting the bread on the table. I had always lived off money earned either by my father or by David. My monetary contributions had been more token than essential. Also, I've gotten connected to the rest of the world. I can relate to a far wider variety of people than I could before, and I love that. Given the choice, I'm not sure I'd ever go back to just my family and art. The entrepreneurial part of my life is challenging and invigorating, and I feel I can help other people — or help *more* other people — than I do with my art.

It's true that fine authentic art does enhance peoples' lives, but it reaches such a small audience. And unless you have sold to a friend, there's no continuing relationship established between artist and buyer. I can imagine being fulfilled as a Tlingit Indian artist, decorating useful objects for a community of people I know, but that's not what being an artist means here and now. Only the wealthy can afford to surround themselves with the touch of the sophisticated human hand. So although I have "succeeded" as an artist (earned a few thousand dollars a year, been shown often, won awards) being an artist only partly satisfies me. I was at a crucial point of having to define what it meant to be an artist when our move forced me into whole new arenas. When I return to art I may allow it to remain my indulgence, free from having to earn more than its own keep, free to be unique and personal, but conversely not shaped and possibly vitalized by the friction and demands of the market. Or I may attempt to synthesize my social, economic and artistic needs.

But for now I'm trying to keep enough air space between jobs to have time to take a walk with Shona, have a night out with David, join Jonathan in his make-believe. The upheaval of our move to Seattle has been a remarkable, if violent and perhaps temporary, cure for the distance our family was feeling within itself. It's exhilarating. It's nerve-racking. A plunge. We're all swimming really hard, together.

III

Now that I am more deeply involved with my work again, the babies are less totally compelling. I am pleased about that; it is the balance that I was hoping to achieve when I first decided to have a child. I enjoy them even more than I did at the beginning, but the major focus of my mental attention is elsewhere.

JANE GREENGOLD STEVENS

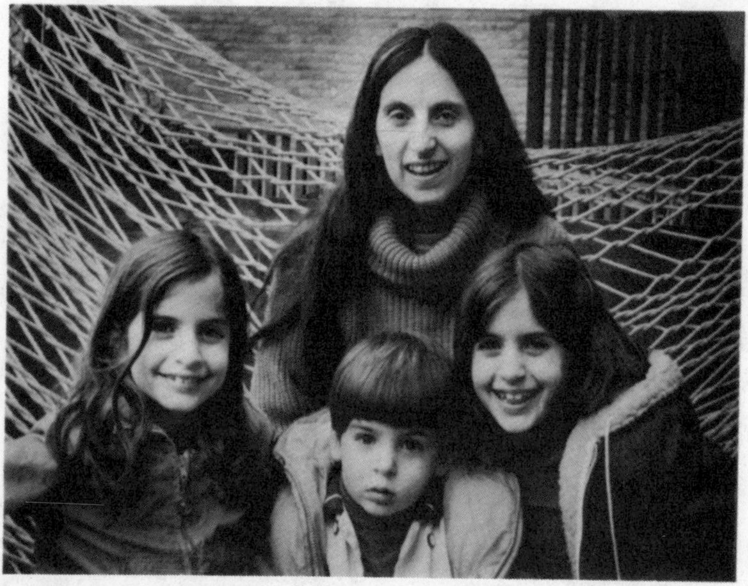

Jane Greengold Stevens

When I was twenty-seven and had been practicing law for three years and painting seriously for two, my husband and I decided to try to have a baby. We had been married for four and a half years. My husband, Ken, was a graduate student, an instructor of design at the Illinois Institute of Technology, and a practicing designer and cabinetmaker. We had established a pattern in our lives that we had maintained for more than a year: Ken teaching part-time and working on various design and carpentry projects, and I working at my law job three days a week and painting for the large part of the other four. We were both enjoying our work, and we felt that we were in relative control of our lives. This gave us a feeling of open space. Although we were both already overcommitted to ongoing and anticipated projects, we had no immediate plans for other radical changes in our lives, and therefore thought that we could carve out a space for a child.

The decision was far from a casual one and was not, especially for me, eased by any assumption that I would have a child. In fact for many years I did not want to have children. I was involved in myself and my legal and artistic careers, and I felt that all my time and energy were well and happily engaged.

I had spent very little time with children; as far as I can remember, I had never done any babysitting and had never even been alone in a house with a baby. I had no experience that made me want children for the pleasure of being with children. My ignorance did not tempt me to romanticize the task of raising children; instead, it left me with no vision of joys.

And yet, while I was still in law school, my friends started having babies and I was confounded by the effect that had on me. I was unable to dismiss the issue from my mind, although at that time I would have had an abortion if I had gotten pregnant. I simply did not want to have a child. I was busy finishing law school, and later studying for the bar exams and beginning my first job as a lawyer. Then I began to work very seriously at my art as well. Too much was changing in my life for me to even consider having a child. But in 1972, when my life was fairly settled and some of my friends were having second children, I could no longer resist thinking about babies. I kept telling myself that I did not want to think about it, but apparently I did.

In July of that year, I saw and held a three-weeks-old baby, the youngest baby I had ever seen or touched, and I was moved and excited by his tiny helplessness. That surprised me: I had expected to be repelled by such vulnerability. My response made me uneasy, but I did begin to have the sense of "wanting one of my own." Yet even then I could think of myriad reasons for not wanting children. Caring for them would involve boring, mindless, repetitive work — all the chores associated with housecleaning, for which I have no tolerance. It would require giving up precious time from my art and would dramatically reduce my ability to act on impulse. It would be a terrifying responsibility to be the parent of a small helpless child. What if he or she were sick? Parents and children so often seem to cause each other grief. It would be the one absolutely irreversible, irrevocable decision I would ever make.

Nonetheless, I thought more and more, seemingly against my will, about babies. This was a puzzle to me, since I believed that I was completely satisfied with my life as it was. Eventually I worked myself up to producing some symptoms of pregnancy (sore breasts and tiredness) hardly an hysterical pregnancy, but enough to push the issue. Finally in August I decided to face the question squarely: why was I so concerned about the whole issue, did I want to have children, and if so, when?

For reasons I did not and still do not understand, I seemed to *want* to decide to have a baby. I felt strongly, though, that it would be crazy to have a baby without trying to assess as best I could its potential effect on my life. I had the ability to make the choice of whether or not to have a child. I wanted to exercise that choice as responsibly as possible.

I had been watching a television series on Leonardo da Vinci, and had been most impressed by his insatiable desire to learn everything possible. And I had just read a book in which the author said that the prime objects of life in Bloomsbury were aesthetic experience and the pleasures of human intercourse. If, as I believed, I too wanted to learn everything possible, and if I too valued human intercourse, surely it would be foolish for me to miss one of the primary human relationships, that of the parent to the child; surely I ought to witness at first hand the development of an infant into an adult. The idea of dealing with and relating to a baby became more attractive.

Once I had come up with these positive intellectual reasons to have a baby, I had to face the critical question of whether and how I could fit a baby into my overcrowded life. I was already pursuing two careers, a time and energy-consuming effort. I had started law school with the simple intention of becoming a lawyer, but my interest and devotion to art became stronger and stronger over the years. If it had been as deep when I started law school as it was four years later, I would probably not have gone at all. By the time I had worked as a lawyer full-time for two years, in a poverty law project in Chicago funded by the Office of Economic Opportunity, my commitment to my painting had become so serious that I negotiated with Legal Aid to be allowed to work only three days a week (for three-fifths my regular salary) so that I would have four days a week in which to paint. I did not stop being ambitious when I stopped full time law work. I transferred my ambition to my art.

This was a major step; it is difficult, if not impossible, to rise in a traditional field like the law without working a forty — or a seventy — hour week. But I was willing to give up the prospect of a successful career as a lawyer because I cared so much about my art. I was not prepared to stop painting in order to make room in my life for a child.

Nor was I prepared to give up law altogether. Although there were days when I passionately wished that I could give it up, there were several reasons why I did not and have not done so. It is important for me to have the sense of political and social reality that Legal Aid clients, the court system, and my relations to the working world as a woman bring me. My artistic efforts are lonely and insular in comparison to my legal efforts, and I am not sure that I would be happy without continuing relationships with professional colleagues and without the kind of public performance that takes place in a courtroom. Also I know that I get a kind of cheap ego satisfaction in being a "woman lawyer" in a man's world. I do not want to need that satisfaction, and it does not mean as much to me as the satisfaction I get from completing a good painting, but in some contexts, it is reassuring. And in the back of my mind, I reserve the possibility of returning to law full-time if I find, eventually, that I am not satisfied with my painting, or if I begin to feel defeated by lack of recognition.

Another, and perhaps the most crucial, reason that I could not give up the practice of law was that I was far from being able to earn a living through my art, and I did not want to be economically dependent on Ken. I did not want to have to support him (except during a short-term project) and therefore saw no reason why he should have to support me. Our marital harmony was based upon a delicate balance of complete sharing of all domestic activity, and it was clear that that balance would shift and perhaps collapse if we were not both self-supporting.

So although my major commitment was to my painting, I continued to practice law. As a result I felt time pressure constantly, despite the flexibility in my part-time office job. I was at the office so few hours a week that my time there was overfilled with work. It was the same with painting. I had enough painting ideas to more than fill a week, so I had to push to fit even a fraction of my art work into four days. Since art and law work are totally unrelated, the transition from one to the other was always wearing and energy-consuming. And I was involved with the other pleasures of living: people, swimming, reading, cooking, my plants, etc. This catalogue of activities was crucial to my thinking about having a baby. I said to myself again and again: I have too much to do now; why add a baby?

Ken was not as tortured as I was by these issues. Unlike me, he had always assumed he would have children. His job meshed more with his private creative interests than mine did, so he could more or less do everything at once.

Also, although he has as many ideas and works on as many projects as I do, he is less driven. He feels less pressure to "get things done" or to become "famous." The issue of time pressure was not so important to him in weighing the decision about children. And his feelings about time pressure were just as important as mine because from the time we first spoke about having babies, Ken and I planned to share baby care.

We already shared all the domestic chores, working constantly to maintain a balance and readjusting the division of labor whenever one of us felt abused. It was not easy, largely because of my recalcitrance. I work very hard at things I care about, but I am spoiled, lazy, and irresponsible about maintenance tasks. My attitudes toward housework closely resemble those of the so-called "average man," to my general discredit. The example of my parents strongly suggested that housework should be beneath my dignity. They paid others to do their domestic tasks and implied through their life-styles that such work was not worthy of their attention. This has made it difficult for me to learn to do my share of the work gracefully. Ken is instinctively much neater and more orderly than I am and suffers from none of my snobbism about housework. While I am less willing than many women to accept responsibility for "the house," he is more willing than most men.

But there have been conflicts. There was a time when our arguments about domestic chores were serious enough that we thought we would never be able to work out a division of child care responsibility. We dealt with our differences with great effort, and by the time I raised the question of having a baby, a satisfactory division of labor in the household had been established. We did much less cleaning and tidying than anyone else we knew, and that seemed to be the easiest solution to the whole problem. What housework we did do, we divided equally.

So when we seriously discussed having a child, we each had adequate faith in the other's commitment to equal participation in the responsibility and the effort. I think that I would not have had a child without that faith. The flexibility in both our schedules, established before we ever seriously thought of having a baby, made significant sharing of the child care possible. And because we were both working we knew we could afford some paid child care as a supplement to our own efforts.

I never considered the possibility of stopping either my law or my art work to care for a baby. I know that I would not have decided to have a child if it had meant giving up either. I wanted to have a baby, but only if I could add him or her to my life without giving up the other things to which I was already committed. All my life I had assumed that when I had a baby, I would also have someone to help take care of it while I worked. It was almost as though I would give birth to a "nanny" at the same time that I gave birth to a baby. The two were inseparable in my head.

I was cared for all my life by a woman whom I in fact called, and whom I still call, "Nanny." My father was a lawyer and my mother was an active politician and then a judge. She was forty when I was born — her only child — and her career was well-established. She added a child to a life that already contained many satisfactions. I think she must have wanted a baby very much, for she braved several problematic pregnancies before she had me. But she never considered staying home to take care of me on a daily basis.

My relationship with my mother was wonderful when I was young. That she was not my only "mothering figure" did not subtract from our closeness, at least as far back as I can remember. So I always assumed without question that I would continue to practice law and paint after I had children. I am a second-generation mother-with-a-profession, and because my own experience as the child of a working mother was a positive one, I had no conflicts at all about the idea of being a working parent. In this I directly followed my mother's example, departing from it only to the degree that I assumed Ken and I would actually care for the child ourselves, and in the consciousness with which we agreed we would share that care between us.

My parents required a full-time babysitter for me because of the nature of their work. They were both out all day and often in the evenings for political functions. As far as I know, the sharing of the little baby care that was not done by Nanny was not an articulated issue between them. In some respects, they had a traditional marriage. My father always earned more money than my mother did and they both liked it that way; they saw the man as the "provider." I am told that my mother took physical care of me when Nanny was not there: diapers, baths, feeding, and so forth. Daddy took me out to play. But I have no memory of my mother having more responsibility for me than my father did, whatever the actual arrangement was. My overall impression of my childhood is that neither parent had any more to do with child care than the other.

However, in all of our assumptions about sharing baby care and having outside help, Ken and I deviated absolutely from the model of Ken's family. One of the first things that Ken's mother ever said to me was that she had never left her children with a babysitter — never, except when she was in the hospital having her other babies; then she left them with her sister. She had worked as a bookkeeper for a few years after her marriage and stopped working when she became pregnant with Ken, the oldest of her three sons. She did *all* the child care and domestic work with no help from any outsiders. Her husband worked long hours as a machinist and was not able to help her very much. Ken believes now that part of his strong desire to be deeply involved with his children comes from his sense that his father was not involved enough with his children. As a result, Ken was more willing to share domestic tasks and to care for children than most men.

Thus our positions on child care appeared to complement each other, and the more we thought about it, the more we felt that we would work well together dealing with a child.

Then, in August, 1972, many of our friends were away, and we had more time than usual just to ourselves. We got a lot of work done. Time seemed more elastic than usual. We were relaxed, and we enjoyed being together. It was this easing of the immediate time pressure, combined with the sense that our marriage was working out well, that made it seem possible to have a baby. I did sometimes think: if things are finally under control, why risk everything with a new and potentially disastrous variable? But in that relaxed month the idea of devoting time and attention to a child became more and more attractive.

I tried very hard to analyze this, to consider it rationally and intellectually. I did not want to give in to a gut impulse without assessing its probable effect on my life. And yet, even as I made the decision to have a baby, I suspected — and in retrospect this seems virtually certain — that it was an irrational, gut decision. I have no other explanation for it. I cannot tell whether it was the result of cultural training or of inherent instinct or of some other factor of which I am unaware. Because I want to be in control of my life, I do not like to believe that I am the passive instrument either of instinct or of society; yet I must admit that my motivation in choosing to have a baby remains essentially a mystery to me.

We decided to try to have a baby. We are so accustomed to controlling our lives that it was very strange to have devoted so much energy to making the decision, and then to realize we did not know if it would ever be possible. And while our decision relieved me of the need to be obsessive about whether or not to have a baby, I was soon equally obsessed about whether or not I would get pregnant. I spent hours, in the office and at home, pondering my physical symptoms, which were increased, I am sure, by my attention to them. My period was late. Tension mounted. I got my period. But we were very lucky, and the next month, probably six weeks after we first had intercourse without contraceptives, I conceived.

It had been an intense six weeks. We had thought a great deal about the possible baby. We had made love a great deal. We are both impatient; when we decide we want something, we want it quickly. We made every effort not to miss the crucial twenty-four hours, and we enjoyed the effort. It was exciting to make love without contraceptives for the first time in our lives. It felt newly naked, newly giving in a way that I, at least, had not expected it would.

When I discovered that I was pregnant, our sense of control returned. For years we had not wanted to have a baby, and with the aid of modern science we did not. Then we decided that we did want to have a baby, and lo, we were going to. Physically, I felt drained — bloaty, with aching breasts, and sleepy, sleepy, sleepy — but we were pleased with ourselves.

During previous years, even though I had not wanted a baby then, I had had romantic images of pregnancy. I had thought that taking care of a child would be a chore but that pregnancy would be somehow luxurious. I would be the center of attention. Everyone would treat me considerately and Ken would be very solicitous. Our culture is full of stories about women who "have never felt better in their lives" than when they were pregnant. I have since decided that that can only be true for women whose every dream is fulfilled by motherhood. It had not occurred to me that one would in fact *need* consideration and solicitousness because of the physical drains of pregnancy. It was not awful, painful, or debilitating, but I always felt less well and less energetic than I do ordinarily.

For the first three months, I was queasy and tired. It was difficult to get anything done; that alone was extremely frustrating. I felt fuzzy-headed, and I worked in a half-stupor, thinking how bizarre it was to give my body and my strength to someone else, to a parasite I had never met. I had moments of resentment, not I think toward the baby or toward Ken, but toward myself for having decided to subject myself to this strain, this drain of my energy. I felt that the strength I normally devoted to myself and to the projects that I cared about was being syphoned off to some stranger. Why am I doing this? I wondered constantly.

Even while I felt sorry for myself, the phenomenon of the pregnancy fascinated me. It seemed incredible that something so drastic could be happening in my body without my being able to control it. How incredible it was that I had to go to a doctor and have laboratory tests to find out if I was pregnant. Throughout my pregnancy I waivered between enthusiasm and eagerness, panic and depression. But when I felt well enough to work efficiently at the office and to paint, I was excited at the prospect of adding another dimension to my life. Ken was consistently enthusiastic. He had moments of doubt, but fewer than mine, and he was very supportive.

After the first three months I felt much better. I was able to do more painting and consequently felt less put-upon. During the fourth month, however, I began to grow at what seemed to me a most extraordinary rate. I had become pregnant in October. In January I did not look at all pregnant, but by the middle of February I looked six months pregnant. My skin ached from the rapid stretch. When I asked my doctor about this, fully expecting him to say reassuringly that that was the way it happened, he agreed that I had grown surprisingly quickly. Indeed he said I was unusually big, and that perhaps I was carrying two babies.

I was overwhelmed. It had never occurred to me that I might have twins. Whenever I had seen a parent pushing a twin baby carriage, I had thought to myself, "Oh, that poor person, what a nightmare!" I had never known any twins when I was a child. There were none in my family. Ken, on hearing this news, revealed that both sides of his family are littered with twins. I was horrified. Trying to squeeze one child into my already overcrowded life was going to be difficult enough; wouldn't it be impossible with two?

I tried to cope with the idea of having twins. How would I ever get anything done with two babies? I had no idea what to do with one baby. I had never changed a diaper in my life. I was an only child, always center stage. I could not imagine being a twin, having to share everyone's attention.

In March the doctor said that I had caught up with myself and was no longer unusually big; he could hear only one heartbeat. I was enormously relieved. In the back of my mind, though, I must confess there was a trace of disappointment: society makes such a fuss about twins, and I generally like to be the center of attention. But I was uneasy about that because I do not at all want to depend on my biological reproductive capacity for whatever specialness I might have.

Between the March and April visit to the doctor I had another growth spurt, and when I arrived for my April examination, the doctor exclaimed at my size. He said that I would clearly have either twins or one very large baby. The chances were fifty-fifty that it would be twins, he thought, and he made an appointment with a radiologist to find out. I was terrified. I was frightened by the prospect of giving birth to one huge baby, and frightened by the prospect of taking care of two small ones.

I went to the radiologist and was x-rayed. He told me he could "see two babies." Two babies. I had to wait several days before I got the official word from my own doctor, during which time I fantasized that there were three. But there were two babies, no more, no less, and my obstetrician said that they appeared to have all their parts correctly connected to all their other parts.

I was overwhelmed. Me, who had wondered for so long whether to have a baby at all, with two! My friends thought it a great ironic joke. To me it seemed like a slap in the face. We had felt so much in control, and now it appeared that nature had the upper hand after all. Yet when we saw the x-ray the amazing reality of two visible bodies inside my one body was dazzling. I became for the first time truly excited instead of terrified.

I got bigger and bigger and more and more bruised from the rapid growth and great activity. But while I was less energetic than usual, I enjoyed being pregnant during those middle months. I was pleased with myself in an obscure way, and I loved to feel the babies thrash. I liked it when Ken and my close friends showed interest in my enormous belly. I was proud of it, despite my feeling that it was absurd to be proud of anything that was not a unique accomplishment.

But the pregnancy was finally more draining than I had expected it would be. From November to May I worked in the office and was seriously involved in my work. I was then Acting Supervisor of a neighborhood legal services office, even though I continued to work only three days a week. During that time I tried to run the office, struggle with its political disputes, and handle part of the caseload of a departing attorney as well as my own. I also wrote a brief for my first case before the United States Supreme Court.

But I had difficulty painting. At the beginning of the pregnancy I was often too lethargic. During the middle trimester I did paint, but less than usual. Near the end I was too big and uncomfortable. It was depressing. I had not expected pregnancy to disrupt my painting or my life in general as much as it did, and I hoped that this was not an omen that the babies would disrupt my life more than I expected or wanted them to.

I decided to stop work in May because the doctor said the babies might well be born up to three weeks earlier than the original date. I had been hoping for a small "vacation" before the babies were born during which I could see some museum shows and work on some paintings. This period was spoiled, however, by the doctor's orders to rest so that the babies would not be born too soon. By the end of May my cervix was completely effaced and one centimeter dilated; the doctor decided that I ought to remain on my back in order to take the pressure of gravity off the cervix so that the babies would have more time to grow.

So I had a real "confinement." I spent two weeks lying down except for frequent trips to the toilet. It was difficult. Once again, as at the beginning of the pregnancy, I could not accomplish anything. And I was too uncomfortable to enjoy the enforced rest. I felt used. My body was not mine. I had to be careful of it, not for its own sake, but for the sake of others. I thought a great deal about the extraordinary fact of lending one's body to another being in this way, an experience unique to women. And the process was taking place without my awareness; I did not feel my cervix dilate. I had to restrict myself without being able to judge from my own response whether it helped or not.

Ken waited on me hand and foot, but I did not like being helpless and dependent. He said however that in a way it was satisfying to him; it gave him an essential role in caring for the babies. After the first week the doctor said that the cervix had closed a bit; that made it easier to tolerate the second week, as it seemed that we were really accomplishing something, preventing a birth when the babies were still too small to face the world safely.

Finally the doctor said that the babies were big enough to be born safely. I was able to resume as normal a life as I could, considering how enormous I was. I had never worried about the process of giving birth, except for the few days before my x-ray when I was faced with the possibility of having one enormous child. In part I felt confident because of our training in the Lamaze method. From the first, we both wanted Ken to be as involved as possible in the pregnancy and the birth. I knew that I would be much more frightened of the birth if I had to face it alone. And Ken wanted to be there. We never considered the possibility of not taking the Lamaze course. I was somewhat self-conscious about being in a group solely because of my biological state, but I enjoyed and was grateful for the classes. I would not have been able to get through the birth as well as I did without them. In retrospect, however, I feel that the Lamaze method understates the pain of childbirth. I realize that I may have had a particularly difficult time, and I appreciate the importance of having women approach the experience in a relaxed mood, but I do think that if the possible pain is understated too much, it can come as a rude shock.

In the early morning of the sixth day after I was allowed back on my feet, I began having strong contractions, and the bag of waters broke. We left for the hospital just at dawn, June 15th. We were very happy, excited, and incredibly, not nervous.

But at the hospital the x-rays taken showed that the babies, who had once been properly head down, were now breech. My mood went from calm to panic; I had not expected complications. The doctor admitted that the delivery of two breech babies might be problematic. It was far from certain that they would follow a normal LaMaze-learned pattern.

The next few hours were depressing because I could not tell whether labor was progressing satisfactorily. Then the contractions became stronger and less regular. All my previous progress was lost, and I began to fear that I would be in labor for days. It was almost impossible for me to stay above the pain. For the first time I understood the meaning of the phrase "a sea of pain." It became more and more difficult to relax, a crucial element of the LaMaze technique. I never thought about the babies at all. Although I still theoretically wanted to be conscious and actively participating in the birth, I began to feel that if the doctors decided I should have a caesarian, I would actually be grateful for the anaesthesia.

But the doctor suddenly said, "You're going to make it. You'll have your babies within an hour." Soon after that I got the urge to push. Pushing itself was an effort, but it was better than lying helpless in pain. With the final pushing came the feeling of bursting, and relief, fantastic relief. Then the doctor said, "It's a girl," and I was so glad, so happy. How much I had wanted a girl! But then he said, "No time to rest yet, start pushing again." They broke the bag of waters, and the whoosh of liquid was so great that I shrieked, "They dropped the baby!" thinking that the second baby had fallen to the floor. The doctor's shoes and socks were soaked. More pushing, another release, and another girl. And then a moment's rest, and then more pushing for the placenta, and the sewing-up of the episiotomy, and the contraction of the uterus, and then I could lie still.

I hardly even thought of the babies. I was totally exhausted, even grateful to be separated from Ken in the recovery room. I luxuriated in lying still. It was the most desirable rest I have ever had.

The birth was without a doubt the most intense experience of my life. In some ways it was also the most horrible. There was no ecstasy, no sexual thrill. I was unprepared for the difficulty and pain of it; for several hours afterward I could feel only pity for any woman about to give birth. But after those first hours I found that my emotional attention was held by the intensity of the experience, and within a few days, incredibly, I could think of other childbirths positively, as a high experience. It is hard to understand. It was, for three hours, an excruciating ordeal; and yet I am glad I experienced it. And if I were ever to have another baby, I would once again choose to be conscious and participating.

When they first brought the babies to me, about six or seven hours after they were born, I did not know how to respond to them. Tiny bizarre strangers. The first-born, weighing four pounds, eleven ounces, we named Vanessa Byrne. The second, who was born only four minutes later, weighing five pounds, seven ounces, we named Rachel Victoria. I felt awe and pleasure, but there was very little passion in my response. Since I had rooming-in, the babies were in the room with me eight or nine hours a day; and each day, as I fed, diapered, and hugged them, I began to love them a little bit more. The "love," whatever than can mean toward such helpless, unformed creatures, grew with the contact.

Ken was ecstatic, exalted, exhilarated. He left the hospital after the birth in a state of high excitement. During the entire week that I was in the hospital, we were both happy and pleased with ourselves. But I was subdued-happy (because of my fatigue and soreness) and he was exuberant-happy. It was wonderful to see his enthusiasm.

It took me several days to come out of my fog enough to remember that there was an outside world; it had faded completely. For those first days I was as disassociated from the rest of my mental life as I can ever remember having been. I had no thoughts about my art, the law, anything — not because I was concentrating totally in the babies, but because I was still sunk into myself, my own body. Whatever small energy I had for things outside myself, I devoted to the babies.

I wanted to nurse them, at least for a while, partly to see what it would be like and partly because the bulk of the reading we had done held that it was healthier for both the baby and the mother. So from the beginning I offered them the breast, but because they were so small, they also were given formula at each feeding. Then, after four days, they became jaundiced, and I had to stop nursing. I began pumping my breasts, not to relieve the fullness (the milk had not really come in yet) but to stimulate them. It was a dull and painful task, but it was the only way I could ensure the future possibility of nursing.

After five days the doctor said that I was ready to leave the hospital; but the babies, because of their jaundice and their weight loss, had to stay. It seemed terribly hard to go home empty-handed, and I couldn't decide whether to stay or go. If I left we would only be able to see them through the glass like any nursery visitor. I tried to get permission to come back for part of each day to be with the babies, but it was refused. The nursery nurses were wonderful and warm, and I had no fear that the babies would suffer if I left. I hesitated about leaving not for their sake, but for my own; I was not sure how I would feel about going home without my babies. But after a week in the hospital, when it was still unclear how much longer they would have to stay, I did go home.

It was a good decision. I had not realized until then how

completely sterile and empty the hospital environment was, how totally devoid of sensory stimuli. I was exhilarated at the sight of the paintings, the smell of plants and cooking, the sound of music. It was wonderful to be back in bed with Ken, even without sex. It felt good to return, for a few moments at a time, to the rest of my life. I did some tentative work on a few on-going projects, and I felt a renewed sense of the non-baby aspects of my life.

But after a few days, I began to fear that I would lose hold of the reality of the babies, that I might begin, in some unarticulated way, to want them not to come home. For the first time we were depressed. Fortunately the babies soon gained weight and four days after me were allowed home. It was a new high.

I had been pumping my breasts dutifully, and as soon as the babies were home I began the effort to wean them from the bottle to the breast. It was a struggle. My breasts required a great deal more effort than the bottle, and the babies preferred the bottle; it seemed pointless to force them. But I continued to try, and after two weeks they began to prefer the breast. But they were agonizingly slow. One baby alone could nurse for thirty or forty minutes. They ate every three hours or more. It felt like we were feeding babies twenty hours a day. It seems incredible to me now that we managed. Sometimes we were up every two hours all night long. Ken got up and changed diapers and brought the babies to be nursed, or he held one while I nursed the other. He was up as often as I was, so we were both always exhausted.

During pregnancy, despite major physiological changes, I essentially maintained my normal intellectual, creative, and professional life. It was diluted somewhat: I did less painting than usual and devoted much energy to thinking about the babies. But to a significant degree my life was unchanged. During the first months of nursing, however, those aspects of my life were totally submerged. My efforts and energies were devoted to my own physical recovery and to the babies. Nursing was the nexus of the two, the actual link between me and the babies, and it was therefore the unarticulated focus of my effort to come to terms with my new identity. I did not consciously realize this at the time, but in retrospect it seems probable to me that I felt so ambivalent about nursing not only because of the physical discomfort or the amount of time it took, but also because it emphasized my new role as "mother." I was not working — I was nursing.

And I was nursing a fantastic proportion of the time. It was an extraordinary confrontation with physicality. Obviously nursing is essentially a physical act, but in our society it is an act imbued with romantic resonance. Nursing two babies, though, has no familiar iconology. At first I nursed one baby at a time, but as they became better nursers I frequently fed them simultaneously. Even pregnancy did not impress upon me as strongly as double nursing did that I am, after all, an animal. To look down at myself and see two tiny creatures sucking at my breasts was something for which little in my intellectual training had prepared me. Ken referred to it as a double-header. I thought I looked like a cow, an image which alternately amused and disturbed me. I wondered sometimes whether I could cope with having someone gnawing at my body ten hours a day. I sometimes felt bruised and mauled and almost repelled by the sense of continuous chewing on me. But I also had moments of enjoying the peacefulness of the nursing, the cuddling that went with it, the feel of the babies' bodies against me; and I knew that in fact it was less work than bottle feeding would have been.

Also, it was seductive, in a way, to be nursing them and thus to be uniquely important to them. That was also threatening because it meant having to be almost constantly available to them. I wanted to be indispensable to them but I also wanted to be able to dispense with the need to be with them. For months I could not simply relax and accept the fact of nursing.

I was never erotically stimulated by breast feeding (and in some odd way it has made my breasts seem unerotic to me, perhaps on a permanent basis) and I do not think that it made a particularly significant difference in my relationship with the babies, at least from my perspective. Nevertheless I am glad that I did it. Although by the time they were weaned (at six and a half months) I had no regrets about the end of nursing, there was a point before that at which I was depressed at the thought that when I weaned these babies my entire reproductive life would be over. To my surprise I felt somewhat cheated because I would have experienced pregnancy, birth, and nursing only once. Although I much prefer non-pregnancy to pregnancy, and although I did not enjoy giving birth, at moments it seems sad to have that part of my life over.

For the first few months of their lives twins are a nightmare. It is tiring but emotionally satisfying to pick up a crying, miserable, wet, hungry baby, change her diapers, comfort her, feed her, and transform her into a quiet, peaceful, dry, full, happy baby. But to go through that entire cycle only to be faced, at the end, with another crying, miserable, wet, hungry baby is devastating. There were many days in which neither Ken nor I did a single thing besides survive and minister to babies. We tried taking naps but all too often, ten minutes after we fell asleep, a baby would cry or the phone would ring. It was more pain than pleasure. Finally we simply resigned ourselves to exhaustion and that acceptance helped.

It was difficult, however, to maintain perspective in the midst of the howling. Sometimes it would suddenly occur to me that I had been carting around a screaming baby for hours, caught up in the rhythm of her hysteria; I would rush to put her down. When they were six weeks old I realized how completely immersed Ken and I had both been in baby care and I was afraid that we had already fallen into the trap of letting the babies take over our lives. Everything else had come to a complete standstill. I was doing very little that was not related to babies, and whatever I was doing, the babies were central in my thoughts.

It now seems inevitable to me that that was the case. I am very deeply involved in my work, especially with my art, and in some ways I consider it the most important thing in my life. But the experience of pregnancy, birth, nursing, and adjusting to two infants overwhelmed everything else. It commanded, for a time, my full attention. It was a rich, compelling experience, a moment of great change, and it took some time to assimilate.

After the first weeks of recovery and baby care, I went out one day into the sun while they were asleep and sketched and watered the flowers and then sprayed myself with water from the hose. The sensual pleasure of being wet outdoors in the breeze was a vivid reminder of how long it had been since my body had been completely my own, serving my own pleasures. It was a wonderful release. As the next days went by Ken and I gradually found tiny bits of time for ourselves. The time away from the babies was both a pleasure, a relief, and a tease. It was dangerous to remember how interesting it could be to read a book, draw, or paint because no sooner did we get interested than a baby would yelp. Still it helped. Neither of us was yet trying hard to work, but we both enjoyed the diversion. It was apparent to both of us very early that absence did indeed make the heart grow fonder.

After my post-partum examination life began to take on a semblance of its former proportions. Sex. It had been a very long time because my vagina had become swollen and sore when I was about seven months pregnant, and we had not had intercourse since. The first time was a big event, but very painful. For weeks it was physically and psychologically difficult for me. It was hard to relax, not only because of the pain, but also because I felt that I was giving so much of myself and my body to the babies. I had never thought of my sexual role as "giving" any more than "taking," but during the time I was nursing, I felt that nursing was a "demand" being made on my body, and that sex was too. Sex seemed like a "demand" partly because it was painful and partly because the location of the pain was the same as it had been in childbirth. Ken's sexual interest in me had never waned during the pregnancy or during nursing, but he tolerated the enforced separation of the last months and the following six weeks quite admirably. Gradually the pain faded and sex was once again integrated successfully into our lives.

When our sex life first resumed, Ken and I both remarked on the fact that when we approached each other, we were shocked each time by the gross size of the other. The babies had become the measure. We were both giving the greater proportion of our energy to the babies, and of necessity for those early months, we each came second in the other's attention. After a year that was no longer true, just as the emotional connection I felt between sex and childbirth faded. But it was almost a year before we were restored to our former prominence in each other's lives.

In terms of Ken's and my basic relationship having babies has been a success. Our lives are fuller since we had the babies, and consequently there is more potential for minor crises and frustrations. We both feel, however, that our essential relationship remains unaltered, except that our practical and emotional interdependence on each other has increased.

That interdependence is sometimes frustrating because

we are each less free to go our own way and to work at our own pace. But it is also an impetus to what are often fruitful confrontations. We each have independent spheres of activity, relationships, and power; but we also share the activity of child care in a very active sense, and we have to be communicating well in order to do it. When one of us cares for the babies in the morning and then turns them over to the other later, we both need to have a good understanding of the moods and interactions of the morning. It is almost impossible to function unless we face problems and irritations at once and work them out. That can be tiring, but it means that annoyances never last or build into insurmountable crises. That has been a constructive result of working together so closely.

I think this is true at least partially because the children have changed both our lives to the same degree and in the same way. If only one of us had had to drastically readjust his or her life, I am sure that we would have felt greater, perhaps disruptive, tensions. I have tried to let the babies change my life as little as possible, although they add a dimension to it that I did not have before. If my life had changed in significant ways and Ken's had not, I know that our marriage would have suffered. But we never considered letting that happen, and the sharing of the efforts and the readjustments has strengthened our relationship.

From the day after the babies were born, Ken and I were both sharing essentially equally in their care, except insofar as nursing necessarily skewed the balance. The supplementary bottles helped restore that balance. At first the demands were so great that we both did baby care all the time. Then when the babies were two months old, we instituted the half-day system on which we have relied ever since. We both participated in the changing and feeding in the middle of the night and the early morning. Then we figured out how many hours there would be between breakfast and the babies' dinner and we divided those hours in half. One of us cared for the babies in the morning while the other painted or wrote or worked on whatever project was in progress, and then we switched in the afternoon. It was a very successful system, as neither of us felt put upon by too many hours with the babies.

School started for Ken in early September, when the babies were less than three months old. He only has to be in school one full day and several part-days a week, so I was not suddenly left completely alone with the babies all the time. But I was alone with them some days, really for the first time, and almost immediately I began to think about going back to work. I wanted to reestablish the balance of child care that we had so carefully created. We both felt very quickly that if he were out of the house for parts of several days each week and I were almost always at home, the responsibility for the babies would be more likely to fall to me. Neither of us wanted that to happen, and we could tell after only a few weeks that the only way to avoid it would be for me to return to work, even if it were only on a very limited basis. I envied Ken the chance to get out, to be away for a little while, and to come home to the babies refreshed. Although I knew that I would be able to work only a few hours each day because the babies were then almost exclusively breast fed, I decided to try to work out an arrangement with the office to work even less than my usual three-fifths week.

That meant we needed to bring in a child care person. I had originally thought I would search for one after the babies were born and have her begin work in the fall, when I would return to the office. (We did make the sexist assumption that the day care person would be a woman. Perhaps if we had had to search for long we would have broadened our horizons.) Because we knew that Ken would be free for the summer, we had planned to care for the babies ourselves till fall. I liked the opportunity to have the summer off anyway. But by chance we had heard in March of a woman who would be looking for a baby care job in the fall, and we had spoken to her, liked her, and agreed to hire her. I knew, although I hardly appreciated it, what a miracle it was to have found a potentially good day care person with so little effort. She had been one of the very first people we had called when we learned that there would be two babies. I called her with some trepidation, fearful that she would retreat. She was tempted to. We negotiated for about a half-hour. She has raised eight children of her own, several grandchildren, and many children of various employers, but she said that she had never taken care of twins. I said nervously that I had never cared for twins either. I offered her more money than we had originally agreed on and as much encouragement as I could (thinking that if I were in her position I would surely refuse) and she agreed to try.

We did not seriously consider arranging out-of-the-house group day care for the girls while they were tiny. We wanted them to have individual attention while they were small. Because we could afford part-time baby care while we both worked, we were not forced to seek alternatives. We did not give much serious consideration to the possibility of five-days-a-week babysitting, partly because we could not have afforded it on our part-time salaries, and partly because we both felt that it would be sad to see our children only on weekends. The flexible schedules that we had previously established as a means to a pleasant and productive lifestyle now made it possible to work and still to see a fair amount of our girls.

For many women the decision to go out to work and to leave small children with a paid babysitter represents a break with their mother's patterns. For me the decision to have less than full-time babysitting was the break. I have tried to analyze why I did decide to have only part-time child care and I think it is to a large extent the result of circumstances. Ken and I were already working out of the house fewer than five days a week, so it was natural simply to have a sitter only for the three days that we were away. I suspect that if I had been married to someone who wanted full-time child care, I would have agreed: I have no principled feelings against it. If at some point one or both of us gets an attractive full-time job offer, we will certainly consider full-time child care. But having begun as we did — able to share and enjoy all non-babysitter time — we have maintained the system.

Even before I returned to the office, I began to be desperate for some time to paint. So in August Mrs. Bush began working three or four hours a day, three days a week. It was a good introduction to the girls and to the slightly peculiar household, and a time for the girls to get to know her. By September she was eager to begin working three longer days and I was eager to get out of the house. Then suddenly I had to write a brief in my Supreme Court case. This development, coupled with Ken's return to work, made it seem as good a time as any to return to the office. The girls were three months and ten days old

It was good to get back to work. I had been given a leave of absence without pay as a maternity leave. Now instead of returning to the neighborhood office where I had been working, I went for the first time to the central, downtown office of the agency. Instead of dealing with many individual clients, I began to work on class actions specializing in welfare and social security areas.

My return to work reestablished the sense of balance and sharing between Ken and me. I arranged to go to the office on the three days on which Ken taught. Mrs. Bush cared for the babies those days, and Ken and I shared the other four on our half-day system.

I never had any qualms about leaving the babies with Mrs. Bush. After all she had raised or helped to raise many children. But the fact of her broad experience presented a slight problem: there was some ambiguity about authority. She was older and more experienced; I was the employer and the mother. For the first month or so, there was a small competition between us about the decision-making power. Also I felt twinges of jealousy and possessiveness when Mrs. Bush first began to care for the babies. I actually felt some hesitancy at the prospect of giving up time with them. Not that my feelings were ever strong enough to force me to consider, even for a minute, the possibility of not working. But I did very clearly feel some twinges of jealousy. I was amazed at myself; this jealousy was hardly in character for a woman who assumed she would give birth to a "nanny" when she gave birth to a child. My unexpected response strengthened my resolve to maintain all my non-baby-related interests: if I had become that attached to the babies in two months, think of how attached and dependent I might be in years to come!

Those feelings of jealousy were the first hints of a low-key, subtle competition for the babies' affection that continued for a long time between Mrs. Bush and me. I wanted the babies to love her, to be as content with her as with me. I wanted them to be happy all the days that she cared for them. And yet I have to admit that in some part of my head I wanted them to be happier with me. What an incredibly selfish perspective. I wanted to be free to do my own work and still to be the prime target of my children's affection. I wanted to be important to my children and yet not so crucial that they would be harmed by my absence. Was I — and am I — asking for the impossible?

Mrs. Bush herself seemed to experience some conflict over this problem. On the one hand she was pleased the girls liked me. It reassured her that I cared for them well when she was not around. But on the other hand I think that she was jealous too. The problem, to the extent that it was one, eased as we all became more accustomed to each other and more secure of our own places in the girls' affections. As their second birthday approaches, I have no regret at leaving them. And I think that neither she nor I now feel any jealousy.

When she first began to work for us I had other conflicts as well. I felt — and feel — awkward about being in the position of an "employer"; I am uncertain about the political ramifications of paying someone else to help me care for my babies and my house, and about the racial issues involved in having a black woman taking care of my children. These are all live issues. But how else can I have babies and practice law and paint all at the same time?

At first I felt very self-conscious about these questions. I wondered, for example, what Mrs. Bush thought of the fact that I was paying her a little more than three dollars per hour so that I could sit in my room and paint blue and orange circles. I asked myself if I was really doing something so worthwhile to me that I should be willing to give up time with my babies and pay someone else in order to be able to do it. The answer was clearly yes.

We are remarkably lucky with Mrs. Bush. In over a year and a half she has missed only one week of work, and then because she was sick. She is thoroughly dependable. It is my fantasy come true: with the babies came the Nanny. We have become utterly dependent on her. During the week she was sick, and during her vacations, we realized that we had already begun almost to take her for granted, and that our lives, as we have structured them, are totally dependent on having some outside help. On our own we simply could not do as much. And we find that as much as we enjoy the girls, weeks in which we care for them full-time tire us, frustrate us, and make us irritable.

I have had only one or two disagreements with Mrs. Bush about ways of dealing with the girls. At the times they occurred, they were hugely distressing because they made me realize that I cannot know of other interactions going on between the girls and Mrs. Bush that I might disapprove. But these incidents have been so rare that they have not in any way destroyed my overall confidence in her.

Questions about raising children are very complex. I often feel insecure about my own ability to make the "right" decision about how to deal with the babies. I have no sense that I know as much as I might know, or have the best instincts that I might have, about raising children. Nonetheless I do not trust anyone more than or even as much as I trust myself to care for my babies. Still, ninety-five percent of the time that I leave the girls with Mrs. Bush, I feel completely comfortable and confident.

As the girls get older they have varying responses to our leaving. I feel certain that they genuinely love Mrs. Bush. When I come home at the end of the day they are playing happily with her and show no marked eagerness to come to me in preference to her. But for several months when they were just over a year old, they cried when we left the house. I hated it. It was distressing to leave them crying. I knew that in just a few minutes they would be fine. (I *knew* this because when I'd "leave" just to go into my room for a few hours of painting I would hear them playing happily after five minutes.) Nonetheless, it is sad to leave them crying.

This stage of routine crying every morning passed and became a rare occurrence. But occasionally Ken or I work at home on a Mrs. Bush day, and then there is a good deal of discontent. It is easier for the girls to relate to Mrs. Bush if we are totally absent.

Actually it is difficult to work in the house with the babies no matter who is caring for them, even if it is one of us.

When they are awake they are distracting, and when they are asleep we have to be quiet so as not to awaken them. If they're playing well with Ken, I feel locked into my room because if I go out to them even for five minutes, there will be a minor uproar when I leave. But a studio away from home would not be a good solution because I sometimes sneak in an hour's work during their nap. And if I worked out of the house at night, Ken would simply be left with the same problems of interruptions and the need to be quiet. What we need is a house big enough to afford more physical distance between us and the babies.

We maintained this system of three Mrs. Bush days, four Ken and Jane days, until January, when the deadline for Ken's Master's thesis in design began to seem too close for comfort. It was becoming clear that Ken would not be able to complete his thesis in the cut-up half-days of our baby care system, and it was important to both of us that he finish. The only solution that we could think of was for me to assume the lion's share of the baby care until the thesis was done, and then for him to do the same for me at some future date when I was involved with a major project. It was sensible, reasonable, and apparently necessary. But I knew that I would not be able to take care of the babies four days a week, with *no* time in which to paint, without feeling resentful and bitter. It isn't that I could not or would not be willing to take care of the babies four days a week, or that I object in theory to being, sometimes, the person responsible for the girls. I do not want to be fanatic about absolute, perfect sharing. But I have so many things that I desperately want to do that I am frustrated beyond endurance if I have no opportunity to do them. If I could paint three days a week and care for the babies four days, I wouldn't mind so much. But to go to the office three days and care for the babies four days would mean no time for my art.

Ken's need for extra time to finish his thesis accentuated the most difficult aspect of our sharing of the baby care — our interdependence. When we split the day in half by hours, our time is our own, and if Ken does something that seems to me to "waste" his time, that's his business. But if I were going to do all the baby care until he finished his thesis, my time would hinge upon his use of time; the longer he took to finish, the longer I would be stuck with all the child care. I knew that I would not be able to sit calmly while he watched the television and the thesis stretched out in front of us.

So we asked Mrs. Bush if she would be willing to work four days a week until the thesis was finished, so that I would have at least one day a week in which I could paint. I thought that if I had one guaranteed painting day I would be better able to care for the babies the other three days without feeling resentful. Luckily she was willing to do it for several months.

It worked. Ken's free time was productive. He worked hard on his thesis and within five months he had finished the rough draft. He felt that he could complete it during his regular share of non-baby time. So we returned eagerly to splitting four days between us.

During that time we both had qualms about having Mrs. Bush care for the babies more days a week than we did. We worried that we would lose our prominence in the babies' affections and that we would somehow drift away from our intense relationship with them. Mrs. Bush had qualms too; she was exhausted by the four-day week and, despite the additional money, she was very glad when it ended. Also some weeks my painting day was problematic. I had moments of real pain when I heard a baby cry. When the girls cry as I am leaving the house, I have to suppress the desire to rush back to them — but then I put the crying and the baby more or less out of my mind within ten minutes. When I am working in the house, I want to rush in at every cry. I know that Mrs. Bush can comfort the baby as well as I can, but *I* need the comfort of contact too.

I bore up very well with my additional child care. There were, however, moments of tension, moments in which I expressed some pent-up hostility that I had not articulated even to myself. And I did have periods of fairly extreme depression in which I wished that I had not decided to have babies at all. I felt overwhelmed and miserable; my worst fear about having babies was coming true — I had no time for myself. But later I realized that it was only because Ken and I were temporarily not sharing the baby care. The return to equal sharing signalled a new period of great enthusiasm for me; I was able to do more work.

Since the babies have begun walking and talking, I have loved and enjoyed them more every day. I feel more and more positive about having had children. My only moments of regret now are in the middle of the night or in the quiet pre-dawn, when I want desperately to be asleep and they want desperately to be awake, or when I have a sudden inspiration and can't act on it because it's my turn to care for them.

There are some situations of continuing pressure. Late afternoon to early evening is a potential "arsenic hour" in which everyone is tired and cranky. It is a tense transition to rush home after a hectic day at the office and try to cook dinner and deal with two tired babies when you're tired yourself. This is the point at which we are most aware of how little flexibility we have in our lives. Even though my job is unusually flexible for a lawyer's there are still deadlines and crises and moments of pressure. It is extremely difficult to deal with work crises and home crises at the same time. One week I had an important brief due in court and Ken got sick. I had to do all the post-Mrs. Bush child care and all the non-Mrs. Bush days plus deal with Ken. I felt as if I had to start rushing the moment I got up in the morning. It was such a hateful week at home that if I had had complete control over my job, I would not have tried to work that week. But there was a deadline that had to be met.

Normally, however, I think that at this stage of the babies' lives and my work, the different kinds of pressure and tension from work and the babies do not conflict unmanageably. I cannot tell whether this will change when the babies are older and making other kinds of demands. The difficulty now is the inexorability of sudden work crises and of sudden baby crises. Neither one will make room for the other. I have learned, though, to steal time and energy from one part of my life for another when I need to. I use office time to run art or baby related errands, art time for crisis law work, bits and pieces of art and law time to write this essay.

Ken and I have agreed, though we never made a conscious articulated decision to this effect, to take time from our social lives in order to have more time to work. We see fewer movies and go out for dinner less often, though we still have dinner guests fairly frequently and we do spend time with our babies with friends and their children. There is so little time that most non-baby care hours are husbanded for work, and our free daylight hours are so reduced that we are eager to work as often as possible during the evening. The girls go to bed at about seven-thirty. Then we eat dinner or have coffee and relax after having eaten earlier with them. It is virtually impossible to begin work before eight-thirty or nine, and after a long day, it is frequently difficult to begin at all. I make an effort to work as many evenings as I possibly can because without that time I am lost.

Actually, the fact that I do frequently begin a three- or four-hour evening of work at nine o'clock is a good example of the fact that having children has forced me to use my time better, and that the price has been the sacrifice of almost all simple relaxation. I remember that before we had children, we often came home from work and sat around and sometimes had a drink and relaxed before starting dinner. By the time we finished eating and were ready to begin to work — it was nine or nine-thirty. Now instead of relaxing, I deal with the kids, make dinner for them and for us, get them to bed — and I still begin to work at nine, trying to forget my fatigue. I feel so much better about myself, my life, and the babies when I have gotten some work done that it is worth being tired. I realize that the greatest proportion of my happiness comes from satisfaction with my art work when it is going well, although I am sure that I would not be able to get such deep satisfaction from my work if my life with Ken and the girls were not as happy as it is. Because I am happiest when I feel that I have gotten a reasonable amount of good work done, the days that feel like pre-baby life plus a few hours of baby care are the good days. On the bad days, I feel as if my life is submerged in an endless and unproductive round of tears, diapers, and bananas. On the bad days, my complaints are all centered around the inelasticity of time. Basically, I enjoy being with the girls. If I could spend time with them and then have the time and energy to paint or write or work, I think I would be satisfied. As it is, I am constantly rushed, pressed for time, and tired.

One incident shortly after the girls' second birthday made me wonder whether I feel more insecure about what having babies has done to my potential than I normally admit to myself. I was browsing in a bookstore, thumbing through a book about Barbara Hepworth, the great English artist, and discovered that she is the mother of triplets. I was absolutely elated. Even now, telling the story, I feel a physical elation. I could not have been more excited if I'd just been told that I'd been chosen for a show at the gallery of my choice. When the joy died down, I realized that my response had been way out of proportion. And the only explanation I can think of is that on some deep level that I do not confront, I am afraid that having children, twins no less, has somehow made it harder (impossible?) for me to become a great artist. When I say this to myself, it does not seem obviously true. I do not feel that I have those doubts. I have been working very hard since the babies were born, and I have had many new ideas, most of which I think have been exciting and which I have been able to work out. It does not seem to me that the children have hampered me, except to slow the pace of my production a bit. But how else can I explain my incredible wild joy at the news that forty years ago Barbara Hepworth had triplets?

I continue to identify myself as I always have: I am an intellectual, an artist, a lawyer, and sometimes a writer. Now I also spend some of my time playing with and taking care of babies. The concept of "motherhood' is meaningless to me. Perhaps it is to everyone, except as a superficial description of a female who has a child. "Mommy" to me still means my mother. When I think that for Vanessa and Rachel I will be the image of "mother," it seems absurd. Actually, the concept of "wife" is equally empty to me. I am married, I live with and share much of my life with Ken, yet I never think of myself as a "wife." In fact I rarely identify myself to myself as a "woman." I take it for granted that I am a woman, and go on to other things which seem more uniquely me.

I do not say lightly that I do not identify myself as a "woman"; I have been reading books by and about women, particularly women artists, and I am making an effort to grasp how their lives and mine are shaped by our femaleness. I think that my life is less formed by my status as a woman than the lives of many other women because I grew up with the clear notion and example that women were intellectually, professionally, publically, and potentially the equal of men. I always believed that I could do anything that I wanted to do. And luckily, I have never had any experiences that taught me otherwise. I have not completely succeeded in everything I have always wanted to do, but I have never failed at anything because I was a woman. And except for conceiving, carrying, bearing, and nursing my babies, I have never succeeded in anything because I am a woman.

Becoming a mother forced me to confront my femaleness as a real factor in making me who I am and what I am able to experience. Being a mother clearly affects my life, but not more profoundly or differently than being a father affects Ken's life; the differences brought on by parenthood do not seem shaped by being a woman. Also, as far as I can tell, the style and content of my art work have not been affected by my becoming a mother. But I am not sure how being a mother has affected me as a person, as opposed to affecting my life. A friend has suggested to me a change of which I was not myself conscious — that I am less self-indulgent than I used to be. I think maybe that is true, but it is really only the result of having become more disciplined in order to get more done in less time. I have no time in which to simply feel sorry for myself; even if I do feel sorry for myself, I have to cope.

I am still sometimes self-conscious about myself in the role of mother, and I do not quite understand why. Several times I have paused suddenly, at breakfast with Ken and both babies at eight a.m., or sitting in the grass with friends and their babies, and felt self-conscious distaste for myself as the young mother. Perhaps it is because the image is too common and I want to be different and not "just like everyone else." I can laugh at myself in such scenes, but

I am not entirely comfortable. I am watching myself, ironically, and I am even more uneasy when I know that other people are watching too.

I am still puzzled about why I decided to have a baby. It occurs to me now, though it did not earlier, that perhaps the pleasure that my parents found in me created in me an unarticulated belief that having children is joyful and rewarding. When I was small, and indeed until I was over twenty, I had the sense that my existence added happiness to their lives. And that is still generally true, though as I've become more independent, it has become more problematic for them. Perhaps that very positive feeling spurred me, unconsciously, to want chilrren.

And I do love my children. There are moments when I am so suffused with love for them that I nearly cry with joy. I am amazed, really, by how much I enjoy the babies, by how appealing, how seductive they are. It is a great sensual pleasure to hold them in my arms.

But sometimes, when the babies wake up unexpectedly in the middle of the evening, or worse, in the middle of the night, I still ask myself, Why? Why have we done this? Why have we saddled ourselves with this effort, this undeniable cry? No other cry is so undeniable. If Ken wants me to do something, and I am working on a painting, I can explain to him why I cannot do it at that moment. But when a baby cries, she will not be patient. Sometimes I almost cry myself with the wish that the cry would stop so that I would not have to respond to it.

And yet as time goes on, and as I love and enjoy the babies more and more, they are clearly less dominant in my life than they were for the first year. I no longer wish that I could spend every waking moment with them and still do all my own work. Now that I am more deeply involved with my work again, the babies are less totally compelling. I am pleased about that; it is the balance that I was hoping to achieve when I first decided to have a child. I enjoy them even more than I did at the beginning, but the major focus of my mental attention is elsewhere.

When I was small, whenever I asked my father how he felt, he invariably answered that he felt fine because he was with me. At the time I thought that he was being insincere, and I often repeated the question, wanting to know how he *really* felt. Now I understand that he was probably not being hypocritical, but that he really felt that way. When one of my babies cries and I am tired or involved in something else, I frequently resent having to drop everything and go to her. On my way to her side, I am tired and sometimes bitter. But once I get to her, and pick her up, and hold her small body close to me, I feel better, feel warmly toward her, and love her. And suddenly I do feel fine, and I am happy to be with her. It seems very odd.

▲

Five years later, it no longer seems odd to me that I am warmed and comforted by my children. The concept of motherhood is no longer "meaningless" to me. I am a mother; I like it: I've even had another child. Now, when Rachel and Vanessa are eight and their brother Aaron is three, I feel very distant from the me who wrote the preceding essay. She seems oddly cool, intellectualized, uneasy with motherhood. I still have bad hours and bad days, days in which I feel overburdened, but I am relaxed about being a mother, and I have discovered that I love it. Now, as the children grow up, I have new concerns about how it is for them to have me as a mother. I am more aware of the stresses and pleasures for them because I am so busy, and as a result I have tried in various small ways to make myself more available to them. I have not given up any of my commitments, but I have softened some edges.

We are a family of five now. It is very different, emotionally, from the cluster of new parents and new children we were six years ago. And yet in many ways the structure of our lives is still the same. Ken and I are still married; we are both still working; we still have a babysitter four days a week.

Shortly after I wrote my first essay, we moved back to New York. We had wanted to move back for several years. Both of us wanted to be at the center of the art and design worlds, and we love the city. Finally I was able to find a three-day-a-week job in a legal services office, and we decided to move on the strength of that, despite the fact that Ken had not yet found a job. My mother had died only two months before we moved; she had been sick for several years. Her illness had been very painful for all of us; her death was a relief. I was sorry that we had not been able to move back to New York before she died, but it was, in fact, less stressful to return after her death than it would have been earlier. (Only recently have I begun to feel acutely how sad it must have been for her not to see her grandchildren more often before she died.)

When we got to New York, the loft we were to live in was not yet empty, so we went to stay with my father on Long Island. It was both a bad and a good time for us to arrive. We stayed with Daddy and Nanny for two months. I commuted an hour and a half to my new job, and Ken commuted to look for a job. It was tense. For a recently widowed, tired, seventy-two-year-old, two rambunctious toddlers and their unsettled parents was a serious invasion, but we survived with our relationship intact.

The year that followed was not easy. Ken found a job in a design office for four ten-hour days a week. But the office was run by a despot, and Ken didn't like it. He was more depressed than I had ever seen him, and we all felt his misery. In the loft we all felt everything that any of us felt; there was too much togetherness. And Long Island City was a bad place to be with little children. We were there because SoHo had become too expensive, but there were no other children, no parks, no good food shopping. It was depressing and isolating.

We had been lucky enough to find a babysitter we liked, an older woman who had been a kindergarten teacher. She had a fabulous trick of arriving every morning with a small special thing in her pocketbook, easing the transition between parent and sitter as we left for work. I felt guilty that Vanessa and Rachel were so isolated that year, because there were so few children in the neighborhood, but I hoped that their own companionship would help.

We were glad to be in New York, but Ken's job, the isolation of the neighborhood, the effort to reestablish ourselves were all trying. That whole transitional year is a blur now; it faded as Ken found a job he liked at the Parsons School of Design, and we moved. I had inherited some money from my mother, and we decided to buy a house. In Manhattan the prices were impossible. We wanted a Yard, a precious commodity in New York. And we needed enough space for a workshop and a studio. After weeks of searching, we discovered that old friends were selling their house in Park Slope, near Prospect Park in Brooklyn. It has a generous south garden, a full height basement for a shop, and four floors. It is small, only 17 feet by 40 feet, but with four floors it is enough room. It felt like a very bourgeois transition, from a loft to a house, but in fact the move gave Ken and me the privacy we needed to work because he has a full shop in the basement and I have the top floor as a studio.

In September 1976, about a year after we'd come back to New York, we moved into the house. The neighborhood was filled with children. Within weeks Rachel and Vanessa started nursery school five days a week, nine to twelve, directly across the street. They began right from the start in separate classes. After only two days of evident anxiety, they seemed very happy there. We were relieved and happy to see them adjusting well to life with other children, and we were emotionally and physically freer to turn to our own work.

We had changed babysitters even before the move because after about five months, our first New York sitter became ill. We all had liked her, and we hated the idea that we might be in for a high turnover in sitters, but the change was a relief to me in one respect. She had commuted to work and needed to leave exactly at 5:30 pm in order to make her train. That meant I had to be home to meet her every day exactly on time. Ken couldn't do it because he was working ten-hour days. It pressured all my afternoons in my new job. So I was glad to look for someone in the city.

We found someone quite quickly, a young woman, only nineteen, immature, somewhat insecure, but very warm and affectionate with the children. It was very helpful, when we moved to the new house and began a new school, that the babysitter did not also change.

That move marked the beginning of a happy, productive stage in our lives. Even before we left Chicago I had begun working on an art idea unlike any I had had before. I began to think about Time as the subject of an art work. It was, of course, a central concept in my life; I didn't have enough of it, and I thought about it a great deal. The beginning of this project marked a major change in my experience since I last wrote here: whereas at first I believed that having children had no effect on the style or content of my art, I gradually allowed this radical change in my life to seep into my art, which became very subjective and incorporated photographs and artifacts of my actual life.

During that first year in New York I began making the rounds of galleries to find one which would allow me to show my Time project, which consisted of paintings, drawings, photographs, collages, a sound tape, a book, a clock collection, and more. It was my first effort at selling my artself in New York, and it was painful. The work had come to be more and more about me, and my relation to my mother's decline and death, and my daughters' birth. Offering it to strangers for acceptance or rejection was not easy. And I had no quick success. One memorable man told me that my ideas were interesting and well developed but that my painting shat; that my intellectual training had clearly been more profound than my visual training. He was right about that, but I was trying to combine the intellectual with the visual, and he was telling me that I had failed.

However, I was eventually offered the opportunity to show my work in a cooperative gallery, as a trial for eventual membership in the gallery. I leapt at the chance, and scheduled the show for April 1977. So when we were at last settled in our new house I had only about six months before my first one-woman show in New York. I had been working on it for a year and a half, but disjointedly. Now I worked like a maniac on the piece itself and on trying to attract attention to it. Ken did a huge amount of work helping me, making frames and supports and display cases. For the last month before the show, the house and family were in chaos. One day, in a desperate effort to get attention, Vanessa and Rachel drew all over our bedroom wall with lipstick.

My degree of absorption during those last few weeks before the show was obviously not good for the children, but as a rare, biennial event I think it was not too disastrous. In some ways I would like to be free to work that intensely on my art all the time, but that is simply not possible with young children.

The girls went to stay at my father's house for two days

while I and many of my friends mounted the show. It was wonderful though exhausting fun, being at the center of such feverish activity, having set it all into motion.

And what was the result? The *New York Times* art critics did not jump for joy; in fact, they ignored it. It is as hard, I learned, to get reviewed as it is to get a gallery to begin with. But I did get good mention in *New York Magazine* and in *The Village Voice*. I did get favorable reactions from many people, and the gallery members were very enthusiastic and invited me to join the gallery, which I did. For a first show, it was a success. I had promise of another show, and my efforts to become a professional artist were begun. I now think the whole show should have been radically edited, but that it had some good pieces in it. I still meet people who saw it and remember it.

When it was over, I felt an enormous space in my life. I was still working steadily three days a week at my law job, as I had been all along, but I had been working intently on the Time project for two years, and now it was over. I could choose anything else to begin. I could try to relax. I could sit back and enjoy Vanessa and Rachel, who were almost four and grown-up and charming. Their twinship had gradually changed for us and for them: they were less often kicking and screaming and more often playing well together. They had become wonderful little girls. I began to hate the idea that I would never have another fabulous four-year-old. Suddenly it seemed as if it might be fun . . . to have another baby.

I was amazed at myself. For years I had sworn aloud that I would never have another baby, but now I was actually beginning to want to do it. I was enjoying Rachel and Vanessa more than I had ever thought I would. And I had been able to put together an ambitious art show; having children did not mean that I could not do my art. Things were going particularly well for us. We both liked our jobs; our new house made things significantly easier. I was feeling powerful and pleased with myself. We could have our family and enjoy ourselves and each other, and earn a living, and do creative work besides. If it was possible with two, why wouldn't it be possible with three?

Our decision to have a third child was different in every way from our original decision to have children. This time, I wanted to do it because I wanted to do it, because it was fun, exciting, cuddly. I wanted another infant to nuzzle, toddler to laugh with, four-year-old to wonder at. I wanted to experience the dynamic of a second child, and to experience a single child. Assuming I would have a single child. We told ourselves we shouldn't do it unless we were willing to face the possibility of having twins again, and we decided we were, though we hoped for only one.

Ken was working full time and I knew that more of the burden of early childcare would fall to me, but to my surprise that didn't seem too threatening. I think that was because we already had our lives structured around the children, we had a babysitter, I knew I loved children, and I had been able to keep working well during Rachel and Vanessa's early years. I would have preferred it if Ken had had a more flexible schedule, but I wanted to have the baby enough to do it despite his full-time job.

During the summer, when I went for my regular gynecological check up, the doctor diagnosed small fibroid tumors and advised me that if I ever wanted to have more children, I should do it in the near future. Once told that, I discovered that I really did want to have another baby. So did Ken. It was amazingly liberating to decide that we could change our minds, that we were free to retract my loud speeches.

I got pregnant immediately. The pregnancy itself went well; except for a cold that lasted two months, I felt healthy and energetic. But we did have several serious family traumas during the pregnancy. Ken tore the cartilage in his knee and was in the hospital for over a week, then on crutches for six weeks. We had our furnace replaced and had to move out of the house for two weeks. Vanessa had an acute asthma attack and pneumonia and was in the hospital for several days. Sometimes I wondered if we were being punished for our greed in wanting a third child. Hard times. But we all survived. I devoted much less energy and emotion to the pregnancy itself than I had to the first, partly because of all these crises and partly because I had been pregnant before, now had two four-year-olds, and in addition to continuing work at the office, I was having a one-woman show about six weeks before the baby was due.

I worked hard putting together a semi-serious show, The Baroque Rolodex, in which I transformed thirty-two rotary Rolodexes — quintessential office equipment — into playful art objects. Vanessa and Rachel had a Rolodex of their own in the show, and frequently they worked with me in the studio. There were times, especially in the last month, when I felt I was pushing myself too much, but most of the time I was enjoying myself. The show was a reasonable success, generating four reviews though, as usual, no sales.

After the show was over, we turned toward each other and concentrated on waiting for the baby. Vanessa and Rachel and I worked hard on a wall hanging for the babe: they drew pictures which I machine-appliqued onto patches of fabric. It was a cozy project, and while we worked we talked about the coming child.

Aaron's birth was very different from Vanessa's and Rachel's. I worked until about ten days before he was due, when I spent fourteen hours in the hospital in false labor. After that I waited, with endless strong but useless contractions. Eventually, three days after the due date, by which time I thought I would lose my mind from two weeks of contractions, the doctor induced labor. Three hours later, Aaron Burckhardt Stevens was born, April 5, 1978, weighing 8 lbs. 3 oz., with a huge head and shoulders.

Until the moment Aaron was born I felt such overpowering loyalty to Vanessa and Rachel that I often asked myself how I could find room in my heart for another child. It seemed that I would always have to love them most, for they were my first children; I'd learned child-loving with them. To my utter amazement, in the first minutes holding Aaron in the delivery room, my loyalties underwent a revolution. This child was so tiny, so helpless, so dependent on me, that my focus shifted almost entirely to him. I fell passionately in love with him. For a year it was like having a love affair, the only kind of love affair that can be tolerated, even encouraged, within the confines of my marriage. I truly longed for Aaron whenever we were apart. I adored him. I revelled in my love for him, though I had moments of anxiety about my radical shift in loyalties. The rest of the family seemed willing to tolerate our devotion to each other.

But I believed that my early passion for Aaron was a function of the postpartum nursing experience, and after a time my loyalties would even out among my children. That is in fact what has happened. I am very happy to have had my third child. I am glad that we are experiencing the more relaxed dynamics of a "second" child, and the more relaxed process of having a single child. Vanessa and Rachel seem to have adjusted well to their younger brother. There were a few over-zealous pats in the first months, and now some annoyed remarks when he gets into their possessions — all well-deserved. In general they seem to enjoy him a great deal. They were almost five when he was born, and they had been, of necessity, sharing toys and attention all their lives. I think that those two factors made it easier for them. Now it is Aaron who exhibits the most jealousy, yelping when I pick up one of his sisters, clutching me and announcing boldly, "*My* mommy only."

I stayed home from work for five months after Aaron was born, and enjoyed him, and the girls, and the spring and summer. My employer was very supportive, and allowed me leave — unpaid except for a few weeks of accumulated vacation pay — without complaint, on the condition that I participate when necessary in work on my ongoing cases, which I did. When I did work, I was paid for it. Ken stayed home occasionally to help out and to be with the baby, but he was actually working full time. I was not on my own, however, as our babysitter was there. I was therefore able to do a moderate amount of art work between nursings. I was sorry that I had arranged to have finished a show before the baby was born, because beginning a new project requires more creative spark than continuing a project already in progress. It turned out to be nearly impossible to begin something new during the first postpartum months. I did do several small projects I liked.

After five months I went back to work. Luckily, my office was very flexible, as long as I got my work done somehow, and they let me return gradually and with erratic hours as Aaron refused to drink from a bottle and I had to rush home midday to nurse him. I nursed him exclusively for about six months, and then in addition to feedings for another seven.

Slowly Aaron was integrated into the structure of the family. Around the time I went back to work, Rachel and Vanessa went back to school, for kindergarten. They returned to the same school where they had gone to nursery school, because we thought that after the introduction of Aaron into the family, other things should remain as stable as possible for them. We all had a good year. Work went well for Ken; he was gradually moving, at Parsons, into a position as head of a new experimental Design Resource Center which was licensing the production of student and faculty designs in the commercial marketplace. He had to travel occasionally, which I hated, and the job had stressful periods, but he was enjoying it. I was satisfied with my law work, but felt somewhat frustrated because I was having trouble beginning a major new art project. However, I was pleased with work on a few minor pieces and hoped that a major project would soon suggest itself. Vanessa and Rachel loved school. Aaron was thriving. There were days when we were all tired, but most of the time our routines were working well for us.

One problem did persist that had emerged during the previous several years. The first winter we were in our house, when Vanessa and Rachel were about three and a half, they each had several bouts of asthmatic bronchitis. Gradually, in the year that followed, we began to see evidence of allergies, and eventually to see that they were having asthmatic reactions to their allergies. Through detailed history-taking and skin tests, the allergist helped us to identify dogs, dust, feathers, kapok, and seasonal allergies as the villains. Both girls have the same allergies, and both have the asthma to about the same degree, though each has had periods of suffering worse than the other.

The allergies and asthma have had a definitely restrictive effect on their social lives, and on ours. Travel is problematic; visiting is limited. They tend to have asthma attacks with colds, so we have had to become more conservative about dealing with colds than we would otherwise have been. For several years, from the time they were three until they were six, they were sick often. We were in doctors' offices or hospital emergency rooms six or eight times; now we can usually avoid that, as we have learned to manage the asthma at home. Largely because of the asthma, Ken and I have not had even a weekend alone since Vanessa and Rachel were three and a half; the homes they might have visited have cats or dogs or kapok or other allergens. Partly because of it we have rarely ventured overnight to new places even as a family. Because of it Rachel and Vanessa have from time to time required extra attention, physical and emotional. Traveling, and during every cold, we have to be prepared to be up much of the night helping to cope with attacks. I think that Rachel and Vanessa have adjusted well to their asthma, and as we all learn to manage it better it limits us less. But it has been a significant and a strenuous factor during the last few years.

In lives like ours, so full and so tightly scheduled, there is little margin for crises. A night of no sleep is a serious handicap at the office. And yet parenthood is full of crises — a household with five people in it has at least five times as many crises as a household with one person. Every childhood illness and crisis puts a strain on our resources of time and energy, reminds us how precarious is the balance that allows us to parent and to work and to make art. For us, the allergies and asthma have added a small but noticeable weight to the crisis side of the scale.

The most radical change in the family since my first essay has been Aaron's birth. But there have been many other changes since. Vanessa and Rachel changed to the local public school for first grade. It was a difficult transition, into the real world of public school and "serious work." They complained strenuously at first about having to sit at their desks all day. But they managed, and they began to learn to read, which they had not done before, and they made friends.

It is a good public school, for New York, but the classes are big and there is of necessity little personal attention. I think Rachel and Vanessa could have survived there and learned the basic skills, but I was afraid that no spark of inspiration or curiosity would be instilled in them. Then a serious problem did arise regarding the public school. The children are supposedly distributed randomly among the classes, but nonetheless there is a wide variation in the quality of both teachers and classes. Unfortunately, for twins in the same grade but different classes, this disparity is glaring. Rachel had the bad luck to be put into a class with a worse teacher and slower students than Vanessa, and it was all too obvious to her that she was moving more slowly. It had a very bad effect on her morale.

The combination of this bad school situation, worsening asthma, and a young brother at home made for a particularly difficult year for Rachel, and her expressions of unhappiness caused me to curtail my art work somewhat so that I could devote more time to her, and to the other children. Ken and I both made an effort to make time to spend alone with each child, and we spent more time all together as a family.

At the end of that year my father generously offered to pay the girls' way in private school. We gratefully accepted, and for second grade they changed schools again, beginning at a private school about two and a half miles from home, to which they travel in a school car. They are full of enthusiasm for their new school. With the change in schools, more attention, and the passage of time, Rachel has cheered up. We have tried to sustain the patterns that helped her, and we have continued to spend much more weekend time on family projects and expeditions. Ironically, as we made ourselves more available the girls grew into a new stage and are now as happy to play with friends on the weekend as to play with us. We have learned that sometimes, if we make ourselves available, we are not needed.

During the summer between kindergarten and first grade, we had another change in babysitters. Our previous sitter had been with us for three years, and while she had always been very good with the children, Ken and I had never had an easy relationship with her. When she finally decided that she did not want to deal any longer with our lack of warmth to her, it was basically a relief to us, though we worried about finding anyone as good with the children. Vanessa and Rachel shed no tears and expressed no regret at her leaving, somewhat to our surprise, but from time to time they still talk about her and see her, so there is clearly some affection between them. We had a terrible few weeks, going through the agony of choosing a new sitter, a process that fills me with terror. But we were fabulously lucky and found a woman we all loved, an intelligent, warm, sensible, twenty-eight-year-old feminist from Brooklyn. It was a wonderful relief to me to have a babysitter who seemed good with the children, and whom I also liked.

Then, after fourteen months, she left, not having liked the changes that came with Ken's working at home. I was devastated when she left, having been completely happy with her. Another panic. Miraculously, we once again found someone we like, a twenty-nine-year-old woman artist. Because of my own experience, in which Nanny became a permanent part of our family, I had unusual expectations of a babysitter. But I am slowly recognizing how different a role the babysitter plays in my children's lives than she did in my own life, because I am around much more than my mother ever was. I am beginning, now, slowly, to adjust to the idea that our babysitter will not stay forever, as Nanny stayed with me.

The other major changes in our lives concern Ken's and my work. After four years in New York, I moved to a new legal services office. It was not a radical shift; at first I did essentially the same work I've done since Vanessa and Rachel were born. The office is closer to home; a brisk half-hour walk which I love. And it is bigger: twenty-two lawyers instead of five. But during the last year I have inadvertently progressed to a new stage in my legal career which has created conflicts in me I have not yet been able to resolve. I have become a supervisor, which increases my salary and my status but also my responsibility. I am officially working four days a week, and though I can at times work three or three and a half days, I have also had some periods in which I work five or more. It has been exciting and challenging, but also very frustrating, because it takes up both art and family time.

I am really not sure why I have let this happen. Partly, I suppose, because success is seductive. I have become a good lawyer, and can get recognition — within my own small area — for my work. The rewards are more immediate than in art, given my relative status in each world. And we need the extra money. But I have less time and energy for art. It is art that loses, as I try to save time for the children. Though they lose, too, in that I get home later in the evening. I have realized, as I did not when I wrote my first essay, how important it is for the children that I do not work five days a week in the office. I would hate to lose the extra day with them. So now I am in a strange period in which I am trying to sort out my commitment to law and art, and struggling to save the art against the onslaught of possible success at the law.

My art life has proceeded since Aaron's birth. I have been in several group shows and have had two one-woman shows: Domestic Impressions, a collection of prints made by pressing forks and toothbrushes onto paper with beet dye, and Line of Sight, presented as work by a character in a novel. The biggest change in my art life is that I have begun to try to write a novel for the first time. I am now devoting a major portion of my small art time to this project. I am not sure I can do a good job, but I am loving the process. During the year after Aaron's birth, I searched and searched for a theme, a direction for a major new art project; when the idea finally came, it was an idea for a novel. I was doubtful about spreading myself out even more, into a new art field, but I also felt I should respect this idea that had been so long in coming and try to pursue it. It is very difficult to write in my fragmented time, so although I have already been working for two years, I have done probably only a third of the book. Still, I love the effort.

The most radical work change, though, was Ken's. His

Parson's job dissolved. The school decided that the Design Resource Center was not making enough money, although that was not Ken's fault. For a while, in dismay, Ken looked for a new job. Then he turned to trying to begin his own design practice at home — which is what he has really wanted to do for a long time. It means his schedule is almost entirely flexible; he is now freer than I am to run errands and stay home when the babysitter is sick. There are problems, too — his presence in the house was such a strain on our babysitter that she left. She said it was not his personality, but the mere presence of a parent in the house, making her feel on stage all the time, that she didn't like. And there is financial insecurity. During the last year we have had to live on a somewhat reduced income. We are still not sure what Ken's income will be in the coming year, though at the moment he seems to have projects enough to match his earlier salary. Ken's work change has meant that we have less money and less security about where next month's money will come from, but he loves the chance to establish his own practice, and he has been producing a series of wonderful designs.

Despite Ken's new availability after years of having a full-time job, the children recently went through a phase in which they all wanted *my* attention. "Go away, Daddy," Aaron would say, "Mamma do it." And the girls, in more subtle ways, said the same. The most virulent stage of this has already passed, but it taught me another valuable and painful lesson. Whatever our theory and plans, the children, through sickness or emotional neediness or whim, may change them. Sometimes it is very hard for me to accept this. During that stage I felt some resentment toward Ken, even though I believed that it was not his fault, because I could get so little work done. I do not bend as gracefully as I should to these demands, but I am learning. In fact, the single most important lesson I've learned during the last seven and a half years is the need for flexibility, the necessity for compromise.

Some days, when I haven't wanted to be flexible or to adjust to the children's needs, I have felt angry and frustrated. But my dominant mood has been very good. I still want to establish myself, eventually, in the art world; I have lost none of my ambition; but most of the time I am comfortable with my slowed pace, enjoying the pleasures of motherhood as I go along. We came back to New York to try to establish art and design careers, and I think there's a reasonable chance we'll succeed.

I think that our children seem happy with themselves and their lives. If they did not, we could not feel as comfortable as we do with the lives we have constructed. As I said in my original essay, I was comfortable about the idea of combining motherhood with career because my own mother had done it with no apparent ill effects for me. But I have finally realized that the lifestyle Ken and I have evolved is totally different from my parents', and undoubtedly harder on the children. I was cared for by a full-time live-in substitute mother, whose only job was to care for me. When my mother was at home, her only job was to be with me; someone else cooked and cleaned. Also, I was an only child.

My children, on the other hand, share all attention among the three of them. And we have set ourselves up as the primary caregivers, with babysitters as part-time substitutes. We are primary, but often not there. And when we are home, we are often engaged in domestic activities, or — harder — our own art activities. My realization of these differences and of my children's resulting needs has led me, during the last year and a half, to relax somewhat my urgent need for time. I am spending longer evenings, more of each weekend, and portions of my "art days" with the children. I can do this and still have at least enough art time to keep me going, hoping for phases when my time will open up again.

For me, the balancing act is a success; difficult, but possible, and enormously more pleasurable than I ever imagined it would be. I know that this life works for me. I love the combination, despite its stresses. I do have the stamina for all these activities. I am less certain that our way of life is desirable from the children's point of view. I hope it is, and I am trying to accommodate to their needs so that it can be, but now I feel that I won't really know until my children grow up and write their own versions of an essay such as this.

POSTSCRIPT, JUNE 1981

I am pregnant.

The history of my conceptions has been a remarkable progression (or regression, depending on your perspective). The first time, when I tried to decide whether or not to have a baby, I thought and thought and considered all angles and tried to be rational. The second time I knew it was irrational and decided to do it anyway, just because I wanted to. This time I just did it. My decision-making was pre-conscious.

Ken and I have flirted for several years with the idea of having a fourth child. We have both acknowledged the absurd extravagance of it; both admitted that it would be terribly hard; both admitted that it would be fun. We have both enjoyed parenting enormously. I would say that we have been trying to convince ourselves that it would be foolish, given everything else we want to do and our less-than-ideal financial situation. But it is also true that we have from time to time admitted that in many ways it was tempting. I have often said that if I didn't have two other careers, I would surely want to have more children, because I enjoy them so much.

So now we feel some fear that it is all too much, concern for the welfare of our already-born children, pleasure in the prospect of a new baby, a new toddler, concern that we will simply exhaust ourselves, and delight.

Delight, and a fear that I must be insane. No one has four children anymore. I am afraid I will have to spend the rest of my life explaining and apologizing for having so many children. But that shouldn't matter. The more important question is what effect this will have on Rachel and Vanessa and Aaron, and on Ken, and me.

I have been trying to measure the probable effect of this baby on the other children, but I cannot. I do know that, according to the lessons I have been learning during the last two years, I cannot responsibly have this baby unless I am willing to plan to give even more time to the children. I wince a little bit when I acknowledge that to myself, but it does not make me want to give up the baby. I ask myself if I am fooling myself, paying lip service to the idea but secretly planning simply to forge ahead. I suspect there may be a little danger of that, a little secret sense that Vanessa and Rachel seem to demand less and less time, and even Aaron somewhat less, so that I will simply be devoting that extra new time not to art, but to a new baby. A little of that thinking is fair, I think. But that is not all. I have tried to sit myself down and confront this fact: I cannot responsibly have this baby unless I am willing to give more time to the children. And I expect this to make my desire for the baby go away, and it does not. I think I am willing to give up more time.

And what does this mean? Partly, that for some reason which I do not at all understand, I feel more relaxed than I used to about the future. The idea has emerged that in the future I will have more time, and to postpone the enjoyment of that time for three years or so is not so bad, and worth the trade-off of a new baby. Perhaps I feel that way partly because I see now for the first time what it means when the children get older and spend all Saturday and Sunday with their friends. So I know it is true that time does open up. But more important, I think, is an insight I had the other night while brushing my teeth and staring at myself fiercely in the mirror, trying to figure this all out.

I have always seemed to measure myself against greatness. Saying, I am an ambitious artist — if I could be either William O. Douglas or Henri Matisse, I'd rather be Matisse. But now for the first time I realize: I will never be Matisse or make a contribution such as he made. I have no idea whether I have the talent ever to have done such a thing, but whether I do or not, it is clear that I have not organized my life in a way that could make such a contribution possible. Ever. I have not made a single-minded commitment. What I can hope for is to write a novel or two or three, and paint and construct art works—if I work hard and am lucky — on the level of Margaret Drabble or Eva Hesse, not Marquez or Matisse. Not even such success is assured, but it is not absurd. And if I am striving toward these realistic or at least plausible goals, another child and more time given to my family should not make their achievement impossible.

Perhaps, in fact, my greatest talent turns out to be the ability to live and to enjoy a very, very full life. And if that is true, I should be using that talent and enjoying it to the fullest. If some part of me wants to have another baby, and if Ken does, too, and if it seems this won't harm our other children, why not? Why not enjoy my extra stamina and energy? Work, and the enjoyment of it, is a very important part of the full life I am enjoying. If I felt that I would have to give up my art for this baby I would think very differently about it. I think I would not want to make such a trade — I know I would not. But I am willing to give up edges. More edges for a longer time.

If I feel any regret at all, it is that we are not in a financial position to enable me to stop my law work for a year or two, stay home with the children and work on my visual art and my novel. I would love to have a chance now to try to really prove myself about the book. I would like to work as hard as possible on it and see what would happen. But in fact I cannot do that, with three children or with four. So choosing against this child does not get me that opportunity.

There are other hard questions. As a result of experience Ken and I both believe now, as we did not before, that the burden of this new child will clearly fall more heavily on me. Not exclusively by any means, since Ken is working at home on a flexible schedule. But more heavily, because of the pregnancy, the nursing, and the fact that the children, at least some of the time, seem to gravitate toward me. The fact that the burden of childcare will fall more to me is difficult for me to accept. I wish it weren't true, and yet, to be honest, the other day when a friend suggested that with proper hormone treatments a man can nurse a baby, I thought, "Oh, no — *I* want to do that!" I really do like being the special Mother, despite my principles and my desire to work. This made me wonder whether I like having children because it is one of the ways to get the kind of total love I had as an only child. I just thought that up the other night, and I have no idea if it is valid. But I am searching to understand this new fact in my life which seems on the surface so surprising.

One other thing I've thought of. I like excitement and drama. I like working hard and putting together a show and then — the opening, the drama, being the center of attention. I like performing in court — the adrenalin, the drama, being the center of attention. Having a baby is the most dramatic thing I've ever done. It has a long prologue; the excitement builds for months, orders my life, gives me a timetable against which to measure events. And then a climax of enormous drama. I don't know, again, how important this is, or whether it is an emotion to be pleased with or ashamed of. It is all too complex.

All I know is that this is something very different for me, somewhat out of control, and I am not afraid or alarmed or horrified. I want to embrace it. A remarkable change from the Jane of the first *Balancing Act*.

IV

I have chosen to defer my intellectual needs to the demands of my husband and children. I have chosen not to change things by arranging for more child care or insisting upon a reordering of Mark's priorities. Instead, I have accepted the ongoing complications of living a divided life.

ANNA SIEGLER

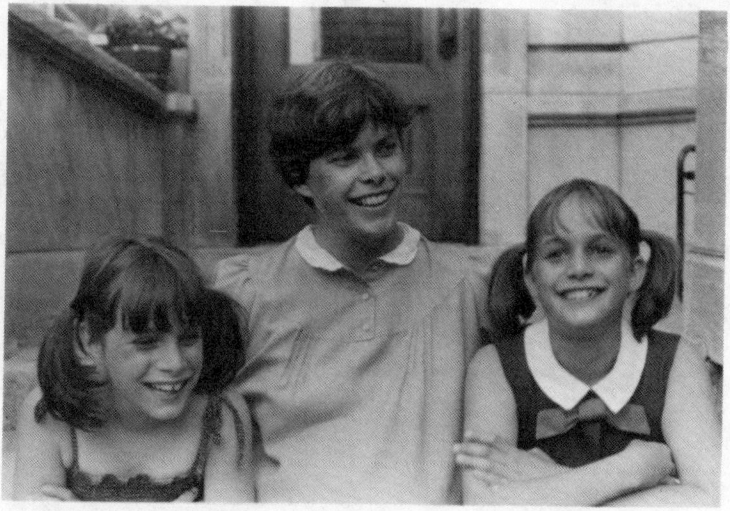

Anna Siegler

"And what brings you here today?" the doctor had asked quietly. I answered that a sense of lethargy and general fatigue was my most persistent problem, that ever since the birth of the twins, I had been beset with an almost overwhelming physiological heaviness. I felt as if I could close my eyes and sleep soundly for hours at any time of day. And yet despite this, I felt as if I should apologize for being in his office, for feeling that my fatigue was worth noticing. I was reminded of Henry James' story, *"The Beast in the Jungle,"* in which the hero senses that a special fate awaits him and so he detaches himself from life. In that cool, asceptic room, I saw myself similarly claiming recognition for a false "specialness" — merely for feeling tired. It only made me feel tiresome.

I have a favorite motto: life is a constant struggle against entropy, which I define as the tendency of all things to revert to a state of greater disorganization. After the children were born, I began to feel that I was losing in the struggle. A sense of failure hung heavy. As days and weeks passed, I never got a grip on things. Papers and correspondence accumulated, the desks became piled high with the refuse of ignored household matters (basic things, like life insurance policies, license plate renewals, income tax records, bank statements), all of which I was responsible for handling. I would pass from room to room with eyes averted to avoid stacks of mail which sat unanswered in silent reproach. Among the stacks were mixed the flotsam of life: a shoelace, three pennies, a displaced puzzle piece.

How had I managed to get myself into this dreadful state of mind? To some extent my depression was simply the consequence of the heavy demands that were made upon my time and energy. I am the hub of the household. The total care of the children and the dog are mine. I plan, shop, and prepare for meals; manage the laundry and oversee the housecleaning; handle bills, correspondence, car maintenance; maintain the social calendar and line up baby sitters; and look after the persistent extras — clothesmending, household repairs and decorating, visits to lawyers, pediatricians, veterinarians.

Even while I have complete responsibility for the care of the household and the children, I am pursuing a career as an historian. I am writing my dissertation for a Ph.D. on the subject of government regulation of industry under Charles I, a problem in the constitutional history of seventeenth century England. I employ a sitter for Alison and Dillan, our two-and-a-half year-old twins, for twenty hours a week. During these hours I go to the library to write. I hope to teach and write in the future.

My husband Mark is a physician who teaches and practices medicine at the University of Chicago. His job is demanding and he works intensely and long, averaging sixty-five to seventy hours a week. Since I am not employed, he provides the total support for our family and our sitter Dorothy. This dependency is uncomfortable at times because it heightens the pressure to spend time away from the children "productively." Otherwise my temporary unemployment is not a concern to either of us. This is our way of sharing. Mark's daily schedule, which takes him out of the house in the early morning and allows him home often only after the children have eaten dinner, does not permit him to take on much child care. But he is eager to have me pursuing my interests.

So in part my depression was simply a question of having too much to do and not enough time to do it in. But hard work was not a sufficient reason. I have always been a hard worker and besides, many women lead far busier lives. My central problem was a lack of insight and a sense of confusion about what I wanted. Although I had structured my days to allow for study time as well as household duties, I had failed to master the delicate balance which made it work. As I tried to understand why a balance was so hard to maintain, I reviewed the features in my background which had left me so unprepared for my dual role as a mother and a professional. I discovered to my surprise that I have long been remarkably passive in the face of life's big moments, that I have moved dreamlike through the years that brought me family and career. The shock of twins brought this longstanding problem to the surface.

I grew up in an exceptionally close-knit and warm family. My mother's strength and wisdom were a vital center to our home. We four children (I was the third) echoed my father in caring for her deeply. Mother has been my conscious model as I care for my own children. Often I find myself using her tone of voice or her touch when I comfort them. The image of her never failing to be patient and calm and tender with us is with me constantly. She was never overwhelming, never grasping in her love. She gave freely, without demanding in return that we tend to her needs. We never needed to reject a suffocating or oversolicitous affection. On the contrary, she maintained a healthy distance which protected her, and us, from unhealthy dependency.

Even now, I wonder at her self-sufficiency and her ability to combine work with family life. She found much satisfaction in her relationship with my father and was extremely attentive to him, at times explaining that she took extra care of him because he was twenty years her senior. Father idolized Mother and not a day passed that we didn't hear one or two stories about their early romance or the miracle of her caring for him. They enjoyed being together and worked closely to run the family's manufacturing business. Father was the designer and machinist, Mother the executive manager. Somehow Mother did all this while totally running the household and raising four children.

Ironically, even this ideal mother has passed on a mixed legacy of loving. She erred only in her strength — or rather, her strength has made her an impossible model for me to live up to. I am finally admitting that I cannot give as much or as well as she did. I cannot shoulder the total responsibility for my children and household with Mother's grace or capacity. I do not succeed when I try, in any case.

My mother worked while we were growing up, but never at the professions for which she was trained. She held degrees as a teacher and a registered nurse, and her example as an educated woman was a particularly forceful one. Perhaps, had she pursued her own careers much earlier, I would have had a keener sense of a mother who lived a separate life beyond the family. Instead, she deferred teaching and nursing, which she has finally taken up since Father retired. I wonder if she might have enjoyed those years of childraising more had she worked at teaching or nursing. I doubt that she would admit to that even now, especially since her cooperation with my father made the business productive and successful.

But Father never tired of praising her accomplishments. His own parents had idealized the educated and cultivated life, and had rejected the cloistered life of a fundamentalist Christian community to study at the University of Chicago at the turn of the century. Mother's example and Father's ideals clearly encouraged me in my love for schooling.

In short my early experience encouraged me to believe that I could, and should, strive to be both a professional woman and a mother. My childhood made motherhood seem highly desirable, as it had been for my own mother. I pictured establishing a family like mine had been, offering companionship and warmth. At the same time, I assumed that I would work as my mother had. Because of her even-handed management, I never considered that combining family and career might be a difficult challenge.

I did anticipate, however, that childrearing would affect at least the pace of my career, if not its continuance. Even before I was married, I made a career choice which would allow me time off during the years I would be raising a family. I chose to pursue a Ph.D. in history rather than study architecture. (I had applied to and been accepted by several schools in both programs.)

I made this choice because I knew a career in architecture would have been extremely difficult to finance and would have required at least two more years of formal class work than graduate school, not to mention clerkship years of long hours and low pay. Teaching seemed a more flexible career, one which would allow part-time work or a personally tailored schedule. Besides, all my schooling as an undergraduate at the University of Chicago made graduate school a more feasible step than architecture school. When I was awarded a Woodrow Wilson and the chance to study at Yale, I made the decision to enter graduate school there.

Architecture was a remote dream, even though I think

of it at times even now as a more desirable profession. It still carries the romantic promise of a more immediately creative life. Perhaps these ruminations are largely the inevitable remnants one carries from a time before choices were made, before pathways diverged, but I begin now to suspect that the same temperament which inclines me to the practical solution and the compromising posture leads to silent disappointment in myself.

After a year at Yale, I returned to Chicago, and Mark and I married. Our patterns were set early, during the five and a half years before we became parents. The rigorous schedule of Mark's training years and my relative freedom (childless and in graduate school) resulted in the total care of the household falling to me. During our first years of marriage (1967-68) when I was twenty-three, Mark was in training as an intern and I taught full-time at St. Xavier College in Chicago. Then while Mark completed three years of residency training, I was teaching part-time and finishing my graduate studies at the University of Chicago. I spent most of my days and evenings alone, free to structure studies, teaching preparations, and household as I chose. I was busy, but looking back on those years of relative freedom, I think upon them as a time of enviable leisure.

We began talking about having a baby after a year of marriage. I had some reservations, since two more years of course work lay ahead of me. I can't deny I had some fears about the future of my career if we had a baby so soon. Even so, I decided that with a few months of trying and nine months of pregnancy, I could put one more year of school behind me. We never seriously considered the potential problems of child care or of my completing my course work. We were confident that we could manage an infant and both our careers. We wanted a family, but it didn't occur to us to discuss in depth how we expected a child to affect our lives and relationship, what kind of parents we wanted to be, or what our mutual expectations as parents were.

I became curious and ready to see what would happen when we tried to conceive. My modest hesitations about course work turned to an anxious craving for pregnancy after a year of trying without results. Besides, by then my course work was almost finished. We sought medical advice and began a concerted program to conceive which was to last almost three years.

Conception was so difficult we barely hoped for success. The pessimism with which we lived greatly influenced my response to motherhood and our mutual adjustment to parenthood. Treatment for conception was a draining and discouraging process, focused as it must be on a rigorous attention to one's body and another's penetration of it at moments prescribed by a third party, the fertility specialist. It always annoyed me that I was a patient at the Infertility Clinic. Why couldn't they call it the Fertility Clinic, thereby describing our goals rather than our problems?

As I look back, I wonder how we persisted so long and lived with the necessary indignities of those treatments. In part because diagnosis and treatment progressed by months rather than by days, the time passed quickly. To isolate particulars of my case, the doctor worked methodically, eliminating first one and then another probable cause. We lived through two years of this, carried along by the logic of the process, expecting each step to offer a solution and success. Mark offered tremendous cooperation and patience; his support never waned.

A final factor in our persistence was a change of scene and doctors. Midway through our efforts (June, 1971), we left to spend a year in England where Mark studied as a fellow in a London hospital. Having qualified by then for Ph.D. candidacy, I spent this year doing research for my thesis. We were encouraged by a referral to London's best specialist, and so we began treatments anew with him. We agreed to defer any thought of adoption until after an evaluation by this doctor. His reputation gave us hope. The flexibility of this year made it possible for me to follow a program often requiring two or three visits to him in a week. It was another nine months before we accomplished our goal: finally I was pregnant, in April, 1972.

Women with amazing fecundity, who copulate and bear fruit with ease, cannot appreciate the distresses of unproductive sex. The emotions falter and intimacy is compromised by the mutual doubts about whether it will work "this time." One cannot escape the sense that something is wrong with a relationship in which, once conception is desired, sex is barren. Infertility exposes one's most private moments to the well-meaning doctor whose treatment requires that he know to the minute the timing of intercourse. At its worst — its most obtrusive — the treatment required me to be in the doctor's office for an examination an hour afterwards.

During this four-year period, conceiving had become the endpoint, the goal. The product and result, a baby, was overshadowed by the process. For all those years, we rarely discussed what our hopes for life with an infant were, never dared to imagine a situation where we were blessed enough to be parents. The subject of life with a child or of our roles as parents was taboo because it was too painful to consider against a backdrop of despairing failure.

I realize now that it is crucial to discuss just these subjects even if the reality of a child seems remote, as it often is for couples who face the birth of a first child. The burden of the taboo colored our responses during my pregnancy, which we greeted at first with jubilation. But Mark's attitude later became more complicated and diluted this initial triumph.

Imagine my confusion and hurt when, finally pregnant

and sporting a fine round belly, I would listen to Mark cast himself as the detached father. Carrying the idea of distance to an extreme, he would describe the scene in which I would present the child only at tea on Sundays, or else not at all, until the (badly-wanted, doggedly-sought, much-loved) offspring reached the rational age of, say, twelve years. I didn't understand why he greeted my pregnancy, the end of our quest, with such negativity. My feelings were too deep to realize that Mark was reacting excessively from anxieties which had never been eased by preparatory discussion, and that his delight was mixed with resentment and resistance to the inevitable changes which lay ahead. And so, despite our intense preparation to get me pregnant, we were woefully unprepared for the birth. We went through pregnancy with only a tenuous grasp of our feelings about the child, our future roles, our visions of the roles we hoped for each other. Not an auspicious beginning, yet not strange in retrospect, considering the barriers we had erected to avoid planning for a child when the possibility seemed doubtful.

The pregnancy for me was delightful, comfortable and comforting. My body was finally behaving in a predictable and naturally correct way. I was one of those who truly blossomed during pregnancy because my spirits were high and I was liking myself more genuinely than I had for some years. I was intensely curious about the birth experience per se. Because it had seemed so remote for all those years, it loomed large in my mind as one of life's most fundamental moments, as necessary to feeling fulfilled as having sex. Far from being fearful of the physical pain, I was eager to know what a contraction really felt like, what being in labor was all about, and how the hell did that baby come out anyway? Even before the years of struggling to conceive my own child, I felt giving birth was a mystery that I had to experience first hand to comprehend. That is why I thought of adoption only as a last resort.

During the last six months of my pregnancy, after we had returned to Chicago from London, I divided my time between working on the thesis and finding a new home. We needed more room and finally moved into a three-bedroom condominium in early December. The birth was very near at hand. It had been predicted for January 1, 1973.

On Christmas, I spent a long sixteen hour day decorating the new nursery. I was climbing into bed at midnight when my bag of waters broke — the prelude to the birth. Within two hours, my contractions had begun and by four a.m., we were driving to the hospital, slowly through quiet darkness, excited and pleased with the regular, mild signals.

The best way to describe my labor is to emphasize the amazing steadiness of the contractions. They were never closer than five minutes apart, and rarely longer than sixty seconds throughout the entire labor. No transitions from stage to stage marked my progress, as the Lamaze training had suggested. The doctors kept me fully informed of the extent of dilation and the position and health of the baby. It meant so much to me that they recognized my place at the center of all that was happening.

Then shortly before I was ready for delivery, a new nurse came on, examined me, listened to my belly, frowned and left the room quickly. She returned with two doctors, having alerted them to the fact that she thought the baby was breech. This was a shock because the baby had been head down for weeks and its position had been verified all that morning as "head is engaged, coming nicely." The excitement began. Maybe there were two babies! Incredible. We had wondered at the possibility of twins because so many women who saw my shape were sure I was carrying two. But each of four doctors had assured us that there was just one rather small baby in there. Besides, I had gained only eighteen pounds.

As the two doctors conferred, their uncertainty moved

them to bet a dollar on whether there were two or one. The small stakes seemed outrageous: it is so like doctors to minimize the drama of other people's lives. With this new dimension of mystery, we rolled to the delivery room, our curiosity mounting. I never even got a strong urge to push, I was so absorbed. The doctors had to tell me when to do it, and then I needed coaching in order to make progress.

Finally, one head appeared. Then came the strongest, most unpleasant sensation of the ordeal: the doctor's hands inside me, pulling on skeletal structures and grasping at wriggling limbs. Then out came Dillan. (We had one name prepared.) Within seconds, the second doctor pushed and felt and said: "There's another one." Just like that, after all those months of thinking there was only one baby. Seven minutes later, our second was born, also head first, slipping easily into the world. That evening we named her Alison. Dillan weighed six pounds two ounces, Alison four pounds fifteen ounces. If there had been only one, it would have weighed over eleven pounds!

We were ecstatic, jubilant, amazed. Twins! What relief. In an instant, our previous debate about whether to have more than one child was resolved. In another instant, I thought: "I only made one bunting." These moments were crowded with joy. The shock of two babies instead of one easily passed. They were healthy, good eaters and sleepers from the beginning. I enjoyed my hospital stay greatly, relishing the specialness of the twins.

I knew that my mother would come to spend the first week. Her visits are a treat under any circumstance, and she was indispensable on this occasion. She helped in those awkward moments when the basic care of an infant (not to mention two) was still strange and worrisome. What a comfort it was to have Mother's company as I nursed babies at night. She would bring me cocoa, hand me one baby, burp her, change the second and hand her to me, burp the second, settle them both, kiss me on the cheek, and send me off to bed. During that first week home, Mark maintained his busy schedule as usual and she and I eased the babies into a manageable feeding schedule.

Mother's visit left me calm and in modest control. The amazing, seemingly conscious cooperation of the babies throughout these early months gave us all a positive start (so memory tells it). Alison proved to be a great sleeper. This allowed me to respond to Dillan's cries, nurse and settle her. Then with one down, I could wake Alison for her leisurely feeding. Our best days followed this pattern. The off days, days of illness, nursing problems, fatigue and boredom were there too. I was too wrapped up in the hourly demands to care that Mark kept his distance, continuing to work long hours and rarely rising in the night. He felt that since I was nursing, his presence would have been redundant. He never even stirred at their cries. Once my mother left, I had no help with the babies. But there was a streak of stubbornness in me which helped me stay in control all during those early months when the demands of infant care were pressing and incessant.

Somehow it all seems far away now. What remains is the reality of our family. Two children. What could be better? Twins have the advantage of both receiving the intense parental energies invested in a first child. At the same time, they grow up with a sibling, inevitably sharing Mother's time and attention. Often, of course, twins are doubly demanding because instead of each getting half of your efforts, their combined demands require twice the output. But I maintain that in the long run twins are raised with one-and-a-half times the energy, the other half representing time saved in terms of total years spent bringing children through infancy and toddlerhood.

But far from coping with two babies with the cool and calculating mentality of the economist who delights in achieving the greatest time/cost efficiency, I have derived intense emotional and aesthetic joys from them. I was eager for children, and by the time they were born, I had nearly completed my Ph.D. Thus, I had a sense of direction in my professional life. This was invaluable because it allowed me to give myself entirely to child care during their first few months. Even though I missed the stimulation of my work, I could do without it so readily only because I knew I would eventually pick up the threads of my intellectual life. I loved fondling and hugging and nursing. I felt great satisfaction in responding successfully to their signals and needs. What joy — I could mother! And nursing too was delightful, not least because of its efficiency. I had a sense that my body was responding "naturally" — that same body which had mysteriously refused to conceive. It supplied ample milk for two thriving babies for over seven months.

I wanted to be a mother. Simply that. I continually take pride in that identity. I refer to myself as "Ma-Ma" and "Mother," as does Mark. When I go out without the children, I am constantly aware of my identity as a mother, taking extra care to drive safely, worrying more about my personal security in the evening or in new neighborhoods. I never feel any twinges of self-consciousness in the role. In fact, when I'm in professional circles, I feel somewhat superior because I am a mother as well as a professional. I see myself extending the chain of warmth and security which my mother gave me. When the children were about six months old, I had a distinct moment of truth which signalled a kind of conversion to this new role. It occurred to me that the special satisfaction I derived from being a mother was taking the place of my need to be mothered. It marked the achievement of a stabler, more self-sufficient identity.

But apparently motherhood was not enough. Gradually

I came to realize that my stability as a capable mother, while fulfilling, was not sufficient. I needed a sense of accomplishment in my personal and professional life as well. The imbalance grew intolerable. I was unprepared for the psychological shock of trying to juggle personal needs with the nearly overwhelming onset of twins.

When the girls were five months old, I had made an encouraging start on my thesis by leaving them for fifteen hours a week to work in the library. I wrote an introduction and outlined my materials in three months. A trip to Europe that September (en famille) and an emergency appendectomy in October combined to create a long pause, but when the children were a year old I renewed my writing, this time arranging for twenty hours a week (four hours, five days) of sitting. Our sitter, Dorothy Oates, was excellent, and I was secure that the children were well cared for and content.

But in spite of my outward commitment to work, the inner tensions accumulated slowly as my unshared responsibilities for child care and household became oppressive. Although I turned to my studies eagerly, the daily, insistent compromising of my intellectual pursuits created a growing discontent which left me exhausted and ineffectual. It was often too difficult to face all I had to do when I could only do it piecemeal. It seems obvious now that I was so frustrated by the limitations on my studies that I often threw up unnecessary obstacles to doing any serious work; I would use my time away from the children to do grocery shopping, to run for the cleaning, or to handle bills and correspondence, even though I could have found other times to do these chores. But the leisure and freedom from the children was so luxurious, and the thesis was so labyrinthine! Even if I spent four hours at my desk, I sometimes found I had produced very little new material. It was hard to be patient with the time spent in rumination if I had nothing concrete to show for it. I shouldn't have been so hard on myself, but when time is short the pressure is heightened.

My energies and interests were divided, yet somehow I failed to grasp the fact that being torn in six directions at once is the "Female Condition." I deflected a large portion of my frustrations onto Mark, blaming him for all the pressures I felt. I resented the fact that he did not change his schedule and habits as I had had to change mine. I wanted him to participate more in the care of the children, to help in the house, or to run a few errands.

But his position was firm; he did not want to be drawn into any domestic responsibilities. He encouraged me to get more household help or have the sitter stay longer if I needed more time to myself. My obstinance in not doing so stemmed from my reluctance to extend babysitting time beyond what I considered a reasonable portion of each day. I didn't want the children to be cared for mainly by a sitter. I didn't want to have to be efficient at their expense.

I never clearly expressed my disappointment about this situation to Mark then, and my passivity proved self-defeating. My brooding sapped energy that I might have channeled constructively. Looking back with the perspective of calmer times, I realize that what I most wanted was for Mark to recognize that my tasks were neither easy nor natural for me, and that if he refused to help with the actual burdens he should at least ease my psychological ones. I needed tolerance for days when the household seemed to be falling apart.

But often in the face my diffuse unhappiness and moroseness, Mark set up defenses. Neither of us came to terms very easily with our problems. We were in a tailspin of recriminating disappointment with each other. We lacked the mutual sympathy that we struggle for now. I failed to sympathize with his difficulties in adjusting to changes in me and to life with infants. He failed to see how overwhelmed I was with the care of the household, him, and the babies. We both denied that these infants were at times like unwelcome and uncivilized strangers disrupting our settled lives.

There were, in short, serious unresolved conflicts in my attitudes toward my childhood, my career, my husband, my children, myself. My strenuous life brought these conflicts to the fore, and they in turn sapped the energy I so badly needed to deal with my strenuous life. It was a vicious circle. What I needed to do in order to deal with the problems which finally drove me to the doctor was to analyze and understand my life and its complexities, rather than berate myself with increasing severity for feeling the way I felt. And that is finally what I did do.

Discussion and introspection have been crucial factors in helping me to grasp more clearly issues which were previously vague broodings. I have gradually come to understand why I felt so burdened by my juggling routine of keeping children, husband, household, and career in balance. While this routine is not easy or fun, it needn't be overwhelming. My feelings of being inundated by household and child care responsibilities were based on fact, but I had heightened the difficulties with my confusion and self-pity.

Discussion with friends about my feelings opened my eyes to other lives and gave me invaluable support. I was startled, and a little abashed, by the realization that my life was no more stressful than anyone else's. Each of us feels drawn and stretched as we struggle to fill the many roles of wife/mother/careerwoman/friend. We are all tired, and we all have reason to be.

The shared writing project that developed into this book was also important because I was encouraged to articulate and order my thought. Mere introspection was not enough because my thoughts needed to be tested against someone else's. Otherwise issues just bounced against each other and continued to generate confusing signals. I would rationalize one day, feel depressed the next, and angry another. Putting these insights into writing was a crucial beginning.

In particular the writing project helped me clarify my differences with Mark. As he and I discussed these issues we began to recognize that each of us had been living with stresses which were hard to articulate. Even though our household arrangements have changed very little, discussion has greatly eased my distress over unshared burdens and unrequited effort. With communication, my brooding passed and my symptoms of heaviness and lethargy disappeared. The present still requires persistent coping, but I am better prepared to live with the acknowledged compromises and limitations of my situation.

First of all, I have had to accept the inherent strictures of a part-time routine. A shortened work period is frustrating because extra time is spent just setting pen to paper after a lapse of a weekend or even after a single day. Worse yet are the periods when weeks are lost, when travels or visits to family introduce longer disruptions. Sustained momentum is an essential ingredient for progress, but I am continually stopping for days or weeks only to spend as many more days or weeks getting back into productive work. It is too easy to let my intellectual interests lapse when I work part-time. Sometimes I feign indifference to the entire thesis project as a defense against caring too much or wanting to spend more time at it than my current schedule allows. When I'm deep into the problems of interpretation and writing, I want to work at it all day, not half a day, and on into the night. Instead I must turn off when it's time to go back to the children, and defer work until after supper and the bedtime routine are finished. By then,

I've usually lost the morning's momentum and turn to something else with a vague sense of despair.

Even so, at this erratic pace, I am making progress and soon will have a completed draft. It is vital to me that I keep at and complete my dissertation. I need to feel I am making a professional identity for myself, one to merge with that other omnipresent identity as mother. When I have earned the degree, I will be able to measure myself against an established, "objective" scale. The Ph.D., though it is tarnished in today's economy, still has a potential luster and marketability. I admit that it will be a comfort to BE something and to DO something as measured by the formal shorthand of a work-oriented society. To be an historian with all the proper credentials, and to teach, would contribute to my self-image and add a proper balance to my secure identity as a mother.

I admire friends who don't need these labels to have a secure identity, but I do need them. To my mind, mothers who find ample satisfaction in, for example, painting, calligraphy, pottery, or puppetry — activities which have no convenient career definition — are very strong. I even admire the garden variety mother whose identity is complete in her homemaking. These women do not need to rely on outward trappings for their sense of self. Maybe it's the image of contentment which impresses me because, by contrast, my spirit is never, or rarely, at ease. I am restless with whatever role I fill, always thinking I might be doing better or something else or something more.

My commitment to myself is to finish and to do well. I have all the education of a scholar and I enjoy using my mind. Writing these things down makes the issue seem pallid. Why should I have to explain my urge to develop a career when throughout my school years, I took my studies seriously and assumed that my education was for a purpose?

I want also to succeed at a personal level because having a career and a family MUST be workable. It must be workable simply because it is what I want. In the past women have done it, and they continue to do it, some with seeming nonchalance and some through overt struggle. I do not pretend nonchalance; the struggle for balance is a continuous one and I am determined to see it through to success. I have committed more than my own time and intellect to this. My husband's emotional support and the money we have invested have been considerable. And the children have given too in a very real way, in terms of the hours of life without Mother and in all those wrenching moments of departure and return which have been a frequent theme of their emotional histories.

Do I fear failure at my work? I keep telling myself that I really don't. I am not given to neurotic hangups and I have always thought I have a very strong ego, yet my inability to quickly finish my thesis and get on with my career has made me question myself, perhaps too harshly. Friends who have been through the ordeal of writing a thesis say that finishing is akin to ecstasy. I have begun to daydream about all that I will do and be when it is over. I want to take up dancing and piano lessons again, to sew more and to study French, to paste photos in albums, hang pictures, resume corresponding — the list is endless and laughably unrealistic. Maybe I've entered some pre-compulsive phase which will firm up my resolve before a final, frenzied push.

But I don't think so. My life does not allow a total absorption in any single activity. For one thing, even if we could afford it, I resist the option of full-time writing. I am not convinced that my productivity would increase to match the numerical increase of hours. I do not want to work full-time yet, and without a Ph.D., any full-time work I could find would barely pay the costs of child care. With the Ph.D. so close, I want to finish and then try to find a teaching position. I want to BE what I've spent so much anguish becoming.

Most fundamentally, I am committed to a part-time schedule now because I want to share this precious, irrevocably fleeting time in the lives of Alison and Dillan. Mark supports my position even though, like me, he has found my work pace maddeningly slow. Gradually, we have both adjusted to a schedule which tries to satisfy my need to get away and work while meeting our shared perception that the children need and deserve a fair allotment of love. He feels this especially because he is absent so much. His days still keep him away from eight a.m. until seven or eight p.m. most weekdays, and half-days on Saturday and Sunday. He values his free time more and more as time to spend with the children. This gives me immeasurable relief. If his professional demands were less, I feel he would be willing to take over regular responsibility for their care. His enthusiasm for more active involvement is a welcome transition from his attitude toward them when they were infants and were less appealing, more difficult companions.

Time is so fleeting. Already the children are enrolled in a nursery school where they spend two mornings a week. They need me now; I need less, in the final analysis, to be selfish now. These years of their early childhood are filled with the excitement of learning and exploring. I want to share these days and to offer my support and enthusiasm for their discoveries. Soon enough the time will come when the children will be independent. I will greatly enjoy my expanded freedom along with theirs, and the prospect of immersing myself more completely in my work is appealing. I feel this because even now my working hours can be exhilirating. They are a source of relief from the pressing emotional demands of mothering.

And still, even during the hardest times, even on long rainy days when the children are cranky and the attractions of offspring very remote, I am glad I have chosen to spend most of my time with them. I want them to have the sense of confidence and security which comes from their knowing, because they feel it through hours and days of my presence, that I love them. I get immeasurable satisfaction from their sparkling, happy eyes and their childish humor. It is gratifying to see the results of my energy as they develop into attractive and intelligent personalities.

I know I need both my children and my work for fulfillment. Therefore, I am left with the challenge of maintaining a balance between the two. Balance means weighing conflicting pressures and desires. It isn't merely a matter of demands imposed by others (husband and children) set against personal desires (more free time to work or to waste). What appear to be demands are in fact the several roles I have embraced for myself. I want to be many things — wife, mother and person — but I must face the limitations of time and of my personality. Balance therefore means compromise.

To some, it may seem as if I have talked myself into a corner of enforced compromise and over-strained commitment. But is this so unusual? Don't we all feel pulled and torn by contradictory demands and limited time, money and energy? Even though we all have some mystic Weberian ideal type in mind, a superwoman against whom we measure our own meager strengths, we all inevitably live with compromises. The crucial determination is which ones, and whether we are able to make choices which do not leave us crucially amputated. The compromises I make of time and energy are ones which I consider worthwhile. Given my commitment to my family, the singleminded pursuit of a professional career and professional status is not possible, although the interweaving of my work with the fabric of my life is. (Yet if I could retrace my steps, I would defer children until after I had completed my degree.)

I have examined and accepted the circumstances which put me at home with the children and leave Mark in the office. My acceptance stems not from any ideological endorsement of traditional male/female roles, but from a personal perception of the kind of mother I want to be, and from my recognition that, given Mark's work and attitudes, the brunt of household responsibilities will continue to fall to me. I also suggest that this is the position of many women who, like me, are socially and intellectually aware of themselves.

The women's movement has added stresses of its own to our lives; it has created challenges, but also threats and reproaches as women are moved to reconsider their goals and place. I have been encouraged to make a thoughtful and conscious effort to define and redefine my personal goals, and as a consequence there has been change and growth in my marriage, especially since the children were born. But I also have had to face certain truths about myself that don't come easily. I am a compromiser; I have chosen to defer my intellectual needs to the demands of my husband and children. I have chosen not to change things by arranging for more child care or insisting upon a reordering of Mark's priorities. Instead, I have accepted the ongoing complications of living a divided life.

Still in place of aimless brooding, I can now at least articulate the frustrations of divided commitments, and I am able to live more easily within the limitations of my choices. It is modest growth but growth nonetheless.

▲

In the five years since I first wrote for *The Balancing Act*, all of us have grown as individuals and as a family. The children, now eight years old and in second grade, continue to be delightful and rewarding. Mark and I have mellowed as parents and become more settled as individuals and as a couple. I personally have resolved some of the central issues reflected in my first essay through a combination of introspection and action. I will try to set out the gradual changes which have brought me to the present.

As I look back, I recall two moments of insight which cleared my doubts about my priorities. In the spring of 1976, I volunteered one morning a week at the university's pediatric hospital. Each time I went I was stunned at the sight of stricken children and anguished parents. Their suffering was hard to be near. One beautiful baby lay sleeping peacefully in a bassinet, after being admitted for observation. Her mother had dropped her. Her father had shot her mother in the head, and the baby had fallen with her. Another day I saw a cancer-ridden eleven-year-old, whining in discomfort and asking for a drink. The impatient nurse shrugged off his request because, as she explained, "He's always demanding something." Sad, sad. The nurse was only mildly callous, I suppose. She had long been inured to particular suffering, and she had lots to do.

This volunteer experience gave me a new sense of myself and my life. It wasn't that I came to endorse the commercial that jingles, "If you've got your health, you've got everything." Rather, I felt chastened by the realization that good fortune, like good health, is a capricious gift. The volunteer job made me ashamed of my self-absorption with small personal setbacks and more appreciative of all that I had. From that time I felt more energetic as I coped with my busy but very normal routines.

I made a second discovery during one of my triennial spurts to clean the closets — which usually lasts through the first half of the first closet. I chanced upon a journal I had written at sixteen. It's the only time I've ever kept a diary, and I had forgotten completely about it. Even now, my kitchen calendar and my monthly cash accounts are my only records of passing months and years. The journal, which spanned two weeks of 1960, was full of embarrassingly romantic and pompous observations. I dare not quote it directly, but I was struck by one entry. On that particular day, twenty years ago, I had watched two young parents load squalling children and bulging grocery bags into a rusty station wagon. I had been put off at first by my sense of the unpleasant tedium of their lives. But as I reflected on this initial reaction later in the diary, I changed my mind. I realized how happy my home and family made me and how much they were the center of my life (even at sixteen). I knew then that I wanted a family to be a part of my adult life too.

It was like meeting a lost relative to discover that part of me from so long ago. I had been totally unaware that as a teenager, I had embraced such an ordinary future for myself. The intervening years of college and graduate school had obscured that earlier perception. It was comforting to know that in my commitment to family in recent years I have, after all, been responding to genuine and deeply-felt desires.

These insights put my personal concerns in perspective and reassured me that my priorities were solid. Even so, the months and years have been filled with very real challenges to my identity. I will indulge in a retrospective view of the central issues which continued to test me as I struggled to balance mothering and working. These issues no longer involved doubts about how the household should be run or about our roles as parents. Rather, they centered on my efforts to finish the thesis and to enter the working world.

I had chosen to divide my energies unequally between home and career. I put my children first, in part because the self-directed work of writing a PH.D. thesis was easy to push into second place. More importantly, it was my choice to put the children first and to raise them myself. This choice meant that I continued to write my thesis at a painful snail's pace, using my time while the girls were at school to revise chapters and pull together a coherent manuscript. Self-discipline was my greatest challenge, and possessing a merely average supply of it was my greatest problem. Every day, I had to wrestle with myself, as if I were divided into two, with half of me dragging the other half to a desk at the library. The thesis was a less than ideal project, in retrospect, because it was lonely work, done in the isolation of the library. Almost any job would have been easier and more stimulating. I would have had structure, compensation and colleagues at a job — a comforting and supportive triad of benefits.

As it was, the slow pace of my work became increasingly frustrating. By 1979, when I turned thirty-five, I was very low for several months. I felt that I was a failure, that I was nowhere in my life and personal goals. Although I had finished a draft of the entire thesis, it needed reworking to make it coherent. After all, I had been writing it in bits and pieces for about six years. The part written first needed to be linked with later parts. The manuscript was unwieldy and would take careful patching before it could be accepted by my three readers. I was afraid I would never finish it, and being thirty-five and still afraid made me feel ashamed. I wanted to avoid people whose successes compared so glaringly with my dull progress. As of January, 1979, then, I still had no job and my thesis — my "work" — was without status as long as it was unfinished.

Employment seemed to be the answer. The only way I could live with myself and overcome my sense of failure was to go out and find a job. I would enter the market, pit myself against the competition, and find a niche where I would be "appreciated." With this nebulous goal in mind, I signed up with a career counseling agency for women.

In the counseling sessions, the counselor first wanted me to air my feelings, particularly the sense of failure which was my dominant mood at the time. She wanted me to get rid of my confusion and to express my frustration and anger. Even though I struggled for self-control, I would burst into tears during each visit. The tears confused me even more. The counselor's presence — her professional, sympathetic ear — was too much for me. She pointed out how unhappy the thesis made me. When she remarked that it was a joyless endeavor, I admitted that I hated it. Mired in unhappiness as I was, I was watching the counselor. She gently prodded me to vent my anger. At the same time, she put me on my guard. I was suspicious of a point of view which might endorse some vague "happiness" mistakenly equated with peace of mind. I didn't necessarily want to be free of pain. What I desperately wanted was to overcome my oppressive feelings of inadequacy.

Even though abandoning the thesis would have brought instant relief, I chose a different solution. My problem was not only the thesis, it was also the loneliness of the work. I was craving more contact with people. An obvious solution was to find colleagues through a job. Spurred by the counseling sessions, I set up interviews with previous employers and acquaintances who might guide me to other contacts. Whenever I spoke with academic associates, their advice was, "Finish the thesis." Each interviewer raised the question, "If you take a job, will that not mean you are giving up the thesis?" Somehow, just getting out and talking to people, presenting my résumé and putting myself in the position of Job Candidate was invigorating. It offered a welcome diversion from my routines, and it enabled me to see myself through fresh eyes. I looked so good on paper! It was wonderfully, though falsely, satisfying to set my résumé before a series of benevolent people. I knew that the résumé would be a counterfeit statement of achievement if I never brought my efforts full circle by completing my Ph. D.

This realization, and the accumulated advice gathered at the interviews, built up a case for turning to the thesis once again. What difference did it make if I began to work that year or the next? Finishing might make me more employable, although I knew that the difference would be only marginal. Mark was particularly persuasive in urging me to finish. He pointed out that, no matter how hard it would be to face the task again, I would be much happier with myself if I completed the Ph.D.

As I struggled with this issue, it occurred to me with stunning clarity that I was repeating a pattern which had been going on for several years. I recalled that for successive springs, I had gone through a similar bleak period, during which I had tried to reject the thesis in favor of work. I had arranged interviews and begun to fantasize, Mitty-like, about myself dressing in tailored clothes and marching out of the door to catch the 8:25. Organized. Employed. Important. (I still puzzle over why our society so ruthlessly links personal worth with remuneration.) But the conclusion of this soul-search disguised as a job search had always been the same: I put off working and went back to my writing.

Another bizarre effect of projecting myself into the world of the Working Woman was that I would have a physical, grief reaction to "leaving" my children. I would watch them play and my vision would begin to blur as I pictured them, the next week after I had started work, without me, with someone else watching them. I would hold them more closely and be infinitely patient with their small trials. *I was not ready to leave them, even in my fantasies.*

Employment as an avenue for rejecting the thesis was clearly not the solution to my problem. Besides my ambivalence about leaving my children, I couldn't imagine myself doing anything in particular that would make my departure acceptable to me. The job search was masking other uncertainties about my place in the world. The process left me aware that I didn't know what I wanted to do. I just had a vague sense of how good it would feel to be a cog in *some* wheel.

Since my problem, the source of my discontent, was in not being finished with the thesis and feeling incomplete as a person, the only way to solve it was to finish. I had to overcome my immediate sense of inadequacy and apply myself once again. The discipline and routine came no easier. My progress was strewn with the litter of ill-disciplined days and chaotic weeks, when the children had chicken pox, when I had back trouble, when school holidays stretched endlessly.

In that spring of 1979, however, having rejected once more full-time employment after my annual orgy of self-pity, I was offered a part-time job which answered all my jumbled needs to be a part of "something" without giving up either my thesis or my children. I was hired to help prepare a scholarly bibliography at the Newberry Library, a venerable Chicago institution. The work was well suited to me. I had background in the field and reading knowledge of French and Spanish. My commitment was flexible: between ten and fifteen hours per week as my schedule allowed. In addition, the Newberry is one of my favorite buildings, full of marbled and panelled surfaces, high ceilings, and rare books. This was a welcome initiation into the working world. I laughed at my simple-minded pleasure in walking through a door marked STAFF ONLY. It was clear that doing something outside my home and getting a paycheck for it were real boosts to my ego. Predictably, since I had less time for the thesis, I worked on it more efficiently and with newly discovered peace of mind.

Six months after taking the part-time job, I proudly delivered my revised 350-page manuscript to my advisor. That same week, I was asked to consider a second job! The local private school where our daughter Alison was in the first grade needed a seventh and eighth grade English teacher. My first response was to say "no" and mumble once more about finishing my thesis. I mused over this for a few days and decided that I didn't want to turn down this opportunity. It meant that I would phase out my job at the Newberry, but I was drawn to the teaching position because it would mean working with lots of people — students, teachers, and staff.

I accepted the offer and in December, 1979, I began teaching two classes an afternoon. My students were bright, and I was challenged by the work. The schedule blended marvelously with the rest of my life. Since my classes were the last ones in each day, I was at the school when Alison was dismissed, and we came home together. Dillan would be waiting for us, having spent an hour at home with a sitter. That spring I directed and produced a play with each class and discovered what I had not known for years; the pleasure of measurable accomplishment. This year, I am teaching a fifth grade class as well, which gives me a full afternoon's work, or seventeen classes a week.

Meanwhile, the thesis had acquired a life of its own, and the stages of its completion progressed with, for me, breathtaking momentum. Three weeks after I gave it to my advisor, he told me it was good, it hung together. Even more satisfying was his recommendation that I show it to my other readers, because he felt it was ready to be defended. The defense is a formal oral examination which is required once all three readers have approved a thesis. It is a two-hour discussion, largely a formality, since one rarely fails the defense. Thus, where the real achievement lies is in being told one is ready for the defense. Shored up by my advisor's approval, I gave the manuscript to my other two readers and turned to Christmas and Hanukkah preparations very happy to be unburdened of this millstone for a while. Within a month, I had learned that all my readers had accepted the thesis and that I should arrange for my defense as soon as possible. I passed the defense on January 28, 1980.

After that, to *really* finish, I was required to present a perfect, typed manuscript to the University Dissertation Secretary who would approve the thesis and allow me to graduate. The prospect of sixteen more weeks of painstaking effort to get the manuscript ready for the typist was not particularly appealing, but it was sheer pleasure compared to all that had gone before. It was to be The Last Sixteen Weeks, after all. Mastering footnote forms and meeting the dissertation office's stylistic requirements was Kafkaesque at times (the first ten footnotes took me twenty hours), but eventually I struck a productive pace.

By the time I had completed all of it, down to the last comma in the last footnote, I was ready to enjoy graduation. Mark put on his academic gown and marched with the faculty. My mother came. The children attended wearing hats and gloves, and they were very proud and excited for me. We threw a big party afterwards with lots of champagne. Friends gave me fountain pens. It was like a cross between a wedding and a bar mitzvah. In all seriousness, graduation resembled a rite of passage. Over the years, the project had become an abstraction, looming in my life like some Herculean task to be performed. I admitted towards the end of the ordeal that it would be wonderful to be "grown up" finally. I became the heroine in all the fairy tales I had read to the children at bedtime.

I speak of the thesis in such personal terms because I have felt divorced from the professional, academic milieu that the PH.D. has prepared me for. I have had little contact with historians in my field, since all my working time was spent writing, and I had no free time to spare. Clearly, because I have given so much time and energy to my family, I lack a solid identification with my profession.

Being a professional had rarely impinged on my identity as a mother. In fact, I had been avoiding the conflict for years. The tension had become clear to me during the defense itself. What I remember most vividly is a great numbness, I was so drained by the relief that the day had come. When I spoke, a part of me sat detached and staring down from the light fixture, watching me perform as an academic. This self-consciousness almost drove every articulate idea out of me. The conversation proceeded like a complex game with rules that I was reluctant to follow. I came from a different world, where children play and quarrel, love me and need me. It was very strange to be talking about seventeenth-century English economic and legal history with four articulate men. They were well-exercised in this mental world. I was overwhelmed.

Thus far, I have sketched out a terrain of concerns, centering on my efforts to consolidate a balanced self-image. This mental terrain is posted with my annual crises: the spring-time job hunt and soul search which resembled an internal closet-cleaning. Meanwhile, what has been happening with the children and Mark? Alison and Dillan are different in all ways, except that they share a birthday. Dillan is quite tall for her age (four inches taller than Alison), brown-eyed, right-handed, good at numbers and logic. She is a quiet observer of the passing scene, except when her vital interests are concerned. She has a quick temper, coupled with a self-assertiveness which she uses to great advantage. Alison is gray-blue-eyed, left-handed, verbal, a voracious reader. She delights in questioning the moral aspects of events. Our ongoing problems center around (ho-hum) sibling rivalry. They understand how to distress each other. If Dillan tries to upset Alison by chanting "witches, witches," (the things Alison fears most), then Alison will hiss back," "robbers and thieves, robbers and thieves" (Dillan's hang-up). And then they run off to play.

They are affectionate, exuberant children. The energy devoted to caring for them as infants and toddlers seems to flow back in their hugs and kisses and declarations of devotion. They fill our lives. They bring so much pleasure in daily conversations and activity. And they continue to amaze and delight me with the sheer aesthetic appeal of their bright eyes, their complexions, their hands, their physical selves. Despite our obvious doting, they constantly seek reassurances of our love, sprinkling the day with questions like, "Who do you like better, me or Dillie?" And there are always the comments which expose other fears and insecurities; for example, "Mommy, when you die, don't let anyone tell me, because if they do, I'll shoot myself." They are bundles of contradictions, wanting most desperately at age eight to have pierced ears, wear high-heeled clogs, and drink from baby bottles. That is to say, they are very normal.

Throughout these years, Mark and I have emphasized their distinctiveness and played down their twinship. Sometimes I hear one say to the other, "Hey, let's be twins today." Then a few minutes later they emerge from the bedroom in matching outfits (of which they have very few). They perceive themselves as sisters who can "become" twins by dressing alike. In an effort to reinforce this separateness, we are sending them to separate schools. This has given them an even greater chance to see themselves as individuals.

We reached this decision the summer before the girls entered kindergarten, when we were impressed with the intensity of their rivalry. Alison seemed always to get the short end of things, since Dillan is physically more powerful and more assertive by temperament. (I tell Dillan that her middle name is "Me First.") Alison had no outlet for retaliating in the face of an overbearing sister. At least this is what we came to understand after Alison went through several months of terrifying nightmares about witches and, significantly, giants. We began to reexamine our decision to send them both to the Jewish day school we had chosen.

As the summer progressed, it seemed less wise to send them to this small school, where they would be in the same classroom from kindergarten through eighth grade. Since we liked the school very much and wanted to maintain our affiliation with a Jewish institution, we decided to keep one girl there and to enroll the other at the University of Chicago Laboratory School. Mark and I independently chose to shift Dillan to the Lab School, because Alison was in a particularly shaky emotional phase. We split them accordingly, and they have thrived in their separate places, although this puts some strange strictures on our schedules when the school calendars don't coordinate. On the other hand, the different holidays give me a welcome opportunity to spend time with each girl alone.

Mark has given them other occasions for separate and individual attention. Four times a year, he attends weekend meetings in New York. Each time, he takes one girl and the other one stays home with me. This has been marvelous for all of us. Mark can give one daughter his undivided and leisurely attention during their travels. Often, he arranges to take the train for the added fun of the journey. Meanwhile, I realize what a pleasure it is to have just one with me at home. It is so peaceful! The child acts like a different person, she is so at ease. The absence of her sister removes the perpetual undercurrent of tension, and the change is almost physically palpable.

The trips Mark arranges with each child are indicative of how he has settled into fathering. His time at home is largely devoted to them. They read and play games together.

Mark encourages them in their school work and likes to give them extra coaching when he can. Recently, he has assumed total responsibility for their wardrobes, a task I was delighted to relinquish. He likes shopping with them, and he does so efficiently and with a sure sense of taste. If they complain about needing slacks or skirts or clogs (Mark would never hear of clogs), I simply say, "Talk to your father about it."

We continue to have a traditional household, in which I oversee the details of running the home, cooking, shopping, laundering, hiring sitters, getting kids to the doctors, the dentist and the piano teacher. To ease the work load, I have hired a college student who helps me from four to six hours a week. I am more comfortable with this now and feel less threatened than I used to. When I wrote my first essay for *The Balancing Act*, I was keenly aware of how much my household departed from the principle of sharing these duties. I felt frustrated and angry because my home did not run the way it "should." Now I am impatient that I should have to apologize for following a pattern which is, after all, still more the norm than otherwise. More important is the point that our arrangements, if less than "ideal," work for us. I see myself following my mother's role model. I have accepted her patterns just as I have always accepted and admired her.

Looking back on the old hostilities of our first years of parenting, I am able to admit that Mark was not the primary cause of my frustration, although he was the likeliest target to blame. Often, what I blamed him for was in fact a projection of my dissatisfaction with myself. I realized this only after finishing the thesis — the task which kept me feeling so incomplete. To complicate the picture, I have always had particular difficulty expressing anger openly and directly, a trait which I share with many women, I suspect. Now that my feelings are clearer, I can get angry more easily. I complain, even rant occasionally, and when I speak up for my interests, I know that Mark will hear me out and help me.

The years have brought changes in both our lives which have made each of us more content, both with each other and within ourselves. Two weeks after I passed my thesis defense, Mark learned that he had been awarded tenure at the University of Chicago Medical School. This was a wonderful and deserved consolidation of his career. He continues to work long hours and spends at least one weekend day in the office. We have accepted the demands of his schedule, although I take comfort in his continuing involvement with the children. Work becomes burdensome to him when it keeps him from spending time with them.

Personal satisfaction is central to our satisfaction with each other. Each of us has reached important goals and we are more secure individuals for it. It is as if I had to love myself again, before I could believe that Mark loves me. To be able to trust in him was a wonderful and comforting realization, as important to us mutually as my overcoming the hurdle of the dissertation was to me personally.

Since I wrote five years ago, three major issues in my life have been resolved. I have laid to rest my uneasiness over the extent of my household and childcare responsibilities. My thesis is finished. The marriage is solid and satisfying. And now, a whole new set of events lies ahead. In August, we will have another child! We are eager to welcome just one baby, which will surely bring fewer strains and unalloyed pleasures. Sharing the baby with Alison and Dillan will add a fresh dimension to the process of raising an infant.

We again needed the help of a fertility specialist, and it took us two years to conceive. Still, the process was psychologically easier this time, since we have our girls. Failure would not have been so sad. Mark was as patient and supportive as before. He was always reassuring in the face of our repeated failures which were announced rudely at monthly intervals. We were reminded of the problems of infertile couples, and again we experienced the special delight of success after our prolonged treatment. This pregnancy also reinforces our feelings that our children, conceived with such difficulty, are a marvelous gift.

Of course the years will not now proceed in a rosy haze. Life will always bring messy emotions, improbable crises, tense schedules. No doubt unpredictable problems will surface. I anticipate having to face more career and work choices. However, an upcoming sabbatical leave, which will coincide with the baby's first year, will allow me to defer these choices. Based on what I've been through, I foresee myself working part-time for a few years, either in teaching or in a field related to history. The work will not take precedence over my family. I have enjoyed my teaching and the involvement with the school in part because I can balance this with my family life. I don't want to lose the luxury of raising my children and sharing time together. And I do insist, despite inevitable ambivalence, that it *is* a luxury.

V

I want it all: marriage and freedom, son and career. I am willing to struggle, because the rewards nourish me. How can I compare my delight in avocados to my anticipation of ripe strawberries? So it is with my commitments to Scot and my career.

Sharon Ladar

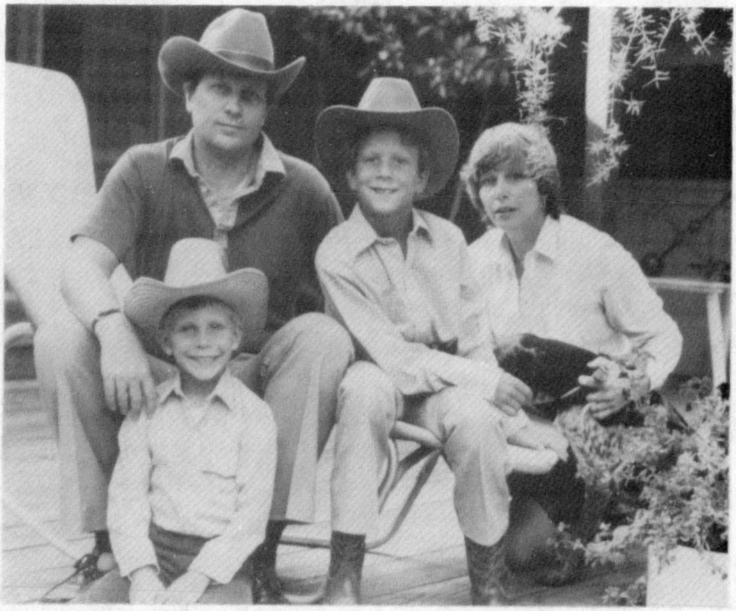

Sharon Ladar

It is only after having plunged into motherhood that I feel free to reveal that I was a closet resister to that laudable institution. I never actually came right out and said that I didn't want children. But then I never really said that I wanted them either. I revealed to a few close friends that I wondered how anyone ever decided that it was time to have a child and that I felt incapable of making such a decision. Now, retrospectively, I understand my largely unspoken doubts and find that they are substantial.

In my family it was presumed that my sisters and I would marry and have children. My three older sisters each had four children; clearly a precedent was set. But I was in conflict with not only the precedent but also the entire idea. Motherhood seemed like a bovine state of docility to me. It swallowed up identity and creativity in endless cycles of maintenance and subservience. My own family was romantic about the very characteristics of motherhood which I found most repellent: the helplessness of the infant with its profound complementary parental responsibility, and the mother as an endless source of compassion, totally giving yet in some magical way self-sufficient.

My parents, a Chicago policeman and his wife, worked hard to provide their children with a milieu that would encourage family life. That our family was so happy was no small feat considering my parents' origins. My mother grew up in an orphanage in South Dakota, and my father grew up on the streets of a tenderloin district in Chicago. They both knew physical and emotional privation. Their coming together, their devotion to their family, and their enduring love for each other seems a tribute to some lost ideal.

They had four children, all girls. I was last by a gap of nearly six years, so in a sense I was raised as an only child. I spent my early years in a vain chase to catch up to my older sisters. Sickly and shy, I played alone a lot and had a rich fantasy world. I remember flashes of dolls, milkweed seeds, bright red tomatoes, the fear of polio, the yellow enamel bed I shared with my sister, but little of substance. I do not have fond memories of childhood. It seemed to last forever.

What was different about my childhood, and what perhaps dramatically altered my direction in life, was that I was bright and went by chance to one of the few experimental grammar schools in the Chicago school system. I took special classes in music, art, and science. I particularly enjoyed the art classes and prided myself on doing things differently — experimentally, I suppose. I found early recognition and a way to distinguish myself.

In retrospect, that interest in art and the need to be "different" gave form and dimension to my life. By the time I was an adolescent, I was already critical of our middle-class neighborhood, the suburbs, and the unexamined life.

My parents' expectations for my sisters and me were rather ordinary. None of my sisters went full-time to college, though one of them went through nurse's training. I think my parents considered education a bit of a frill for girls who would, after all, marry and bear children. My father was dead set against any of his daughters remaining single and making her way alone in the world. Despite this, they were proud of my intellectual achievement and supported as best they could my determination to go to college. At that time they were approaching sixty and planning for retirement, so they were unable to finance my education.

I decided to go to the Institute of Design at the Illinois Institute of Technology because of its fine reputation. My father was surprised at my decision because of the cost of going to a private school and because of its location — southside Chicago, a ghetto. I went to school that fall with enough money to pay for tuition and room and board for one semester only. I was gambling that I would find a way to pay for the second semester, and I did. I went through school on a combination of scholarships, government loans, twelve hours a week of clerical work, and what assistance my parents and my fathers' sisters were able to offer.

The financial struggle toughened me and helped me to forge an early sense of independence, both economic and intellectual. I consciously sought to escape from the conformity of middle-class America. I was interested in giving some form to my life which was congruent with my character and needs rather than living out some role blindly assigned to me by an anonymous historical force. Studying design and, later, practicing and teaching design, helped me to do this.

As a designer I occupy the space that lies between ideas and people, for designers give visual form to messages. The form may be a symbol or a system of symbols, a book, an exhibition. Not only does design require the practical application of perceptual psychology, learning theory, and aesthetics, it also demands a knowledge of typography, photography, illustration, and production techniques. Its measure of success, a tightrope walk between originality and intelligibility, is its impact on the audience — specifically whether or not its message effectively communicates itself to the audience.

As a designer, I publicly practice my profession; as a design thinker, I privately generate theory. Between the two is my role as teacher, in which I theorize and criticize in a semi-public context. It is the connection between these public and private dimensions that provides me with new ideas for work. I wish I could be single-purpose — a painter or a printmaker or a photographer — but I cannot. I trade intensity for generality; I bore easily; I am impatient. I am really a sprinter in spirit.

What I am trying to make clear here is that the practice of design is not, for me, simply a way of earning a living. On the contrary it was the interest around which my life took form. I was not about to give up my profession (really *could not* have given it up) in order to become a mother. Morever my career required, and will continue to require, that I be current in diverse disciplines and technologies — a time consuming proposition. This time could not be entirely given over to child-care without undermining my performance. And finally my profession demands that I be to some extent a public person, that I put in hours outside of my home as well as in my study. Someone else was going to have to be watching the baby during those hours.

In short, the addition of a child to my interests implied major psychological and practical adjustments in my life. I wish I had been as clear about this before the arrival of Scot as I am now.

During college I met Rex, the man I married. We met on a blind date nearly twelve years ago. I was intrigued by certain unusual characteristics — his poetry, his tatoo, his fierce independence, and his sense of structure and nature. He was studying architecture and I was studying design, but despite a similarity of interest, we were quite opposite in our perceptions of the world and life. He was a rationalist and I was an empiricist. That we married, eight years ago, seems both inevitable and surprising — we were so alike yet so different. During the years together we have changed. Rex has become in some odd way more subjective and at the same time more pragmatic, and I have become more objective and logical. We have not leveled each other to a mean, but we have catalyzed each other into new perceptions of the world.

From the beginning, we each cultivated our individuality, and preserved our equality. Our parents presented healthy models in that respect. Both members of each couple were well matched in determination, willfulness, and sometimes guile. In my childhood, the vigorous arguments I witnessed clearly showed my mother's strength and fortitude. I did not assume that I was passive or that Rex had higher status than I. I never was tempted to play the role of charming wife, social appendage, cherished mate, and housewife.

Rex respected my professional commitment and understood my need to have time for myself. He was not threatened by me; he was perhaps the most self-sufficient person I knew. We were able to share professional concerns without being in competition. His commitment to architecture was easily equal to my commitment to design.

Even before the development of my career, I formulated for myself a relationship between happiness and creativity: I was more productive when I was less happy. If my personal life was well adjusted, I was content to enjoy it; but when my life was torn, beseiged, and incomplete, then I worked to create the missing satisfactions. Before we married, Rex and I agreed that I should be unhappy about thirty percent of the time. That was not unreasonable or unworkable. In some unexpected and precarious way we pushed each other aside, we withdrew from our relationship in order to assert an enlightened selfishness. Yet this kind of enforced separation only made the connection in our relationship more complete.

Even with that kind of closeness, Rex and I approached our roles and responsibilities within our marriage quite differently. We married on the edge of a value transition. Friends who married in the early sixties were definitely more entrenched in traditional family roles than we. But friends who married in the late sixties were definitely more progressive. I remember early in our marriage, before the women's movement had really gotten off the ground, we attended a party in Chicago. We were introduced to a young woman who was discussing women's liberation. Rex wandered off to get drinks for us, during which time she launched a penetrating inquiry into the equaliy of our marriage. Was Rex liberated in his attitude toward women? Yes, I replied, he intellectually supported the movement. Did he vacuum, cook, do dishes, iron, and market? (She quickly moved from the theoretical to the practical.) No, I replied. I was irritated with her tactics. She had hit a nerve — I was already chafing under the traditional expectations of my young marriage and of both Rex's and my own upbringing. I was beginning to understand what Rex's devoted, live-in grandmother had done to pervert his sense of domestic responsibility. Rex's mother had worked from the time he was four. Superficially this seemed like a good childhood model. But in reality his grandmother, who took care of him, was basically sexist (which is not surprising), and Rex was the oldest son. That combination ensured him a privileged position in his own family, a position he expected to carry with him into marriage.

His job complicated things even further. He was — and is — an architect for a large corporation, so he kept long and traditional corporate hours. He did not have the flexibility to share equally in domestic chores. My work, on the other hand, allowed more flexibility, and as a consequence I ended up doing the housework, even when I was working full time.

I was certainly not altogether content with this arrangement. After all, Rex could have rejected a traditional full-time professional involvement, even if he was programmed from early childhood to accept it — and maybe that is the real point. It seems to me that boys are raised to be single-purpose, one-thing-at-a-time people while girls are raised to cope simultaneously with several things. One needs only to observe a woman cooking, watching her child, and talking animatedly on the telephone to understand the awareness skills she has mastered.

So partly because of his job and partly because of his assumptions about marriage, I found that the delegation of domestic responsibility consisted mostly of me delegating to myself. Rex did manage the household accounts, a job I found frustrating, tedious, and dull. He also half-heartedly washed the kitchen and bathroom floors and made an occasional weekend breakfast. I survived this division of responsibilities because I stubbornly refused to give up hope for more sharing of maintenance chores and because I found I could think, daydream, or focus on odd sensory relationships while I did housework. I also developed a much more casual attitude toward cleanliness in our apartment.

From the beginning of my marriage I dodged questions about having a baby by saying it was too soon, we were too young, not while Rex was in the Army, not before he had adjusted again to civilian life, and so on. I was never at a loss for excuses. This went on for five years, during which time Rex and I learned to cherish our relationship and our individual freedoms. I had been working all that time as a professional designer and had started graduate school. I was in my late twenties. It was therefore increasingly difficult to imagine staying at home, relinquishing a satisfying career to raise a family.

I viewed the situation as demanding an either/or decision. I knew of no woman who had successfully combined motherhood with a profession. My own mother went to work when I was eight to improve the family finances, but she never quite overcame the guilt. I can remember the neighbors referring to me as a waif and an orphan. After all, the families with whom I was familiar were typical in their distribution of traditional roles: father was the provider (absent much of the time), mother was the homemaker/caretaker (present nearly all of the time), and the children were the focus of the family; their needs, both real and imaginary, took precedence over the needs of the adults.

Nevertheless, the issue of whether or not to have a child was omnipresent, and the pressure from my parents and sisters to begin a family continued to grow. We did not approach a decision about this rationally: we could not. We did not discuss the practical implications of having a baby other than deciding to employ a child-care person. We didn't try to anticipate how we would manage with a child. We just felt in the abstract that we wanted one. I never doubted that I would be a fine parent. After all, I was responsive and genuinely liked children; I enjoyed being around them as well as interacting with and observing them. I was not so sure that Rex would be a good parent, but I knew that he would try and that he would not take the responsibility carelessly. He himself never doubted that he wanted a child.

I made the decision to try to conceive a child without resolving my conflicts about motherhood versus career. It was time that pushed me over the edge. I had already squandered many good fertile years and didn't really have all that many left. I also knew that once I finished graduate school, it might be impossible for me to interrupt my work. I felt it was best to insert a powerful life experience such as birth within the framework of a strong, existing commitment — my commitment to my studies. Then that baby could not blow my life to bits. The event would be contained.

What a crazy logic, born of fear and self-apprehension. I was less than honest to myself about my ambivalence, hesitation, and fear.

But we took the chance and abandoned the birth control we had practiced so rigorously. For two years I awaited my period each month with anxiety, only to be curiously disappointed and simultaneously relieved when it arrived. Well-meaning friends and family who were privy to our plans offered advice and watched me eagerly for the least sign of indigestion. I felt like a butterfly being scrutinized by a collector. Was I a *good* specimen? It seemed ironical and unfair that many species give remarkable physical signs when they are in heat while the human female is secretive about her physical state. If only my belly button could have turned green at the appropriate time! I charted my temperature month after month and became inordinately aware of every twinge and tingle. It was absurd Needless to say this was a difficult time for Rex and me both sexually and emotionally. We were like two machines performing on demand, the spirit missing.

During this time, a number of good friends as well as one of my sisters conceived and bore children. I was acutely aware of pregnant women and those with small children. I can remember looking at them for some particular sign of health, robustness, earthiness — I didn't really know what — something they had that I obviously lacked. Coming to grips with my inability to conceive changed my self-image. I suppose that my womanliness was at stake. I was like some ripe, succulent navel orange with no seeds, a reproductive fraud. My connection to the earth, my spontaneity, and the life-force which had in some poetic way seemed to define me before were now illusions. It was painful for me to be around my pregnant sister; I avoided her with considerable determination. Only after the birth of her daughter and our subsequent adoption of Scot was I able to share my feelings with her.

After a year of this emotional chaos, I sought professional advice, only to be reassured after a number of tests that nothing should prevent either Rex or me from having children. I was disappointed that some minor, reparable difficulty was not found. I knew that the cause of infertility could be psychological, and it occurred to me that my inability to conceive may have been related to my high-strung and impatient disposition as well as to my unresolved feelings about motherhood.

Toward the end of the second year I took fertility pills, which intensified my anxiety. If I could barely entertain the possibility of one, what if it were a multiple birth, a genuine side show event? At that point Rex and I began to discuss adoption. We had always considered this possibility. When it came to nature and nurture, both of us placed the emphasis on nurture. Without a belief in the importance of environment as a life-molding force, adoption would have been inconceivable for us.

We had not really seriously considered it at the beginning of our efforts. We were reluctant to admit our biological inadequacy; theoretically, conception was always just a few weeks away. We held no fashionable position concerning zero population growth that we wanted to flaunt. We were curious about what we could produce (egotists, to be sure). But once we began to seriously talk about it, I felt a little better. Considering adoption meant postponing a decision on motherhood. I could peruse both adoption and conception over a few years and wait to see what happened.

But we found ourselves unable to commit ourselves to adoption or to give up the idea of having our own child. Somewhere along the way, we had become increasingly interested in *having* a baby, but we didn't know when or how or even if we would succeed.

Caught between adoption and a continued attempt to conceive, I spent a fair amount of time reflecting on the meaning of having a child. It seemed to me that children could be a physical manifestation of a couple's love, could provide a physical sense of immortality for the parents, or could be ego-extensions of the parents. My inability to conceive made me grieve for the loss of a biological link to the future. Since I did not believe in an after-life, a child became the only meaningful kind of immortality to me. My speculations brought me face-to-face with the tenuousness of "my life." Its fragility was shocking.

Discussion of adoption continued. Concerned friends assured me that even discussing adoption sometimes brought on the desired pregnancy. And if the adoption was completed, then frequently within a year or two the desired pregnancy would occur. Adoption was like a magic potion — a new and unusual means to assure the old end. I refused to entertain it on such a basis. The adoption had to be an ultimate commitment, not an expediency.

I tried to develop a thoughtful awareness of the implications of adoption, more so than did Rex. It was difficult to try to imagine a baby given up at birth and transferred to other people who said they would love and care for it. What a promise. Certainly a more binding promise than marriage because of its implicit dependency. And a promise with no more substantial basis than a simple desire to have a child.

Finally we began adoption procedures. We agreed and disagreed at predictable points. Since we were both aware of the importance of early childhood, we wanted to have an infant free from experience; that would also give us a total experience with parenting. We both wanted a healthy, normal child. That was particularly important to me; I had no desire to become a devoted mother to a special child.

The disagreement centered around what kind of baby to adopt. At that time white infants were scarce, so we discussed other options. I felt I could accept any normal, healthy child, but Rex wanted to get specific. Frankly, I found his attitude insupportable and embarrassing. I was reluctant to discuss it with a social worker as it seemed irrational and bigoted. But in retrospect, Rex might have been more realistic than me in examining his attitude and his ability to cope with a child who was clearly not our offspring. Another problem concerning the adoption of a child with mixed parentage was the grandparents. Everything I read about adoption stressed the desirability of total acceptance by the extended family. At the time I did not appreciate this conviction, but I did recognize that the grandparents might have difficulty in accepting some children. Yet another obstacle was the issue of religious affiliation — we were unwilling to establish a tie to an organized religion solely for the purpose of adoption.

The whole process of adoption, with its uncertainties about time and the availability of an appropriate infant, made the reality of living with a child both immediate and remote. Day-to-day care, the fitting together of our lives, the practical realities of a child did not concern us because we did not know how long it would be before we could actually adopt. We had trouble even imagining ourselves as parents. Perhaps because my reluctance and conflicts about motherhood were not dealt with openly, they were obstacles blocking thoughtful preparation for parenthood. We approached it with naive trust in our commonsense, without questioning the traditional child-care arrangement — the mother as primary caretaker. After all, intimacy with children was foreign to Rex's experience. I was not certain that he could accept an adopted child even though he said all the right words. Perhaps I did not push for the sharing of responsibilities because I was more certain of my own skill and commitment. Perhaps I felt the adoption would be a success from Rex's viewpoint only if he were given the time to find his own way to the child.

Then suddenly, within two weeks of deciding to adopt, we were parents. It happened so fast that there was no time to meticulously weigh alternatives, procrastinate or rationalize. We made a spontaneous decision and were committed. We were told of a white woman who was expected to deliver in two weeks and to give the child up for adoption. We were assured that she was in good health, had had excellent pre-natal care, and was expected to deliver a healthy, normal child.

The anticipation was intense — as was the fear. We now had only two weeks to rehearse in our imaginations what having a child would be like — how he or she would enrich (impoverish?) our lives. We were excited in a controlled way, reminding ourselves that the woman might decide against adoption after the birth.

Scot was born.

In the nursery, he was tagged "baby boy." He was a week old when we picked him up. As soon as I knew he was ours, I couldn't wait to get him out of the nursery — I knew

I could give him something that was not to be had there. Secretly, in my gut, I was a mother. I was filled with curiosity and awe when I first saw him. He was crying and kicking and had bright dark eyes and surprisingly well-articulated hands. I cried, Rex cried, and Scot cried. The nurse cried. It was an exquisite moment that changed our lives.

Scot was an easy, contented baby and an eager eater. I wondered how I would have managed with a more difficult child, but I was convinced that I had everything well under control from the start. After all, he was a strong and adaptable baby, and I was not really as green as many new mothers; I had become an aunt when I was ten years old and had eagerly tended numerous nieces and nephews.

At first I overplayed the "mother-of-adopted-child" role. I was painfully honest with the most casual stranger concerning Scot's adoption. This may have been due to a need to put some psychological or emotional distance between Scot and me, but it may also have been due to a need to rehearse and become comfortable with the reality of having an adopted son. Or perhaps my honesty was a defensive tactic. It identified me as a special kind of mother, and it deterred from comment those people who believed that an inability to have children was preordained, a retribution for past sins, or the result of some inscrutable emotional selection to prevent potential child-abusers from having children.

Because Scot was not our natural child, I felt a great need to be a "good" mother. I wondered if others knew from observing us that, at the very first, I did not love him. I cared for him lovingly but for the first few weeks there was no real bond between us. He was my child but also a stranger. Nevertheless the bond was quietly growing. When Scot was between three and four months old, it occurred to me that I loved him deeply and never wanted to lose him.

Adoption provides a somewhat unusual perspective on the relationship between parent and child. Scot is not an extension of Rex or me; instead, he is a unique individual whose growth and development has been entrusted to us. He is a surprise package, an unknown quantity. We cannot preconceive a result based on our own appearance and character; what happens will be the result of an interaction of great sublety — that of his character with the climate and environment we provide.

The adoption itself took place with a month left of teaching before the holidays. We picked Scot up on Tuesday and I had to teach on Wednesday. And teach I did, with my mother happily pinch-hitting for me until I had time to make other arrangements. She disapproved of my continued working, and while I was acutely sensitive to her criticism, I nevertheless held my ground. I knew I had to make motherhood work in a new way for me.

On Wednesday I arrived at school, cigars in hand, to announce Scot's adoption. I needed to be a bit iconoclastic, but I didn't conceal my joy and perhaps a tremor or two of apprehension at this sudden adventure. I believe my colleagues were genuinely stunned by my disclosure since I had never discussed a desire for a family. Much as I had expected, two outspoken male colleagues began to banter about the forthcoming ascendancy of my hormones and descendency of my intellect. I was already on guard, but their comments brought a tremulous emotion close to the surface. They had hit their target squarely. A challenge like that couldn't be ignored, particularly since they were men I respected.

My colleagues and family clearly expected the traditional abandonment of work in favor of motherhood. On one side, colleagues rang a death knell for my spirit and intellect, and on the other, my mother and family urged me to relax, accept the joys of motherhood, and abandon my professional involvement. I rapidly formulated an intellectual stand in opposition to this traditional trade-off. My own argument revolved around three variables: the different needs of different women, the variety of ways in which a child's needs can be met, and the quality of mothering as opposed to the quantity.

I needed the stimulation of my profession; I knew that I could not continue to grow if I confined myself to my home. I felt I had a somewhat higher than average amount of energy to dispense and I thought I could handle more than the typical domestic situation. Further, I thought it was important to help a child to love and trust beyond the nuclear family, to learn that different people have different priorities and different ways of caring. It is important for a child to develop a strong and independent self-image that can complement the skills necessary for adapting to life's complex requirements. I never believed in an idyllic childhood which protected a child from the realities of life and promoted dependency. As for quality of mothering, I was more sensitive, responsive, and appreciative of Scot if I was able to get away from him, take perspective, and feel good about my own identity. What was good for me affected my ability to be good for Scot.

Rex respected my needs and reasons for wanting to remain active in my profession but he also went on record encouraging me to drop out for a year or so. We both realized the importance of early childhood, and if Scot had been a difficult child or had had some disability, I might have had to reverse my decision. Basically, the decision to combine motherhood and career was mine. I was unable to turn away from my commitment to design. Teaching two semesters with a long vacation in between meant that I would be absent from the home about eighty days out of the year. I did much of my teaching preparation in the evening.

Work on my Master's thesis proceeded slowly but regularly after Scot was three months old and began to sleep through the night. That I taught, was a graduate student, and was also a mother without sacrificing any dimension of my life was not the simple product of determination and energy. It depended on the satisfaction and personal growth that teaching afforded me, the excitement of an intellectually challenging thesis, Scot's easygoing, positive nature, Rex's intellectual and emotional support, and my conscious and careful juggling of roles. Further, it depended crucially on the availability of good mother-substitutes.

I knew how difficult it could be for a child to adjust to the absence of his or her parents. As a child I had been timid and anxiety-ridden, and I remember becoming physically ill when my parents went out. I used to check their closet to see if their clothes were still there — if they were, I knew they would return. I did not want Scot to suffer that kind of anxiety. As a consequence I tried to be sensitive to his sense of security and well-being. That meant simple and predictable arrangements, one mother-substitute over a long period of time, basically one teenage baby-sitter, and no regular, extended periods of absence on my part. As a result, Scot has developed a healthy sense of security and a readiness to be on the go and away from me.

The decision-making concerning Scot's child-care situations and his time spent away from the family was left to me. Under no circumstances would I have left him for a forty-hour work week. (I doubt that I could ever again work on such a traditional and inflexible full-time schedule.) I would not have left him for more than the twenty-four hours a week that I did. On the other hand, I would not have left him for fewer hours. If our family finances had taken a dive, I would have tried to economize in areas other than child care. If I had not been gainfully employed the child care might have diminished somewhat, but my professional projects would not necessarily have suffered since I do my best work at night.

Although I was initially apprehensive about the difficulties of leaving Scot with someone other than myself for concentrated periods of time, my child-care arrangements have worked out well for us both. I think it is probably more difficult to leave a child with someone after being its constant attendant for a year or so. It may be even a greater shock for the child. Scot has always known that I would go and return again — it is a part of the pattern of our lives. But there were difficult times, times when Scot would cry to see me go. Both the child-care people and I were positive about my going: as soon as the separation anxiety seemed to subside, we began elaborate goodbyes, hugs, kisses, waving, etc. I was amazed at my ability to submerge myself in the day's rigors of teaching and research with hardly a thought of him. But the homecoming was sweet. I anticipated seeing, holding, and playing with him.

Rex, though he did not participate in our child-care arrangements, has vivid memories of his early caretaking of Scot. I do not share these memories, but I admit my recollections of Scot's infancy are rather vague. Rex did handle the six a.m. feeding and he played with Scot frequently. He was never a genuine member of the sanitation corps but he did do his share of rocking and floorwalking a cranky baby. However, it was only as Scot grew older that Rex became really active in his care.

From the first, I was fortunate to find good, dependable, and loving women to care for Scot in my absence. During his infancy, we had a rotund, jovial grandmother, herself a mother of five boys. She cuddled, laughed, and talked to Scot endlessly. We shared his development, and she shared her experience with me. I did feel some resentment toward her occasionally, as Scot was so obviously content and happy to be with her. But, due to illness, she decided not to continue caring for him. It was during the Christmas holidays and I had only two weeks to make a new arrangement before the next semester. I was panicked. I had come to depend on her; Scot knew her and was comfortable with the arrangement.

I felt defeated for the moment. Where would I find another good woman? I got on the phone with a neighbor and the following day found another child-care person: Grandma June, young, dynamic, mother of five, easygoing, outdoorsy, and positive. Scot acquired with her a new family as well, since they were neighbors. Papa George and two of the kids were also part of Scot's days away from me. I welcomed the chance to share childraising with an experienced and loving mother. I learned a great deal from June, carefully observing her relationship with her twelve-year-old son, the shape of things to come for Scot and me. Scot loved her and her family and I was not at all jealous.

I trusted both Grandma June and our earlier babysitter to act in Scot's best interest. I had faith in their judgment and gave few specific directions concerning their care of my son. The proof of their success was Scot's attitude toward them. I feel strongly that children need to adapt to expectations different from those of their parents. But just as I observed the mother-substitutes, they observed me and sensed my own priorities — few treats, no wanton destructiveness, no giving in to tantrums; and in a more positive sense, much love, praise for goodness, and encouragement for trying out new skills. Between me and our mother-substitutes, Scot was exposed from the beginning to fairly consistent values and reactions to his behavior.

Looking back now, I can see that Scot has unquestionably altered my life. On the positive side, he has provided a connection to the lost child within me — he is a connection to life. I think there are two times in life when one puts the loneliness of living aside. The first deep, moving love affair makes oneness seem remote and impossible ever again. The intimacy of an infant or small child is the second enveloping connection, the second vital and dynamic escape from loneliness. Scot is a creator of surprise, a stretcher of imagination, a stimulator of childhood's lost memories. He brings me new connections of mind and spirit.

Even when he was an infant, he enhanced my understanding with his unfolding perceptions of the world. For instance, I read somewhere that infants express pleasure and try to control their environment by sucking. When Scot was about three months old, and cranky, I showed him the art in the apartment on the rather curious theory that he would give it a spontaneous suck-rating, thereby cueing me into his visual sensibility. Puckered up, intent on the pacifier, he looked at Eskimo prints and sucked, at contemporary serigraphs and sucked; but the prize accolade of fourteen sucks went to a photograph by Aaron Siskind. Scot, you had primitive but good taste.

There are times, however, when the frustrations of raising a child outweigh the stimulation. Although in a real sense Scot enriches my life with new perceptions, at the same time I yield up to him precious hours from my work time. Since Scot, there has been a trail of started, half-done, and nearly-but-never-done projects. He is a distraction.

But it is the contrasting rhythms of the mother and designer/teacher roles that has posed the greatest problems for me. Finding a way to integrate these diverse rhythms and finding the energy for the counterpoint has not always been easy. Adaptability and flexibility are essential to life with children. Our son, for example, has a certain rhythm to his life which requires from me a slower pace and a patience which is not really part of my nature. The rhythm of mothering is hypnotic and seductive, causing energy and ambition to submerge. I recall the hours I spent with Scot in the rocking chair or pushing him in a swing and realize the sense of endless time, the measured moments, the repetition, and the stupor that I struggled against when he was very small.

I feel the ebb and flow of my energy and try to use it effectively and harmoniously, but I wish there were more of it. Since Scot, I fantasize that I can steal energy from others directly. I occasionally ask Rex for a power-hug and imagine that I am drawing energy from his physical strength.

The description of a typical teaching day will help to focus the juggling act between work and parenting which I find stimulating yet frustrating and enervating. The morning begins at seven-thirty, when Scot gets up. I have never been a dutiful wife who rises to cook some incredible breakfast for her husband. Rex gets up around six and is gone by seven. Scot and I have breakfast; then I dress him and turn on "Sesame Street." That entertains him while I make beds, dress, and drink lots of coffee. At nine-twenty Grandma June arrives to take over for the day. We have a quick cup of coffee together and then I leave, between nine-thirty and ten o'clock. Frequently I run errands downtown on my way to school, or I might spend part of the morning in the library. A noon I have lunch with colleagues, and I begin to teach at one o'clock. Around five-thirty (having missed part of the rush-hour traffic) I leave for home, a drive that takes half an hour if the traffic isn't too bad. I get home around six and, depending on how wound up I am, I might have a beer with June before she leaves.

Returning marks the most difficult part of the day. I am tired and have yet to face dinner and the nighttime routine. Dinner is simple—a casserole, or spaghetti prepared on a less hectic day. While I get dinner together Rex, who arrives at six-thirty, plays with Scot. Since the age of one, Scot has fed himself table food and has eaten with us. I've always thought of dinner as a social occasion for the family, though admittedly I would occasionally enjoy an intimate dinner with Rex. After dinner, we all flop on our bed to cuddle, play, and talk. Frequently Rex bathes Scot and picks up toys while I do dishes. Around eight, Scot goes to bed with juice, bedtime stories, songs, and cuddling.

Now *my* evening begins. The problem is to come alive again. The coffee is brewing and I am fighting fatigue. I spend the evening in my workroom preparing material for the next teaching session or working on some project of my own. Around midnight I make a drink and flop on the bed with Rex. If he is already asleep, I simply sit quietly by myself. I am a night person, but after the rigors of such a day, I find small energy reserves for the evening. I use coffee and liquor (if I am dependent on either, it is the coffee) to stimulate me and to speed the ups and downs. There are two cycles to every day. I peak out around four p.m. and by six I am in a slump. If I know that the evening involves crucial concentration or a deadline, I hold back during the afternoon high in order to save energy for the evening cycle.

As this typical day illustrates, the addition of Scot to our lives has brought a certain density and overlap of activities and emotions. Our fears about the potential clash of activities have proven accurate. Although in theory we do not want to exclude Scot entirely from our work activities, in practice this separation is necessary. He does occasionally accompany me on errands to school, just as he occasionally goes to work with Rex on Saturdays. I never hide his existence from professional associates. But until recently I was uncomfortable with the idea of being a mother. I felt I wanted to keep that role separate from my profession: my general concept of motherhood did not include proficiency or creativity in any other context. For just that reason, I wanted to insulate my professional contacts from Scot. I didn't want to force them to face my personal life because it might diminish my professional credibility.

But often this separation of child and profession is impossible to sustain, no matter what my views about it. There is for example the telephone sprint. The ringing of the phone signals the start of a race to see who can answer first, Scot leaping vertically as well as moving horizontally, screaming, "I'll get it!" However when he gets it, he listens intently, breathes heavily, and says nothing. It is the heavy breathing routine in reverse. I don't mind that family, friends, colleagues, or students get this unexpected treatment on occasion. But when I am involved in getting quotes for professional services over the phone in order to finish a project, my frustration soars. These are calls during which I have to quickly establish my credibility. It is disconcerting to concentrate on a business call while Scot throws balls at me or demands juice. It is even worse when clients return calls and Scot and I race for the phone. If I win, Scot loudly and articulately voices his displeasure; if he wins, the caller gets heavy breathing. I am annoyed by my inability to muster even some semblance of a professional demeanor on the phone.

Since Scot, life has required a logistical plan. Where I previously operated spontaneously or waited for some crisis to spur me to action, now I see the necessity of anticipating what might happen so that I won't lose control of my environment. Children throw curves and are experts at the fake-out. It is sometimes impossible to anticipate their next move. At times I resent the energy and thought that I put into facilitating operations. I have evolved routines for making telephone calls, going to restaurants with Scot, and such; but as soon as I take a routine for granted,

Scot outgrows it and I have to evolve a new one. Scot has forced me into what sometimes seems an energy-consuming, self-conscious way of functioning. A sudden vacation, an impromptu night out for a film, love in the afternoon — all now require a logistical plan that eliminates spontaneity.

This has unquestionably been one of the more difficult adjustments for me. For awhile, I simply assumed that Scot added another dimension to my life. But in fact he has dramatically altered my sense of self, my sense of time, and most important, my relationship with Rex. Children inevitably skim the cream of love away, leaving parents to neglect or take for granted their own relationship. Rex and I are certainly capable of taking each other for a commodity as reliable as a summer heat wave. Since Scot, we have less time together and are less aware of each other's involvements. We lavish less affection on each other than we did before. The special times for us have diminished; we have less time together, less spontaneous intimacy, less communication. Our limited ability to be impulsive, and our real need to be together and away from Scot, prompts us to take vacations — "getaways" — without him. Just as Rex and I separate to connect more fully, we have found we need to separate from our son on occasion in order to enjoy the connection.

On the other hand, if we had not had a child, our marriage might have ended. This doesn't imply that Scot was the adhesive for a faltering marriage; I was always free to pursue my independent interests, and I loved, trusted, and respected Rex. Our sex life was good. But is it possible to sustain a vital human relationship over years without fallow periods? (Courtship in its most romantic and intimate sense should begin after five years of marriage.) Marriage is a concept like motherhood, clothed in impossible ideals and media distortions, touted as a cheap panacea for loneliness, lack of appetite, and irresponsibility. I have outgrown the romantic illusions of marriage but at times I miss them. It has been our separations that rekindle intense longing and bring to the surface of our busy lives a sense of our relationship.

Scot has altered our sense of autonomy. Whatever we do, it affects the whole family and not just ourselves. A good example of this is my thesis, which I began before Scot was born and finished when he was two-and-a-half. In order to finish and at the same time continue teaching, holding down an eight-room apartment, doing meals, laundry, etc., something had to give. The process of elimination determined the priorities. The quality of domestic duties went first. This was no great problem as Rex has even greater tolerance for environmental dirt and mess than I. The next to go was any pretext of having a growing relationship with Rex. At best we had a holding action during that year. Scot got his full measure until the last month or six weeks; then he too went on hold while my thesis took first priority.

There were times during that year when life for me became rather humorless and passionless. Humor or passion would appear at odd moments of stress as reactions, but I felt I was responding to my environment rather than demanding from it. Was this woman's estate? I was adapting but I did not choose the direction of my change. I had believed until this time that I made my life, but while I was finishing my thesis it appeared that life was making me. I felt that I was losing control and that my energy was being drained by a fight for control. Relationships with son, husband, and students were sucking the marrow from my bones. What was left for me? Where had I gone? I had no time to live gracefully. Except for an occasional insight, I put out fires, I prevented fires. I was tired.

At those times I felt defeated. When my energy was gone,

I was a shell, an automata, a nonentity. I would sit in the dark and wonder what had happened to me, what I had done to myself and what I had let others do to me. Rex was unsympathetic and I resented him tremendously for this. He would deliver an ultimatum: something in my life must yield. I would be too beaten to argue or even to think about what facet of my life was expendable. I would give up. The end of energy, my tears, Rex's ultimatum was like a recurring theatrical piece played out each time to perfection. But the act of giving up would make the energy flow again, and a new and longer cycle would begin to build.

There were days when I was physically present but mentally absent. Scot was especially sensitive to this and he reacted with frustration and anger to my lack of enthusiasm and response. I had an interminable sense of waiting during the day, waiting for evening and work. I tried to save tasks which could be performed with Scot present — those which required little concentration — but they were precious few. Rex was aware of the superfluity of his presence during the evenings. But when the crunch really came, he was unbelievably supportive. In addition to doing more child-care, he proofread and drew and inked most of the diagrams (based on my sketches) for my thesis. Without that kind of grassroots physical and emotional support, I might have collapsed under the stress of time and the scope of the material, even though I never doubted the significance of my work. What had been a valued individual activity became a valued cooperative one.

Inevitably, during the year that I worked on my thesis, I reproached myself for not being more productive. Occasionally I would try to step back and evaluate the substance and direction of my intellectual and creative growth since Scot. I had been on guard against being mesmerized by mothering from the beginning, but was my strategy working? On his first birthday I reflected that I essentially had been coasting on previous groundwork and that that could not last forever. But by his second birthday, I had resolved some intellectual and visual problems relating to my thesis; it seemed that my juices were still running and that I had attained a degree of maturity.

Nevertheless, I often felt fragmented and diffused. Was there no way to integrate the facets of my life? Was there no center to teacher, designer, mother, mate, thinker? As my thesis progressed and as Scot matured, I began to understand that I needed to search out connections between exactly those areas I had separated and protected from infringement. I needed a connection similar to the one I had made between Scot's growing perception of the world around him and my understanding of psychology and visual design. I needed to develop broader categories for what I did and to find a way to be really energized for more consecutive hours during the day. I needed to stop making value judgments about when I should or should not be energized. In short, I needed to be more fluid. But where was I to find that kind of grace when l was desperate for more time and energy?

After I finished the thesis, Rex admitted that he had been uncertain about whether I would finally get it done. I had never been uncertain. My thesis gave intellectual focus to a difficult time in my life — Scot's infancy — and failure to finish would have made my professional commitment suspect. If my priorities had remained fixed, if Scot and Rex had always come first, I might have scuttled my work out of overwhelming frustration.

For Rex, the year was full of his own work and the pressures and tensions related to it. He hadn't really missed me much, although he had occasionally missed clean underwear and hankies. As for me, the time was both frustrating and exhilarating. It was frustrating because of the time pressure, the desire to do more than was possible, and the conscious decision to approach teaching in a more cavalier manner in order to concentrate my energies on the thesis. I also missed some important opportunities with Scot that can never be recaptured. But it was exhilarating in that I experienced a new understanding of what I could do in a given space of time. I was alone a great deal that year, but I grew from it.

When we had reassembled a more conventional life, I found that the three of us still had something special after time on hold. A minor bonus was that sex became once again sexier. Sexiness seems to require a certain peace of mind. A major bonus was that while I worked on my thesis, Rex developed a new sensitivity and appreciation for Scot, and Scot got to know his father in a new way. Because my thesis had consumed both time and money, additional outside child-care for Scot would have been a strain. The crisis of my thesis drew Rex squarely into his parental role, and he had a new pride in being a father.

Previously his traditional work hours had created a situation in which it was easiest to act out the mother/father stereotypes. Rex had spent fewer hours with our son than I, and had inevitably failed to develop certain sensitivities to him. He was a bit of a novelty for Scot, a curiosity who brought out only Scot's best behavior. I on the other hand was relatively commonplace, and Scot's worst behavior was saved for me. In order to protect my sanity, I had become immune to the petty irritations Scot devised. By dinnertime, I reacted only to the most gross behavioral abberations. I was simply worn down, and stagnating in my function as primary parent. I needed help. Rex came through, as much as he could given his inflexible work hours.

I have to confess that at first I found it difficult to leave well enough alone when Rex began taking more responsibility for our son. If Scot did an exceptionally good job of cleaning up toys before bed, Rex didn't praise him warmly enough to suit me. So I would wander by the bedtime activity to add my compliments and reinforcement. Rex also had a way of getting Scot's clothes on backwards that I found to be sheer perfidy — almost a studied effort to confound and frustrate me. Perhaps I had a cultural hang-up: I could leave mother substitutes (females) alone to interact freely with Scot, but I wanted Rex (male) to be more and better than was possible. It got absurd. I felt that Rex was inept. I took over. Rex lost an opportunity to grow with Scot. The next time he was still inept and I took over again. At the same time, I was afraid that Rex and Scot would be strangers to each other, and I wanted them to find in each other a rich and satisfying relationship. Finally I learned to leave them alone. It was a matter between them; I could only intrude.

The patterns of parenting, working, and sharing that Rex and I had evolved up to this time were a product not of plan but of chance. But when my education was complete and we had some breathing space, we began to reflect on how we ought to structure our family life. As it stood, Rex was responsible for about seventy-five percent of our income and I brought in the remainder. During the time I was a graduate student, this had seemed a reasonable arrangement. Rex's income had grown over the years while mine had remained stagnant. I must admit that in the deep recesses of my mind I considered myself free to squander time and energy on professional play for meager reward. Rex not only supported this traditional expectation, he also seemed happy with it.

Money just had never been a substantial problem for us. We never kept separate accounts and we never differentiated in any way between what money either of us brought in. We operated on a simple system: each contributed according to ability and received according to need (and Rex and I are generous in understanding each other's needs). I had never felt financially dependent on him even though in fact I was. But with my thesis out of the way, I developed a desire for some money of my own, and I felt I was ready to become more involved in my work.

However, I was in a bind. Without more sharing of child-care and domestic chores, I was not free to do much professionally other than a few freelance design projects out of my apartment studio. Where was I going to find the time to do more? Rex's work hours were long and inflexible, and neither of us could accept the idea of more paid child-care for Scot.

The way out of this difficulty, theoretically, was for me to liberate Rex financially, and to thereby liberate myself. If I could earn more money, he could feel free to accept a lower paying job that allowed him more free time. Or at the very least, he could feel less driven by the job he had. As it turned out, he had become less than satisfied both with his relatively complete responsibility for the family income, and with his rigid work hours. He was ready to entertain the idea of changing his life so that more sharing would be possible, and he agreed, although grudgingly, that he ought to take on more of the practical responsibility for Scot.

Once we had settled these matters, I took the first step toward more equality: I accepted a full-time faculty position at the Illinois Institute of Technology. This was a satisfying step in terms of my professional development, and it allowed me to earn about two fifths of the family income. What remained to be worked out was an equitable division of the child-care and domestic responsibilities.

Progress in this area was much more difficult. Rex did not in fact change jobs, and I continued to be left with most of the child-care and the housework. My new schedule was only possible because Scot had by this time become a resourceful little boy who did not require constant mothering, and because much of my class preparation could be done at home. I had not expected a formal division of sharing between Rex and me; we had tried such arrangements, and they failed because our needs were continually in flux. But I had hoped for spontaneous assistance, a true spirit of cooperation. I wanted Rex to perceive what needed doing and to simply do it. (Once, after Scot picked up toys, Rex actually, without prompting, pulled out the vacuum and cleaned the rug.) There was, however, some cause for hope because we had at least reached a theoretical agreement, which we could struggle to put into practice.

Once I had finished my thesis and Rex and I had settled as clearly as we could the issue of sharing, we began to feel the folk-heat for a second child. How could I possibly be so selfish as to deprive my child of the intimacy and rivalry of a sibling? And no doubt my family and friends wondered why the adoption-conception miracle had not worked for me. In truth I had been rigorously practicing birth control. But when my thesis was finished, the time was ripe to reopen my conflicts with motherhood, to understand where I had been and where I was, and to decide if I wanted another child.

I approached this new decision with an understanding of myself as a mother that I had not had the first time, so I had an intellectual edge. I was enjoying motherhood and Rex had an increasing appreciation for being a father. It would be good for Scot to share parental attentions with another child. I was curious about being pregnant and giving birth; I felt I'd like to have the experience. If I didn't try to conceive, I'd always wonder if I could do it. These were just a few of my reasons for wanting a second child. But I also had reasons for not wanting one. It would require more time and energy; my professional involvement might falter; I would have to really face up to my (his/our) lack of fertility. The infertility was no small albatross.

Actually, intimations of a decision were apparent the previous summer, when I planted an herb garden in a large window box on the back porch. I discovered there numerous caterpillars eating the parsley. They were voracious eaters and beautiful creatures, a yellow-green with intense warm yellow and black stripes. I called the Field Museum for help in identifying them and learned that they would become black swallowtail butterflies if I supplied them with adequate parsley, dill, or carrot tops. I thought that Scot and I (he was really too young) would enjoy the experience of seeing them change. They ate all my parsley, so I put them in a glass coffee pot and bought parsley for them. We watched the mystery of the chrysalis; I drew and studied them. Six metamorphosed and became elegant black creatures which flew out our window on some unknown sojourn. In a sense, I had been midwife to them. For me, they became symbolic of the blind but awesome turnings of nature.

During this time, my period was extraordinarily late, even though I was practicing birth control. I secretly hoped that nature had overtaken me and caught me unawares. In some curious and inexplicable way, I had been moved by the butterflies. But as I entertained the possibility of being pregnant, all the old unresolved conflicts reemerged. I was again simultaneously depressed and relieved to find that I was not pregnant.

So it was clear that for some time I had been tempted to have another child, but it was also clear that my conflicts about motherhood remained. Of course, we might have adopted another child. I liked especially the idea of having a daughter, there was so much I could share with her. Scot's maleness had caught me off-guard. Having grown up in a predominantly female family, I found Scot mysterious and had to play him by ear. He was concerned that I had no penis. While showering one day with him, he announced that he was going to the store to buy a penis for me. Truly a fantasy of American consumerism! I asked what I would do with a penis. Scot replied that I could take off my furries and put on the penis and be just like him. What male egotism — this, even in the face of my example of equality.

The idea of a second child persisted. After all, I had survived and even flourished while being a mother. I was surprised that it had worked. I was able to fix the frustrations in my mind and dismiss them. I was able to laugh at the image of myself cautiously becoming a mother even though, looking back, my original resistance to motherhood seemed understandable. I no longer insisted on defining myself in purely professional terms. Scot and Rex had brought me to the realization that simply enjoying and savoring the life I was living was as important and in its way as defining as my professional role. My family had drawn me into the larger cycle of life and human relationships. I had a new sense of continuity, and an acceptance of a femaleness that I had previously used only for devious ends. I felt strong, whole, in control, and accepting, all at once, and I felt extraordinarily lucky to have a cherished son and to have kept my identity. But I could not resolve the issue of a second child. The chance I would have to take with my professional commitment still seemed unreasonable.

It took a chance encounter on the street to put an end to it. One night after dinner with friends, I was shot in an attempted robbery. The incident lasted only a minute but its impact on my life was considerable. The facts of what happened are less surprising to me than my internal reactions to the situation as it played itself out over that night and the following months.

I saw the comic strip flash of white, yellow, and orange; the sound rocketed in my ears. I felt the explosion, a physical kind of expansion in my body. I felt the pain. "Oh God, I've been shot."

It felt as though I had been shot in the chest, just below the left breast. I lay down on the dry winter grass. Surely I was dying. But strangely enough, my mind was amazingly alert, and I began to imagine the consequences of my death: Rex would manage, he would remarry. My conference paper would not get done, too bad. But Scot — how could my little boy get along without me? Suddenly I was filled with an astonishingly intense desire to survive, not for my own sake, but for the sake of my child. This powerful feeling, mingled with the pain, flooded my mind and body, and revealed to me in no uncertain terms the depth of my attachment to Scot. I had not known that I was capable of a desire so quintessentially maternal and selfless; but there it was.

A doctor leaned over me, opened my coat and shirt, and said, "Shot in the arm." In the arm? Why, the cowboys just wrapped an old bandana around their arm wounds and rode off into the sunset.

As it turned out, however, my arm required a good deal more than the old bandana treatment. The bone was broken and there was a lot of pain. But worse than this was the fact that instead of riding off into the sunset, I had to return from the hospital to a home situation that showed signs of coming apart. My relationship with Rex was a shambles. The interest he had developed in Scot while I finished my thesis had begun to fade before I was shot; for weeks Scot's standard question had been whether daddy was coming home for dinner. I had begun to feel that Rex regarded our apartment as a boarding house.

After the gunshot incident I was desperate for tenderness and support, but Rex continued to be deeply involved in the culmination of a project on which he had spent four years. His indifference threw the character of my marriage and family into a new and colder light. I was the emotional center, the primary giver. It was my tenderness and caring that held us together; and now that I was in the position of needing to receive with little to give, now that I was the primary taker, my husband was unwilling or incapable of reaching out to me.

I considered ending the relationship and played out alternative scenarios in my mind. I thought I could make it as a single, working parent. It was my choice; after all, I had been emotionally abandoned. I was glad there was only one child.

Time passed. I shadowboxed in silence, unready to face the question of divorce squarely. Then, to complicate matters further, my carnal desires resurfaced. Rex was a reluctant lover. There I was, arm in cast, painkillers at the ready, and bitterness between us. But I insisted. I needed to assert my sexual existence, to physically celebrate life.

Of course, the world being the ironical place that it is, I became pregnant, almost immediately. It took me quite a while to believe it: my late period could easily be explained by the shock I had experienced, the surgery, and the pain killers I had been taking. And Rex and I had not been very active sexually. But there was no arguing with the test result; I was pregnant. The crazy turns of life.

It could not have happened at a worse time. I was still weak and sick from the wound in my arm, I was behind in my work, and I was angry enough with my husband to seriously consider dissolving the marriage. I was not about to accept the emotional burden of raising an additional child unless Rex committed himself to a larger share of the parenting and to more emotional support for me. In taking this position I did not spell out my ultimatums. I wanted genuine action and commitment rather than cheap words.

Rex accepted the bargain. He was excited by the pregnancy and he wanted the child. After all, we had finally done what we had been trying to do for years. The prospect of another child forced some issues between Rex and me out into the open and allowed us to begin to rebuild our relationship.

Then, just as suddenly, I miscarried.

I lay in a sunny room studying the cracks in the ceiling and the brilliant daffodils Rex and Scot had brought me the day before. Why this? Why now? Hadn't I been through enough? Nature had picked me up and then abandoned me. I grieved again for the loss of a biological link to the future.

I kept asking myself what sense the whole thing made. In a little under three months, I had been shot and survived, had seen the disintegration of my marriage and put it together again, had conceived a life and lost it. I had never been so high as when I realized that I would live. The pain had been meaningless — I would live, and life was so dear. And then a gift of nature had been given and taken back. I was a hang-glider sailing off the cliffs only to crash on the rocky bottomlands. But I had learned that I was a survivor. I was tough and resilient, and I felt ready for the life that was flowing around me.

I left the hospital. The cottonwood seeds were blowing, the leaves were turning and flashing in the sun. I sensed that I was arriving somewhere, putting ideas together — fluid ideas about living with Rex and Scot, teaching and practicing design, and being open with myself. I was ready to accept some risk and seek out challenge. I could put away old ghosts and anxieties; ancient bugaboos had been laid to rest.

And now, months later, I think that I have finally molded motherhood to my form. It fits — it feels good. I have met and continue to meet women who are mothers and more. They are fascinating people struggling to combine a deep human commitment with self-realization. They encourage me, and I appreciate them in all their variety as I have never appreciated any other group. Since becoming a mother my emotions seem to run more intensely. Motherhood seems to soften many women; why, then, should it have tightened my perceptions and laid a fierce honesty on me? It seems impossible to escape being changed by mothering, but the nature of the change is unpredictable. I have toughened. I no longer push aside or excuse what makes me uncomfortable or offends me. I face things squarely.

I want it all: marriage and freedom, son and career. I am willing to struggle, because the rewards nourish me. How can I compare my delight in avocados to my anticipation of ripe strawberries? So it is with my commitments to Scot and my career. They are not comparable; they are simply different. It amuses me to consider Scot the avocado in my hand and my profession the anticipation of strawberries.

I have no regrets.

▲

Let me pick up the thread and continue. The pattern is a variation; you will find the colors brighter, the rhythm and form more integrated, the edges less raw, less apparent.

Following the miscarriage, we had been advised to wait a few months before trying to conceive. I expected to become pregnant and decided to deal with its impact on my job as a full-time faculty member at the Illinois Institute of Technology when I had more details concerning the due date, leaves of absence, and so on. The completion of the first *Balancing Act* manuscript in September of 1975 marked the beginning of my pregnancy. It was as if the writing were cathartic; my apprehensions vaporized. Writing was a way to work out my ambivalence and confusion. Pregnancy was now a serious goal. I pursued it with a casual abandon born of confidence.

I discovered I was pregnant after the fall term began, and the baby was due after the end of the spring term. The timing was perfect if only my body would behave reasonably well. As it happened, the pregnancy was difficult in the early stages. I started to bleed; the doctor decided that I should remain in bed for a week. Both the thought of another miscarriage and the forced inactivity were trying. I knew that I could not endure a long confinement. I was willing to exercise some caution and manage my energy carefully, but my life couldn't come to an abrupt halt even for this sought-after stranger. Fortunately the bleeding subsided and the remainder of my pregnancy was ordinary. I did succeed in teaching to the end of the term and found that college students were more at ease with my reproductive state than were my colleagues, who observed my overripe condition and joked that they had string and Swiss army knives — just in case.

Rex had agreed to go through Lamaze classes but didn't commit himself to being present at the delivery until the end of the pregnancy when his protestations diminished. The baby was due at the end of May and during that month my doctor repeatedly said I could give birth any time. We were eager to "do it," to see what had been cooking, but the baby was in no hurry. I went into labor the first week in June. The labor was slow and erratic — most of all I remember feeling a weird combination of excitement and boredom. I arrived at the hospital at six a.m. and didn't give birth until after eleven p.m.

I found the act of giving birth to be remote from real life. It will not integrate; it remains a special almost alien event. Perhaps if I were to do it again I could better understand it and tune in on the experience. In a funny way I feel cheated; not that I don't have a beautiful child as the result, but that the experience itself was not as spiritually moving as I supposed it would be. Expectations!

The delivery itself was exciting. Rex was present. He cradled my head and shoulders and reassured me while we watched the classical moves in the mirror: the crowning, the head, the shoulders, the body. Jay was born quietly — purple then red then pink — a chameleon with a hesitant cry. It was an event too rare and too common for words.

I had wanted to nurse Jay, and during my pregnancy, to compensate for sensitive skin, I had pulled on my nipples to toughen them and had on hand a supply of bag balm, a lanolin product used on cow's udders. (I rather enjoyed the symbolic touch of the bag balm.) While at the hospital I saw the beautiful yellow colostrum dripping from my nipples — what an exotic fluid. Jay was eager to nurse and my breasts filled as if by magic. Nursing was not at all disappointing, but positively pleasurable, even sexual.

During the time I suckled Jay, I was personally wrestling with the difference between birth and adoption. The bond between Jay and me developed more quickly than my bond with Scot had when he was an infant. I felt some guilt over my stronger feeling for Jay during our first hours together, but I reassured myself with the thought that this time I had had nine months of anticipation and the confidence of having experienced motherhood before. But I worried about Scot's reaction to the baby. I did not want him to have to deal simultaneously with his adoption and the painful realization that he had to share me with his brother. I proceeded slowly in telling him about his own birth and adoption, guided always by his questions. I did not want him to draw comparisons in that climate already fraught with his jealousy, sense of abandonment, and curiosity.

I still feel that Scot's understanding of his adoption must be a process that unfolds in bits and pieces over time. I can already mark milestones in this process even though we are still at the beginning. At breakfast recently Jay announced that he came out of my body when he was born and so did Scot. I looked across the table at Scot, wondering how he would react. Scot calmly corrected Jay, saying that he came out of another woman's body, that she couldn't care for him, and that we wanted a baby, a son. This was the first time I had heard Scot discuss it in his own words. In years to come he may want to know why he was offered for adoption, who gave him life, why we adopted him. The process will unfold as far as his curiosity and need take him. We do not fear or dread his need; his adoption is a separate matter from our love, and it cannot possibly make us any less important to him. Scot now reads to Jay. Jay torments his brother, but Scot has told me how at night he hears Jay breathing quietly in his sleep and, "I just know I love him."

The difference between the boys is fascinating. I can see in Jay resemblances to us both physical and temperamental. In Scot I see our attitudes and values. There is no substantial difference in our love for them. In fact, I almost expected to feel something more for Jay, but Scot was our first child and the power of that first experience in parenting has never paled.

When Jay was a little over a year old, Rex received an attractive job offer in Kansas City. My instinct was to dig in my heels and resist leaving Chicago. How could I shatter the vital network of grandmother, aunt, neighbors, and friends who sustained and supported me as a parent? Despite the difficulties of urban life — the violence, the public school problems, and more — I was not eager to move. We eventually made the decision to move after a careful consideration of our collective options and an evaluation of Kansas City. As it turned out, Kansas City was not the crude ugly cow town I had expected. Instead we found a charming small city with hills, trees, culture, easy access to almost everything, and a much less stressful and violent urban situation.

We found a house in Kansas and moved after the holidays. I didn't work for about nine months; I stayed home in order to get the children and myself accustomed to a new environment and to help Scot find new friends. In retrospect, the time spent in getting settled was well worth it, but after a few months I started to feel bored and anxious about my own professional life. My days of full-time childcare and housekeeping made me recall that as a child I played endless and elaborate games of "house" complete with too many dolls, rotting food borrowed from the kitchen, and truly sick house cleaning binges. I was even eager to learn to iron. Whew! Perhaps this extensive rehearsal burned me out for the reality of "house." Three months of intensive homemaking was all I could muster. In September of 1978 I accepted a tenure-track position at the University of Kansas. Once again, life became complex, but complexity was definitely preferable to boredom.

Scot was in the first grade and I arranged for a teenaged sitter after school on the days I would be gone. Jay came with me to a daycare center which was affiliated with the university and where early childhood research was sometimes conducted. It was a model center, probably the best of its kind. This was my first experience with daycare; Jay was just past two years old and needed playmates and stimulation that couldn't be counted on with a sitter in our home. The daycare center combined physical warmth, holding, hugging, shared activity and structure, with opportunities for individual play. They even used a very gradual approach to toilet training. When I first visited the center it was naptime and I observed a row of cots with toddlers, each more beautiful than the next, sound asleep. Jay adjusted easily to the center and I was pleased with the arrangement. I never once doubted that the center had the children's best interests as their goal.

Before this, I had never actively thought about daycare. It was a necessity for people with little money. But after our move, daycare became an attractive alternative for several reasons: Jay could commute with me to the university (the distance between there and home is forty-two miles, or about an hour driving, through pleasant pastoral countryside). I felt uncomfortable with the idea of Jay being an hour away at home while I was at school. In an emergency or in case of sickness, I was five minutes away if we were both on campus. Besides, the commute was an opportunity for us to sing, talk, and be silly together. I had confidence that the affiliation with the university would ensure a responsible and progressive program. Finally, our last in-home sitter arrangement had turned painfully sour.

In Chicago, when Jay was an infant, I had employed our last babysitter. I looked at that time for another woman such as Scot's Irish grandma, Mrs. Ryan, and just as before, the search for a warm responsible childcare person for my infant made me feel vulnerable. Luckily, I found a peppy, attractive Hungarian woman who agreed to care for Jay and for Scot when he came home from school. Alice cared for Jay with positive zeal; she sang Hungarian folk tunes to him, walked him in the park, and played endlessly with him. However, Alice and Scot never got along. Because Alice was terrific with the baby and Scot was primarily at school, I thought we could get by. I tried to help Scot and Alice become friends but I never succeeded. Alice had one child, a girl. She was unable to respond to Scot's childish animosity toward his brother or toward her. In many respects Alice was a child herself; she would structure situations in which Scot would fail to say or do the right thing (according to Alice) and then she would pout. I suspected that the problem she had with Scot would reveal itself in her relationship with Jay once he became more assertive and less of a baby. She finally overstepped the bounds of acceptable criticism of Scot in front of me. Then she became critical of me, charging me with neglect of my baby and an unreasonable love for my adopted child. She quit. I was both relieved and furious. I knew we were moving and I knew that I would never again want to open my family to the emotional burden of such an intense involvement with a stranger.

The problem, I decided, was that Alice had been looking for more than employment. She wanted love and family. We were willing to deliver more than impersonal employment, but I could not allow her to dominate any of us, to manipulate us according to her image of how we ought to live. Only Jay in his dependency and innocence could deliver the kind of love she wanted. But Jay was eighteen months old when she quit. He was becoming a determined handful as he learned to exercise the power of his personality, and soon he too would have challenged Alice. Scot, even today, intermittently talks of Alice. He remembers the injustice of her games and recalls his own petty pranks designed to make her mad. He still wonders why she didn't like him. The experience was sad for everyone save Jay, and it made me highly aware of the problems of private babysitting, especially the blurred line between such a sitter's paid responsibilities and her emotional ones.

The advantage of daycare lies in the professionalism of its staff, but one disadvantage is that no center will take care of sick children. Rex and I have agreed that I take full responsibility for Jay in sickness and in health. If Jay suddenly becomes ill, I stay home. Fortunately, this hasn't happened often. On the other hand, if Scot becomes ill during school, Rex is to be called, since he is five minutes from home and available in any emergency. This year Scot, who is nine, can stay alone if he is not too sick; he is reliable and Rex can come home for lunch to check on him. Meanwhile a neighbor is alerted, and we call him periodically. I know Scot sometimes feels lonely, but he also feels competent and grown-up staying alone. While these arrangements seem complex, they are workable because Rex is increasingly willing to care for the children, and because we live in a comfortable, safe suburban environment. Here I can give my children a freedom and independence I would deny them in Chicago.

Despite our satisfaction with our present childcare, next year when Jay enters kindergarten, our arrangements will change again. Jay's current preschool at the university goes through kindergarten; however, I would like to see him begin at the neighborhood school. The local school has an excellent kindergarten and Jay is eager to join his brother in school. But the typical public school half-day program presents problems. My plan is to condense my teaching schedule to two days a week and find an in-home sitter (here we go again) for those two afternoons. If Rex cooperates by delaying his morning departure for work, this routine can succeed. As I make these plans, I realize again that my commute has dramatically affected Rex's role as a parent. The fact that I am forty miles away when I am at work has forced his participation in parenthood in a way that passionate urging on my part would not.

My work also exempts me from some of Rex's work-related social obligations. This is another way in which my career impinges on him more than his career impinges on me. The asymmetry reflects how deeply social expectations are ingrained. If my department is having a gallery opening, it is not uncommon for faculty wives to be asked to pour punch. So far no one (except in jest) has suggested that faculty husbands pour. However, the corporation for which Rex works expects wives to be available for cocktails, dinner, or other functions. If Rex is entertaining city officials on behalf of the corporation, there is pressure for me to be at his side. While I am not indifferent to Rex's social obligations, I am too busy to be actively involved in helping out. I do not spin off my excess energy on elaborate dinner parties or tennis tournaments at the right club. We work separately and lead very private lives together. I enjoy the autonomy of this arrangement. We share our lives selectively by desire rather than necessity.

Sharing responsibility and being responsive to each other's professional goals has profoundly changed our marriage. When I was offered an opportunity to become chairperson of a respected department in an eastern university, we had a revealing discussion. Would we move for this? Was my career as essential in its own way as his? What impact would such a move have on Rex's career? To my surprise, Rex indicated a willingness to move, a recognition of the value of my professional involvement.

As I have become more confident of my professional status, I have become much more aggressive in anticipating and seeking out professional opportunities. Recently, I submitted a research proposal to a corporation in the east that, if accepted, would allow me to do research that interests me, and would allow Rex to do a fast-track executive MBA at a prestigious university nearby. Another opportunity I have pursued is an opening in Australia to head a Visual Communication program. This also Rex has supported, despite the fact that it makes very little sense financially. An adventure for the family at this particular time is very attractive, and it pleases me that I can provide the opportunity and initial financial resources as well as Rex. I consider this equality to be an index of our changing relationship.

This past fall, in the midst of my restlessness and the headiness of my new feelings of professional competence, I found myself facing tenure at the university. It was a dilemma. I didn't believe in tenure because of its calcifying side effects, but I liked the idea of increased salary and better academic rank. The system forced me to go after something I didn't value — to go through the paces of preparing my dossier. I had six weeks to document, organize and write a defense of my professional life. I had begun the process even though I considered it unworthy, but as I got involved I saw that the project could give me a clear sense of where I had been and where I was now. It forced me to evaluate the different contexts in which I had worked: studio, design office, freelance, public and private universities. It made me reflect on and articulate my teaching and research goals, not in vague generalities but in specific terms. I saw the pattern I had been weaving; it made more sense in retrospect than when I had lived it. As I went through old correspondence, examined graphics done a decade ago, I felt like an explorer on an ancient dig. Aspirations, frustrations, false starts, flashes of brilliance were all before me. There was no doubt that this was the work of a serious, committed person.

I finished my dossier and passively awaited a decision concerning my immediate future. I hated submitting myself to measurement, most of all measurement against some impossible ideal. Could one be a fine teacher, involved in research, a practicing designer, a responsible faculty member (committee work, spontaneous advising and counseling), and also be a family member? The university might find my performance inadequate, but I could not allow my profession to squeeze me further. I refused to let the balance tip in their favor.

I submitted my case for tenure to the review committee. I patiently rewrote, clarified, amended, expanded the case based on their suggestions. On one point I held firm and refused to modify my position. Last on my list of teaching objectives was to be a role model for women students preparing to enter a male-dominated profession. I included my *Balancing Act* essay in the dossier. Both the teaching objective and the essay became controversial points in my tenure case at the departmental and the school level. The committee was divided: some accepted the significance of the essay and were open to the subtle teaching function of being a role model, while others strongly urged me to remove this material from my file. The material remained. I insisted that the university deal with me as a complete person. I have struggled to integrate my life, and the idea of presenting myself as a rigidly defined fragment troubled and offended me.

My stubborn insistence that the university accept me on my own terms paid off. I was awarded tenure in the spring of 1981. I had successfully overcome a major professional hurdle and had won a personal victory. It felt good to get the recognition, but the tenure decision did not resolve my ambivalence about teaching as a profession. I am a good teacher, as I had proved to myself when I received an award for being an outstanding educator during my second year at the University of Kansas. This award reflects my sincere commitment to teaching design and my interest in and accessibility to students. But the emotional demands of teaching studio courses — often one-on-one — are draining and I return to my family empty. Half measures don't seem to work for me. Teaching is slow. What do I have to show for it? I sometimes feel as though I am dragging weights behind me, pulling the students where I want to go. Like so many other teachers, I am a candidate for burnout and must learn to address *my* needs.

On the other hand, the flexible academic schedule gives me the time I need for my children. I love the free summer to write an article, do research, play with my children, drift with them through the long bright afternoons. I love the long winter holidays when we ski together. My schedule is in tune with theirs; I work intensively about thirty-six weeks out of the year. I believe that somewhere in the recesses of my mind, I knew that being an academic would fit with parenting. I would never consider a conventional work schedule. I may complain about the intensity of my work and the difficulty of finding vital time to spend with my family during the school year, but a regular day-in, day-out, fifty-week a year job is out of the question.

As an alternative to an academic position, I have been considering setting up a project-oriented design practice. In the process of teaching I have educated myself well. The practice of design produces tangible results which are quite attractive to me. My doubts center on the fact that I am not a good business person, and I would hesitate to take on the responsibility of running my own business. In addition, I would have to work at home, and I am afraid that I might be unable to get my family to respect my professional time if I were still accessible. My own design practice is not an impossible prospect, but I have learned that any change in my work life requires serious thought and considerable patience. By the time Jay is in first grade, I could begin to consider more freelance design work at home.

Even if I decide to remain in an academic setting, the advantage to being a designer is that I can surface from my self-effacing role as teacher and turn my attention to my own work. To illustrate, an idea crystallized in the heavy atmosphere surrounding the tenure decision, an idea that captured my imagination because of its whacky sincerity. I decided to document key moments in art history by photographing cows (nothing could be more remote from "art" than cows). I would bridge the gap between art and life with images found in the rural countryside I crossed every day in my commute. Many images leaped into my mind — the Henry Moore reclining rear haunches of a cow set in an evenly textured field, the Barnett Newman black cow against a dark barn in shadow, cows a la Constable or Turner as a first image in the series. It was exhilarating to begin the research. I took my first field trip, documenting with camera and diagrams the herds, locations, shooting opportunities and difficulties. Anyone finding my notes might conclude that I rustle cattle! The next step is to meet the farmers. I believe they will be amazed and delighted that I have the good sense to want to photograph their cows. The project feeds my spirit, allows me to produce images, and legitimately puts me in a solitary context.

Finally, this period of taking stock of my professional life has convinced me all over again that my work and my relationship with my husband and sons are of primary importance. I have become increasingly casual about our home and the details of our physical lives. This trade-off is essential, but it affects the orderliness of our lives according to my waxing and waning interest and time for cooking, cleaning, and thinking about the visual details of our home. These visual details — the plants, the flowers, and the space — are important to me but often neglected. Objects appear and disappear as they migrate with small dirty hands. We are constantly locked in a frustrating battle with the second law of thermodynamics: order decreases, chaos increases. This past week our gas (read heat) was turned off and our phone service disconnected because we forgot to pay the bills. For two months I have been trying to get my car licensed. The state police took the plates, claiming that I was not insured. I had mailed my check too late. The university parking service is after me too. I have been issued seven tickets, four of which I refuse to pay. In seven short months I have received more tickets from the parking service than I received as a garageless motorist in Chicago over seventeen years. I am beginning to think big brother is lurking behind every bush, lying in wait for me to take a calculated risk. More than ever we need a keeper. I have not quite made peace with the disorder of our daily lives. Perhaps I never will. I do not know, any more than the family knows, when I will suddenly have a fit of anger concerning the mess, complete with shouting, throwing, and idle threats. But I do get action: Rex and the boys momentarily straighten up and help and I get the anger and frustration out. But in the end my priorities are fairly clear, and being a keeper is at the bottom of the list. I do not regret this — I have no desire to be a drudge.

Tonight we looked at slides, hundreds of slides beginning with Scot's adoption nine years ago. We laughed at the silly baby pictures and we remembered our feelings as we adjusted to family life. The children enjoyed seeing their early history, separating memory from hearsay. Jay, whose memory is shortest, wanted a blow-by-blow description, a complete story for each image. Rex and I saw the continuity of our lives as parents. The sequence of events leading to now seems inevitable.

As I look back I can say that it gets easier to be a parent: independence slowly comes to children and is regained by adults. The time of intimate bonding is brief. Jay, at four, is in love with me. I love this and will miss it as the boys look more and more to their father for interaction and approval. And Rex has become a responsive parent. Before we had children, I was not sure how being a parent would fit Rex, and I think now that in the early stages I was too critical of him. He found his own way through the maze of emotions and conflicts that marked our transition into parenthood.

As the boys have gotten older we have moved from traditional parental roles to a more equitable sharing of responsibility for our children. For example, disaster struck last winter, while I was in Boston on business for two days. This was Rex's first solo emergency. Scot's nine-month-old pup was struck by a car in front of our house. The dog had congenital cataracts and limited vision, but we were attached to her despite her disability. The pup was still alive but suffering terribly when Rex called me for advice. I could hear the sadness in his voice, his concern for the dog and the children's perception of the event. No matter how badly I wanted to be there to help comfort the children and say good-bye to our dog, Rex had to manage alone. The dog had to be put to sleep. This event brought death to our door for the first time, and Scot's fears, questions, and outrage at the idea of death all came tumbling out.

I understand my earlier conflict and ambivalence regarding the combination of children and a career. But, after nine years, the anxiety is gone. I've done it, completed my biological destiny without being submerged by it. I didn't lose myself. But I recognize a limit in myself, a limit that balances expectations with reality. I want to participate in my children's lives and for that I need time; I must be present. There is no consideration of more children because I would not subdivide the time I have for two to include a third. I would not decrease my commitment to my work, and it is only on occasion that I can create time where none existed before.

I am constantly amazed at the way we submit to the whims of fashion. It has become fashionable to be childless. Common wisdom would have it that women must make a choice between family and career or run the almost certain risk of making an abortion of one or the other. This is bunk. A simple and artificial separation of home and work diminishes the whole woman. I stubbornly maintain that it is possible to have both children and a career so long as the myths of perfect childhood or parenting or housekeeping or stellar performance in a career are put aside. I have to ask myself constantly which goals are real and which are illusory or artificial. The answers are not always obvious. Professionally, I try to maintain a view of my teaching that values dedication and competence rather than an unrealistic image of "success." As a parent, I can only say that I am trying to meet my children's needs and enjoy them as they grow and change.

This past year marks the beginning of a dynamic balance. It is not fragile, but it is not tremendously elastic either. I have an honest commitment to both family and career without too many preconceptions about how to meet that goal. It is difficult to be honest with oneself—to recognize foibles, illusions, and facts. One fact is that I am trying to prepare my children to be responsible, independent individuals as early as possible. Another fact is that I'd love more time to myself, a weekend vacation alone or a solid week to immerse myself in the cows project. While I cannot be single-minded, the prospect of free time to develop some of my ideas rapidly is very attractive.

In the meantime, if you happen to run into me on the street, don't be deceived by my handsome and wily children; don't look for answers in the grocery bag; don't be misled by my cool blue gaze. Beneath this calm exterior there is a juggler, an artist who with fanfare and a sense of accomplishment keeps an enormous number of plates dancing in the air. As one plate slows down, I give it another spin—now another, and another. I am skillful; I have observed no cracks. My energy does not fail me.

Conclusion

Our first *The Balancing Act* essays were written from inside the fog — in some cases, from inside the panic — surrounding our efforts to adjust to the drastic impact of new motherhood. Now we are more distant from that crisis, and we have each made our separate peace with our roles. We can no longer indulge in spontaneous relaxation or single-minded work sessions, but we have found a new pleasure in the feeling of energy and resilience that comes from meeting our responsibilities capably. Our lives are not as simple as they were before our children were born, but they are immeasurably richer.

In contrast to the air of crisis that pervades our first essays, our updates are for the most part reassuring in tone. We intend to be reassuring. The balancing act is possible; we are accomplishing it and enjoying it. All of us have achieved professional milestones in these years when we were also becoming parents. Linda has devoted long hours to seeing a small business prosper. Jayme has continued to have gallery showings and to receive national recognition for her ceramics. Jane has moved on to jobs of increasing responsibility in her law career and has had four one-woman art shows in New York. Anna has finished her PH.D. thesis. Sharon has been awarded tenure in her university teaching position.

On the other side of the balance, every one of us has gone on to have a second or third baby. Not all of us would have predicted the birth of additional children at the time our first essays were written, nor perhaps would those who read about our earlier crises. But after the initial shock, we all discovered that motherhood can be wonderful, that our children had become much-prized sources of joy, pleasure, and comfort to us. Their physical beauty, the sweetness of their voices, the simple intensity of their love for us made us want to pursue the experience of motherhood and to see what new challenges and pleasures another baby would bring.

We take it as an affirmation of our choice to commit ourselves equally to children and career that all of us are still married, when according to recent statistics at least two of us ought to be divorced by now. We attribute our stability neither to special luck nor to special forbearance in the face of life's problems. All our marriages have been tested as we questioned traditional assumptions about family life. Sharon has written here about her fears for the survival of her marriage, and Anna has spoken of her struggle not to blame her husband for her own disappointments. But we entered our marriages knowing, as did our husbands, that we wished to pursue our careers and that we had our own lives to lead. For their part, our husbands, however short they may have fallen of a theoretical ideal, have all assumed that they want to spend more time with their children and enter more fully into domestic responsibilities than their own fathers did.

Our professional successes, our growing families, our

lasting marriages are gratifying evidence to us that the decision to combine work and motherhood is more than viable — it is desirable and worthy of imitation. Yet it is also true that no amount of experience or good organization has made our lives easy. The balancing act is never static. We must constantly be prepared to readjust our schedules and priorities to meet the changing demands of growing children, larger families and developing careers. All of us have felt the difficulty of meeting the psychological and emotional needs of a growing family while at the same time meeting increasing professional responsibility. Parenthood is stressful simply because it increases the number of people in whose lives we are intensely involved — people who frequently get sick and who are constantly facing difficult developmental milestones. The more children we have, the more frequent crises become. We have all learned that to be a good parent requires almost constant readiness to help children cope with crises, and when that responsibility is combined with the need to be intellectually available for work, the result is a serious drain on one's energy. Perhaps this is the inevitable and permanent bottom line of combining motherhood and career.

And there are other problems. None of us, for example, has found the perfect solution to the problem of childcare. Those of us with babies or very young children still rely on sitters who come to the house, partly because we feel that our children need more individual attention than they would get in a nursery or daycare center, and partly because daycare for infants is almost nonexistent. The more closely a sitter shares our values and tastes, the more likely we are to be happy with her. Despite our best efforts, however, babysitters come and go, and all of us dread the task of finding or replacing a sitter.

Those of us with older children have moved more and more in the direction of all-day nurseries or daycare centers. They are less expensive than private sitters, and they have the advantage of being professionally run and of providing playmates for our children. However, a good day-care center can be hard to find or hard to get into. In addition, if a child gets sick or school is closed, the entire family must juggle commitments and make special arrangements. This can be hair-raising. In general, we try to choose the best from our limited alternatives, and we find it helps a little just to recognize that no arrangement is likely to be permanent, or even suitable for very long.

The issue of sharing domestic responsibility with our husbands is also still very much alive. At the time our first essays were written the five of us fell into two widely separate groups: those couples who, whenever the babysitter was off-duty, shared responsibility for the children equally as a matter of principle, and couples who had no principle of equal sharing, so that when the sitter went home the burden of childcare fell almost entirely upon the woman. During the intervening six years, our positions have moved closer together. Sharon's and Anna's husbands, who originally shared least in the care of the children, have taken on more responsibility. Linda's husband now shares less in the childcare than he formerly did. Jane and Jayme are now sharing equally with their husbands, as they did in the beginning, but for most of the last six years their arrangements were more conventional, with the women taking greater responsibility for the children and the men working at full-time jobs.

In spite of good intentions on the part of the husbands and tireless urging on the part of the wives, none of us has been able to sustain a pattern of equal sharing for the long term. We hate to admit it, but we all have backed down on the issue of equal sharing, at least for specific times and in specific circumstances, and it has made life easier when we have done so.

One of the great problems of the equal sharing ideal is defining exactly how it ought to operate. We approached parenthood assuming it meant equal sacrifice — an equal number of hours at domestic tasks so that no one felt like a slave. Now that we regard domestic undertakings less as sacrifice and more as pleasure, it is harder to use that rule, and we try to define sharing more positively: each parent should spend as much time as possible with the children.

But that still leaves the question of specifics. Should both parents devote strictly equal numbers of hours to work and home? Or should they simply divide the responsibilities at home so that neither parent shoulders the entire burden? Or ought the goal to be equality over the long term: one parent works full-time one year, the other parent full-time the next? In our own cases, Jane and Jayme have learned that for both parents to have flexible, part-time careers means dramatic sacrifices in family income, and making ends meet becomes a more and more pressing problem. Those of us who now rely on at least one parent's full-time salary have faced the reality that a secure income still means full-time work. We have had to take it month by month, constantly readjusting as each parent completes one project and approaches another, as families move to new cities, as babysitters come and go, as school schedules change, as children grow older.

That constant readjustment is itself endlessly fatiguing. Linda finally decided to take on the major responsibility for her household, delegating individual tasks to her husband when necessary. Anna and Sharon, who knew from the beginning that their husbands were establishing demanding careers and could not take responsibility for the household, may actually have followed a more straightforward path. Anna is now catching up, achieving more work time for herself, and her husband is finding ways of accepting responsibility for the children without disrupting his work schedule. Sharon, on the other hand, simply went ahead with her career plans and let necessity dictate what household responsibilities her husband would have to take on. Jane and her husband have devoted enormous energy to reapportionment of responsibility as their work schedules change, and they have been startled to learn that even with equal availability, children sometimes make unequal demands. Both Jane and Jayme have voiced their frustration at the sacrifices in efficiency that come with the effort to share responsibility at home.

Despite our scattered successes, we still agree that equal sharing of responsibility ought to be an objective for working couples. The burden of parenthood is too great for women to shoulder alone, especially if they are trying to maintain independent lives. However, we must not deceive ourselves about the difficulty of the task. For many people of both sexes, equal sharing means relinquishing power in a known realm (domestic life for women, the world of outside work for men) for power in an unknown realm. And even when equal sharing is a conscious goal for both the husband and the wife, pressures of the workplace and demands of children do not always permit equality. We have not resolved this issue, but we all agree that we cannot afford to squander our precious emotional energy in feeling that we have failed. Surely each experiment in equal sharing helps; each gesture toward that goal counts.

As we look for connections between our original essays and our updates, we realize that since the birth of our first children we have faced the continuing psychological challenge of combining into one balanced identity the separate roles of worker and mother. On the one hand is the professional person, ambitious, busy, shielded from worry about domestic matters. On the other hand is the mother, generous, loving, putting her children first. How can we embody both those roles when they seem to demand different, even antagonistic, traits of character? We see that we have worked through that dilemma by constantly viewing ourselves from different angles, by trying on different identities, by imagining how we look to other people.

In our original essays all of us are highly preoccupied with self-image. Anna and Jayme, who felt at that time the most comfortable with their role as mother, worried about their professional images. The rest of us, Linda, Jane, and Sharon, felt confident in our professional identities but did not always feel at ease with viewing ourselves as mothers. Linda describes going Christmas shopping after Sarah was born, looking at her reflection in store windows for reassurance that she was the same "serious" person she had been before she became a mother. Jane admits that sometimes, sitting on the grass with friends and their babies, she felt distaste for herself as something so ordinary as a young mother. And Sharon describes the embarrassment she felt at having her small son beat her to the telephone when she was expecting business calls.

In our updates, Linda and Anna admit that they still find themselves living in two worlds. Linda tries on the role of the glamorous career woman, making business calls from the maternity ward, but the performance seems comical and false to her. Anna talks at some length about her experiments with self-image. She is moved to tears by the fantasy of seeing herself kiss her children goodbye to go to work, yet takes conscious pleasure in walking through the door marked "Staff Only." Similarly, as she defends her thesis, she sees herself transported from a world where children play to one where she sits among grown men, expounding English economic history.

Jayme in her update senses even greater fragmentation,

living in what she sees as three worlds: home, the world of work that brings in money, and the world of her art which she sees as her true professional identity. She finds herself trying to reconcile all these roles by looking at herself through the eyes of her father, her children's eyes, the eyes of the outside world.

Jane and Sharon, on the other hand, see themselves in their updates as having laid to rest their self-consciousness about being mothers as well as professionals. Jane, in fact, sees the integration of motherhood into her identity as an important element of growth between her first and second essays. For Sharon, facing tenure at the university was a turning point in which she realized that she no longer felt secretly apologetic for devoting energy to home and family as well as to career. Yet even the balanced identities that Jane and Sharon have forged for themselves face tests in their new essays. Jane studies herself in the mirror as she brushes her teeth, wondering how it "looks" to have four children. Sharon fights the tenure committee to keep her original *The Balancing Act* essay in her file, and she ends her essay admonishing her readers not to be misled by the grocery bag she carries on the street.

We attribute our self-consciousness as we attempt to combine career and motherhood to our lack of models after which to pattern ourselves, and by whose standards to set our goals and measure our successes. We have all consciously rejected the male model of success, which depends on overriding concentration on a career sixty hours a week. None of us has been willing to pass up that much of the experience of our children's growth. Yet we resist the assumption that part-time work lacks seriousness, and we have absolutely rejected the possibility of full-time motherhood. Jane and Anna have discussed here how they have relied on their own mothers as models for their lives, and the rest of us have been conscious, especially in our first essays, of reorganizing and amending the models our mothers have set for us. Jane, perhaps the boldest of us all, has used standards of "greatness" — Barbara Hepworth, artist and mother of triplets, William O. Douglas, Matisse — to try to understand her goals. But all of us wish we did not have to expend such energy in seeking examples that express our ambitions and legitimize our choices. We hope that the five of us can serve as models for younger women, and that our book will encourage both men and women to think and write seriously about how to create enriching adulthoods for themselves while sharing their lives with children.